Digital Geishas and Talking Frogs

THE BEST 21ST CENTURY SHORT STORIES FROM JAPAN

Edited by Helen Mitsios

CHENG & TSUI COMPANY

Boston

16 15 14 13 12 11   1 2 3 4 5 6 7 8 9 10

Published by
Cheng & Tsui Company, Inc.
25 West Street
Boston, MA 02111-1213 USA
Fax (617) 426-3669
www.cheng-tsui.com
"Bringing Asia to the World"™

ISBN-13: 978-0-88727-7924

Library of Congress Cataloging-in-Publication Data

Digital geishas and talking frogs : the best 21st century short stories from Japan / edited by Helen Mitsios ; introduction by Pico Iyer.
    p. cm.
  ISBN 978-0-88727-792-4 (pbk.) -- ISBN 978-0-88727-793-1 (ebook) 1. Japanese fiction--21st century--Translations into English. 2. Short stories, Japanese--Translations into English. 3. Japan--Social life and customs--Fiction. 4. Social change--Japan--Fiction. 5. Japan--Fiction. I. Mitsios, Helen. II. Title: Best 21st century short stories from Japan. III. Title: 21st century short stories from Japan. IV. Title: Short stories from Japan.

PL782.E8D55 2011
895.6'3010806--dc22
                            2011000255

Credits:
Front cover illustration by Nikolai Larin © ImageZoo/Corbis
Back cover photograph by Tony Winters

Printed in the United States of America

Contents

Acknowledgments

First things first: I would like to convey my heartfelt gratitude to the authors and translators who made this book possible.

In addition, I would like to acknowledge Alexandra Jaton and Eavan Cully at Cheng & Tsui Co.; Yurika Y. Yoshida at Japan Foreign-Rights Centre; and Amanda Urban at ICM.

Thank you to friends and family who added wind to my sails while I was working on this book, and especially to Karen Callahan who once upon a time gave me her copy of Yukio Mishima's *Forbidden Colors* to read; Hitomi Shimada, both a beautiful person and wonderful friend; Karrie Lawlor for her support and optimism; Dr. Howard C. Cutler for his generosity, wisdom, and humor over the years; and Lisa Krug for unparalleled friendship and our standing Friday lunch date over the last decade or so.

Most of all, my gratitude extends to Tony Winters, my *samurai, sensei,* and husband.

Foreword

It was hard to believe twenty years had gone by. I was on the phone having almost the same conversation with the same person on the same subject. Two decades had passed since I first edited *New Japanese Voices: The Best Contemporary Fiction from Japan,* and now my good friend, Keiko Imai, founder and director of Shonan Universal Design Institute in Tokyo, had just asked me, "Why don't you put together a new version of the book?   One for the 21st century?"   I answered, "Let me think about it." And in her indomitable manner she responded, "No need. Just do it."

Once my decision to put together a "sequel" to the first collection was made, one event led quickly to another. I had just written a book review on Natsuo Kirino's novel *Real World* for *The Philadelphia Inquirer* and knew she hadn't published a short story in English translation. When I asked her if she would contribute a story to my new collection, she said yes. I also contacted Haruki Murakami. He had been the first person to agree to contribute to my first collection when I met him years ago in the seating area of a swank hotel lobby overlooking Central Park East. He said yes again. I phoned Masahiko Shimada, who happened to be on an extended professional assignment here in Manhattan, where he was staying with his wife (within convenient walking distance of Lincoln Center so they could watch their beloved operas). He too, said yes.

And so this new collection was underway. But as the stories, each so fresh and unusual, crossed my desk one after the other, I began to feel less like an editor than an anxious host trying to create the perfect guest list for an engaging dinner party. I hoped the whole would be greater than the parts. I hoped that each guest would find commonality with the others yet be distinctive enough to hold his or her own. Perhaps one would spin a yarn, share a secret or even misbehave. They did not disappoint.

The writers in this collection are master storytellers, and I am honored to share their work with you. Several writers have seen their stories translated into English before; others make their debut in English translation here. Many of them have won the highest literary accolades such as the Akutagawa Prize, the Mishima Prize, the Kawabata Prize, and the Tanizaki Prize, as well as other awards and distinctions. In Japan their fiction is read and admired by millions. Now, thanks to a distinguished group of translators, these stories can be enjoyed in English.

Though some of these literary works defy genre, all recognize the importance of their subjects' inner lives. The stories often address the dilemma of characters who find themselves lost in a complex world of accelerated change. In Japan, a Confucian reverence for ancient traditions rubs shoulders with a desire to experience all the boundless wonders our 21st-century technological world has to offer. The philosopher's tenets live on: a respect for social harmony, the here and now, man's relationship to his fellow man, and most importantly a proper balance in all things. The latter is reflected in a Confucian maxim: "If you do not want to spill the wine, do not fill the glass to the brim." However, as these characters negotiate their way between the traditional and new, and the sense of isolation that accompanies the use of technologies designed, almost ironically, to bring us closer together—wine is most definitely spilt.

And speaking of wine, the table has been set for our dinner party. I'd like to invite you now to join me and meet our most illustrious guests—and feast at a table of literary delights.

Helen Mitsios
New York, New York

Introduction

"People like to put us down," The Who screamed while I was growing up in England, "just because we get around." Not long thereafter—in "Won't Get Fooled Again"—they were snarling, "Meet the old boss, same as the new boss." The Empire was gone, they knew, and all that was left to them were empty bottles and peeling alleyways, in which to pick fights with other restless teenagers. In time a full-throated revolution would arrive with the punks, desecrating the Union Jack and portraits of the Queen, but until that absolute rebellion all that was possible was a shouting in the void.

I think of that, sometimes, when I read and reread some of the stories in this collection, rich with the numbed and occasionally desperate sound of a child whose Confucian father has been thrown out of the house—and allowed few visiting rights—and whose American-style mother doesn't know quite what to do with the post-nuclear mess. "I don't care," "I'm not taking it," "I want something else, but I don't know what it is" are the cries of the kids left behind; and just underneath their words you can hear the plaintiveness of a generation that has buried the old order but not yet found its way to a new, and so finds itself adrift, in a kind of limbo, somewhere between one of the oldest societies on earth (in terms of demographics and invisible traditions) and the youngest (in terms of mix-and-match fashions and high-tech conveniences).

The celebrated "Big Three" of postwar Japanese fiction were all after-midnight elegists of a kind, so concerned that Japan might lose its soul (and become just a suburb of the West) that they retreated to old corners and ideas, determined to hang on to what they deemed "authentically" Japanese. But the writers of the new century in Japan—Generation X.2, you could say—are notably contrary, even Oedipal in their determination to show how far they live from the verities of Yukio Mishima, Yasunari Kawabata and Junichiro Tanizaki. They are the children of U.S. army bases and parents who grew up in the rubble of the old; they are the grandchildren of the soldiers who lost the war and came to wonder why they'd been fighting it in the first place. If their elders—as described in the first story here—longed to be permanently "entranced," they strive to be permanently unenchanted.

How perfect, then, that this anthology, so artfully put together by Helen Mitsios, begins with a story about the unsettled daughter of a famous author (based, we gather, on Tanizaki). The very inheritance that is the source of her public fascination is also the center of her private sense of exile and abandonment; the much-admired novelist that all the world is so eager to hear about was cold to her and selfish and ready to jettison even his daughter in the pursuit of his art. While not yet out of her teens, she is already flinging one of his precious letters to her into a fire. But even as she does so, she knows that his blood flows through her and that his face peers out through her own. Her very act of destruction, in fact, suggests how much he has passed his "evil spark" down to her.

"I hate writers," she cries, and in those three words we hear the rallying-cry and the starting point for the unapologetic stories that follow.

If I had to come up with a secret title for this anthology, in fact, I think it might be *Absent Fathers and Lost Kids* (or even *Lost Fathers and Absent Kids*). It's startling how many of the pieces that follow Natsuo Kirino's opening tale turn upon fathers who are gone, and not only in the haunting tale of childhood wishfulness called "The No Fathers Club." In another story here, two very different young characters have fathers who are dead—and a third ends up stabbing the father who abused her when young; in another, a middle-aged man dwindles, quite literally, into an absence, and in yet another an older man is imagined as a mummy, strangled and wrapped up naked in a plastic bag.

Traditionally, and even on my arrival here in 1987, Japan has defined itself through its mothers and the air of reassurance, public warmth and nurturing that suffuses its shops and streets; one psychoanalyst even wrote a famous book on its "Anatomy of Dependence." But the Japan of the new century, for all the dutiful mothers at its center, seems dominated by fathers who have abdicated their responsibilities, leaving children with more time than love and more money than direction.

Again and again we see lost souls here, of both sexes, who cannot tell if they're dreaming or awake; one man who decides to abandon his death-in-life would rather waste away than return to an existence in which his only real connection is with an unmet female announcer on an FM radio station. In more than one story we see older men with underage girls; one teenage object of desire is not only trafficking in her own body, but in those of her friends as well. Even when she finds a boy she likes, she tries to woo him by telling him she'll sell her body for him. "You'll get to wear cool suits," she promises, "and I'll let you ride in a Porsche."

When guidance comes in this anthology, it comes only from a six-foot-tall frog; many characters in these tales are weirdly passive, just killing time until a tsunami, a pregnancy or two dangerously seductive girls appear on the horizon to shake them out of their stupor. "Despite my youth," the narrator in one story says, "I always felt I was living out the rest of my days." In another, a young narrator confesses, "There's nothing for us to do today, and no plans for tomorrow either." It's no surprise that Haruki Murakami has become all but the global laureate of suburbia, dislocation and what is described in a story here (though not by him) as "aimless plenty." His characters are jet-lagged even when the flights they take are internal. An "absolutely ordinary guy" in his story here, as in many of his stories—"no wife, no kids, both parents dead"—more or less floats through life, not doing much good (or much harm), unsure if he's running in place or just, like a worn-out instrument, running down.

Lest all this sound too gloomy, I should stress that Japan today, on its surface, is as seamless, fashionable, fast-moving, reliable and attentive as when I first arrived; go into a convenience store and the apparently disso-ciated kids of this anthology will gently cup your palm as they hand you back your change and seem at least as shy, courteous and helpful as their grandmothers did. Indeed, the writers featured in this collection have exercised extraordinary resolve and clarity in simply giving their tales of a modern floating world such structure and definition. In a story such as "My Slightly Crooked Brooch," we get a vision of everyday human emotions in a sleek modern landscape that has all the polish and absolute confidence of a 19th-century classic.

Even more important, the central perspective behind and inside many of these tales is that of a woman, often a girl. The "Big Three" loved to dwell on the beauty of pretty young things, and all the ways such idealized creatures could be used by older, backwards-looking men to symbolize purity or innocence. In this collection, the objectified young women get their own back, and point out how tiresome it is to be fussed over by creepy older guys, and how much, in fact, they're in control of the men who think they've "conquered" them. Hitomi Kanehara, whose story "Delilah" is included here, won one of Japan's most prestigious literary prizes, the Akutagawa, while she was just twenty, having dropped out of high school and written a novel while in San Francisco; Natsuo Kirino and Yoko Ogawa are both winning ever larger international followings with tales that are the opposite of reassuring and often as direct and unflinching as two of Kirino's titles: *Out* and *Grotesque*.

The landscape through which their characters move is, of course, one of anonymous streets and red-light bars, of look-alike "family-style" restaurants and places drably called the Tokyo Metropolitan Art Space or the Tokyo Station Gallery. Their people think nothing by now of going to Finnish movies or relaxing on a beach with the stories of the Shanghai-born British master of dystopia, J.G. Ballard. Their problem is not—as we lazily imagine of Japan—having too much work, but too little; their predicament is not that of having too great a sense of national pride, but rather too weak a sense of affiliation. Pinball wizards and quadrophenics, they drift through days that are as weightless as a video game, with everything (including themselves) about to dissolve with the next click.

When the precursor to this volume came out, twenty years ago—*New Japanese Voices: The Best Contemporary Fiction from Japan*—it was already apparent that the writers of the new Japan had no interest in apostrophizing geisha (unless they were anime figures—or being impersonated for a day by platinum-haired girls with Hello Kitty bags); and the home-made nationalism upheld by the likes of Mishima had been seriously thrown into question by several national defeats.

But what has happened since is that Japan has found that a hybrid identity composed of disparate aspects of the outside world fits about as well as the "almost illegal miniskirt" and the crazily oversized Utah Jazz t-shirt we see in one story here. All the iPhones and hand-held devices and portable TVs of the past twenty years have not begun to offer a lasting solution to loneliness and confusion and doubt.

A new generation of "freeters" wanders through a labyrinth of part-time, go-nowhere jobs and "hooks up" with new partners every hour; one boy here is called "Joe" and in another story one of his contemporaries complains of being asked by a girl from Saitama to call her "Jennifer." To a striking degree the people in these pieces are defined not by what they have, but by what they lack: it only makes sense that one protagonist is shown literally eliminating himself, and a fractured account of a tsunami emphasizes for us that everything that was here two minutes ago is now gone. And it's no coincidence, I suspect, that one piece ends with a young tough beating up a friend's abusive father—and replacing his "shiny black leather shoes" with Air Jordans.

As I write this, the quiet ancient capital where I live, Nara, is celebrating its 1300th anniversary all around me. I turn on the TV, and see a Japanese couple getting married, apparently with delight, by a robot; I open the newspaper and read of agencies in Tokyo that rent out actresses to visit old couples on Sunday mornings and call, "Hi, Mom! Hi, Pop! How are you?" because the couple's own daughters are no longer ready to perform their filial duties. At the same time, the misty pavilions, the local gift for listening and the public cheerfulness of the place are often as impressive and humbling as they ever were. My Japanese father-in-law lives in a traditional wooden house down the street from a fox shrine and recalls his wartime years in Manchuria and Siberia; my Japanese mother-in-law has never set foot outside Japan. But my Japanese wife—a contemporary of the writers in this collection—resolved at an early age that she would look beyond the boundaries of her forebears (hence my place in her life) and her daughter now lives in Spain with a Spanish-Ecuadorian fiancé. I can only wonder what "Japan" will mean when the next generation of the family, no doubt delightedly mixed-up, comes upon the scene.

"Where is the terminus of the Tokyo Loop Line?" one character asks himself in this book. It's a resonant question that reverberates on many levels, of course, and the "Loop Line" might almost be a modern, industrial parody of the natural cycles that have traditionally kept things in place in Japan—an old Confucian idea lost in American translation. Things go round, yes, but for some Japanese in this young century a loop suggests the ceaseless, pointless rotation of a treadmill.

The joy of this anthology is that so many writers, often with a keen sense of the world outside Japan, can still muster the courage, eloquence and energy to ask where courage, eloquence and energy have gone in the society around them. The Who, after all, were shouting out, "I hope I die before I get old" almost half a century ago—and yet here they still are, senior citizens now, their time kept by Ringo Starr's son on drums, shouting out their cry of impatience in our midst, even though they know now that it can never come true. If anything, their power, intensity and popularity have grown even greater as their singer and songwriter near their seventies.

I know this, as it happens, because I saw them in concert not so long ago, in a 16,000-seat arena in the shadow of Osaka Castle. As the fans around me—all Japanese—shouted out the angry slogans of their youth, they might as well have been saying that they, like the band, were not about to fade away or give up "talkin' 'bout my generation." Loyal, leather-jacketed and clearly thrilled to be in the company of the disaffected foreigners who had given them their life's soundtrack, they looked to me a little like the writers of the stories in this memorable collection.

Pico Iyer
Nara, Japan

Digital Geishas and Talking Frogs

Natsuo Kirino

Natsuo Kirino quickly established a reputation in her country as one of a rare breed of mystery writers whose work goes well beyond the conventional crime novel. She is a leading figure in the recent boom of female writers of Japanese detective fiction. This fact has been demonstrated by her winning not only the Grand Prix for Crime Fiction in Japan for *Out* in 1998, but one of its major literary awards, the Naoki Prize, for *Soft Cheeks* (which has not yet been published in English), in 1999. Several of her books have also been turned into feature movies. Kirino's work often addresses social issues such as the plight of women in Japanese society, constriction of their domestic lives, and discrimination in the workplace, as well as discrimination against immigrant workers.

The Floating Forest

Translated by Jonathan W. Lawless

SINCE THREE OR FOUR OF HER HUSBAND'S SEMINAR students were coming over tonight, Aiko Itō was measuring out rice. Young students always drank a lot of alcohol and ate a ton. During the winter, Aiko's strategy was to prepare cheap pot-luck stew and second-rate alcohol, and afterward bring out loads of rice balls. But her husband, Ryūhei, would insist otherwise, saying things like, "Let 'em have the good stuff!" Although he was a professor at a private college, having published next to nothing Ryūhei's salary wasn't nearly enough to be constantly having guests come home for dinner. His love of entertaining house-guests was exactly like his uncle, Shōkichi Akagi. Aiko remembered her own mother, who had remarried with Akagi, complaining that even when they had no money he still called guests over without a second thought, and she was embarrassed when she couldn't put anything out on the table. This brought a wry smile to Aiko's lips.

1

It was February, and the kitchen, which faced north, was freezing. Their traditional Japanese-style home (with the exception of the single Western-style octagonal drawing room) suited the tastes of the ever-fashionable Ryūhei. He was also similar to Akagi in his insistence upon a particular style of house, clothes, and other small items such as stationary. That same Akagi had collapsed in his house in Shinjuku Ward's Yarai-cho and died a year earlier. To uncle and nephew, so similar in features and interests, went mother and daughter, respectively. This unusual relationship, too, as time went by would likely become a simple, single line, like entangled threads coming undone. Thinking such things, Aiko turned on the small gas stove at her feet and began rinsing eight cups of rice. The water from the tap was cold as ice, and her fingers numbed while sloshing the rice around in it.

"Mom, a visitor. Want me to turn on the stove in the drawing room?"

Her second daughter, Naoko, came to tell her. Naoko, in her third year of junior high, was nearing the time for her high school entrance exams. She seemed to be suffering from lack of sleep and didn't look well. Her study room was directly above the front door, so she usually became aware of visitors before anyone else.

"Oh, I wonder who that could be?"

Aiko wiped her hands on her apron and asked her youngest daughter. Aiko's hands were bright red, so she hurriedly warmed them by the stove.

"He says he's from a publishing house. He says he wants to talk to you."

Naoko answered, eyes sparkling. *Here we go again*, thought Aiko, and after she undid her apron she told Naoko to go ahead and light the gas stove. With numb fingers Aiko picked off a pill or two of wool from her heavy, sand-colored cardigan and straightened the hem of her dark brown wool skirt, which had turned up. Walking along the hall to the front door, she wondered, *how many people does this make?*

It had been half a year since her father passed away. At first newspapers and weekly magazines came to her house looking for interviews one after another, but she didn't respond to any of them. Aiko's real father was the novelist Keiichirō Kitamura. However, while she wouldn't necessarily have called their relationship "estranged," they had not frequently visited one another since she married Ryūhei Itō before the war. On Kitamura's side, his third wife Sachiko, her sisters, and her other children were nestled in fast. After getting divorced from Aiko's mother, Kitamura remarried twice, and it was the wife from his third marriage, Sachiko, whom he loved most of all, and he loved her until he died.

An elderly man wearing black-rimmed glasses was standing with his back turned to the stained-glass front door. He had a black coat in his hands, and his navy blue suit with white-patterned black tie matched his white hair perfectly. The man met Aiko's eyes with a warm expression.

"Miss Aiko, you most likely do not remember me. My name is Kaname Ishinabe."

Ishinabe held out his card reverently. It read: "The Literary World Press – Publication Director – Kaname Ishinabe." Aiko was familiar with the name Literary World Press, but to what extent Kitamura or Akagi had dealings with them, she couldn't be certain. Aiko tilted her head. She did feel as though she had seen Ishinabe's face before. But she had no recollection of the name. Ishinabe smiled and watched on as Aiko fell silent, attempting to remember. Although he was reserved, there was a calm about him that suggested self-assertiveness. Little wonder that Naoko, who was usually rather absent-minded, thought to ask if she should turn on the stove in the meeting room, thought Aiko.

"Mr. Ishinabe? Well, could it be that we've met before?"

"We have. When I met you, I burned my right hand . . ."

Ishinabe showed her the small remnants of a burn on the back of his right hand. It showed visibly white on his sun-tanned skin. "Ah!" Aiko gave a small cry, then looked up at Ishinabe's face. *Could it be? That man I met more than thirty years ago?* At the time, Aiko had just turned fifteen and Ishinabe was a newspaper reporter. His black hair had turned stark white and his body had become much heavier, but the core of the person hadn't changed. At the very heart of Ishinabe was an almost unbridled curiosity. Perhaps with the passing of years he had learned to hide that strong curiosity smoothly behind a smile.

"Yes, now I remember. It's been a long time."

"Indeed, and the great number of years since we met is entirely my fault. At the time I was a reporter, but I always wanted to try my hand at editing, so I transferred to Bundansha after the war."

"Oh, is that so? My apologies for not knowing. Please, do come in."

To cover up her inner excitement, Aiko bent over and arranged the slippers. Her instincts told her that a formidable opponent had just come. Those many years ago, too, she had lost her temper in the face of the persistent Ishinabe. However, Aiko waited for him to come in without showing the slightest trace of her mind's workings, and then she showed him into the drawing room. Ishinabe had apparently been checking her height as she walked ahead of him, for he spoke from behind.

"You haven't grown much since then, have you?"

"It's true. I'm short."

"Kitamura wasn't very tall either, was he?"

Aiko paid no attention to his words.

A large bookshelf was built into the wall of the drawing room, its shelves full with the works of Kitamura and Akagi. The gas stove that Naoko had lit was rapidly warming the room. Aiko stole a glance quickly to the plaster wall where moisture had gathered. A guest had once warned her: "Humidity is bad for books, you know." As usual, Kitamura's works were simply haphazardly shoved onto the bookshelf. She had been told that the books were all first printings, limited editions, and so on—all books that would make a dilettante dance with joy to see—but having been brought up surrounded by books since the day she was born, Aiko didn't see it as anything special and couldn't appreciate them, and in fact didn't even care to think about it.

However, it seemed as though Ryūhei had a particular idea about books, so the collections of poems and other writings by his own uncle, Akagi, he lined up precisely, beautifully in order by year. Ryūhei's reason for not attempting to rearrange Kitamura's books was probably either due to hesitance because Kitamura was Aiko's real father, or because he didn't care for Kitamura as a person. Aiko guessed that it was the latter. Kitamura was surprisingly cold to those he had lost interest in, so it was only reasonable for the entire house of Akagi, Ryūhei included, to eschew dealings with him. The Akagi family came from a wealthy house in Wakayama, for generations lovers of culture, who excelled in music, and who believed deeply in friendship.

However, in the house of Ryūhei and Aiko Itō, there was no evidence beyond this bookshelf to suggest a profound relation between such men of letters. Since their oldest son left for Fukuoka to take up his new posi-tion, the two of them and their two remaining children, with the excep-tion of the occasional visit by students, maintained a peaceful daily life, punctuated by life's occasional turbulences. It was Aiko's wish, as well as her way of life.

Aiko placed a wooden ashtray, which Ryūhei had bought and brought home from Jakarta, in front of Ishinabe. Informing him, "I'll prepare some refreshments," she left the drawing room momentarily. In the kitchen Naoko was boiling water, having felt it the appropriate action for the situation. She seemed unhappy to see her mother come back.

"Let me bring it out to you."

"I will bring it out."

"Come on, I wanna hear what you guys're talking about."

Naoko whined, her voice filled with disappointment. Aiko knew that her daughter held a great interest in her grandfather, Keiichirō Kitamura. Kitamura, who a few years earlier had been awarded the imperial Order of Culture, had written books since his school days and had left behind innumerable works. Nearly all of his writings were praised as master-pieces, and he also published many works overseas, enough even to have scholars of his literature outside of the country. What child wouldn't feel excitement at knowing they were a direct grandchild of Kitamura, an author known by everyone throughout all of Japan? Furthermore, her father's uncle—no, her grandmother's partner—was Shōkichi Akagi, he, too, was an author who was awarded the Order of Culture as a poet. However, the older children had all become taciturn upon learning the fact that Kitamura and Akagi had battled long over their grandmother's affections, and after they broke away from each other Akagi and their grandmother had remarried and were then estranged from Kitamura. Aiko's oldest son, Shōhei, and her oldest daughter, Kyōko, whether they were overwhelmed by the complicated relationship between Kitamura and Akagi, or that of their grandmother and mother, they never said anything about it, and they feigned indifference toward their grandpar-ents. But Aiko's last child, Naoko, perhaps because she hadn't yet grasped the situation, seemed to be proud of her grandfather beyond belief.

"This is an adult conversation, so you must not come in the room."

Aiko clearly stated, placing the green tea she had very carefully poured out onto a tray and lifting it up. When she returned to the drawing room, Ishinabe was there with his eyes closed, apparently thinking about something very intensely. He sensed her presence and turned around, bowing his head deeply.

"My apologies for coming unannounced. Please don't trouble yourself."

"No, I am very sorry for what I did back then."

"That's all in the past now. Besides, I think of it as a privilege, so please don't bother yourself with it. I met you then quite randomly, and I was desperate to make you talk."

After gazing at the back of his right hand as if it were an honorary mark, Ishinabe continued.

"I've watched you from afar as you grew up. Now you seem to be happy, and I'm truly relieved to see that. The truth is I saw you at both Akagi and Kitamura's funerals, but I didn't talk to you. Still, the fact that the year after Akagi died Kitamura passed away as well gives me the feeling that there was some kind of connection."

Aiko nodded gracefully. Kitamura didn't attend Akagi's funeral, supposedly due to health, and only sent a telegram. However, immediately after that one of his works was to be made into a movie, so he was on television together with the actresses that were to be in the film. It goes without saying how Aiko's mother, Hideko, or Aiko's husband must have felt at such cold, heartless treatment. That was the kind of person Kitamura was; disregarding the feelings of others, he put preference on the most important thing to him at that moment.

In his later years, Akagi poured great passion into writing school songs, and he didn't write a single novel—no, he became unable to write them. As if to compensate for this, he invited writers to his house and formed a literary salon which came to be called the Akagi Faction. For a second an image of Kitamura's face flitted across her mind, of him raising his voice in high-pitched laughter and saying, "After all, he's a poet, and poets are pure, see? You have to be a villain to write novels!" Kitamura hated exchange among literary persons. Ishinabe, too, assuming he'd been an editor for a while, should be well informed about the arrogance and condescending behavior of Kitamura in his later years in his disregard of Akagi.

No sooner had the conversation stopped than Ishinabe brought his hands to his knees and lowered his head.

"Miss Aiko, the truth is I came today to ask a single favor of you."

"What would that be?"

She had a pretty good idea what he wanted, but she responded as if she couldn't guess. Ishinabe grinned as if he wanted to tell Aiko that he understood her resolution.

"Is there no possible way that you may be persuaded to write your memoirs? Please, I beg of you to do this for me. There is no one else in this world that could draw as heavily on the blood of Kitamura. Besides, you are a woman who has lived her life walking along a checkered destiny. Calling it 'checkered' may be rude, but I don't know of any other woman who's been handed a fate such as yours. And, being the daughter of a writer you must've had to experience some unreasonable things, am I wrong? But, if you'd been just any writer's daughter, you wouldn't have had to go through all that. It was because you were the child of the great Kitamura. So from your perspective, would you be willing to write about Kitamura as your father, Akagi as a second father, and how you perceived your mother? Of course, about yourself as well. Truth be told, I wish to know about your feelings at this moment more than anything else. The year after next I will leave the company due to my age. Before that would you please allow me this one last job? Your memoir—no, even an essay would be fine—if I could but receive that, I would have absolutely no regrets about my work as an editor. I've been thinking about this for a long time. I came here thinking that now, half a year after Kitamura passed away, I could finally visit you. How do you feel about it?"

Ishinabe spoke in one burst, a serious expression on his face. Aiko, only half-listening, forgot even to answer him. A checkered destiny. *That's how people think of me.* She felt as though she'd just been given a new perspective, and she was ruminating over the words.

When Aiko was fifteen, her mother was divorced by Kitamura and then ended up marrying Akagi, and Aiko followed her from Kitamura's house. Even though Aiko pleaded, saying she didn't want to go, somehow in her own way as a fifteen-year-old she knew that Kitamura would never be persuaded. Kitamura did as he liked; he became immediately entranced with whatever he took interest in, and his wife and child cleanly, completely disappeared from his heart's desire along with all the rest. He was the kind of person who wished he could always be infatuated with something. Aiko's intuition told her that this time, too, he was absorbed in his plans to throw away Aiko's mother and hand her off to Akagi. While watching her parents keep a distance so cold that they didn't even fight, at some point even in Aiko's heart resignation came creeping in. She'd even prepared herself for the fact that her parents' attitudes and feelings would never again return to what they once were. And she didn't think it would be particularly bad living with Akagi, either. That was because Akagi, an old friend of Kitamura, was like a kind and dependable uncle for her, who had often written her letters since she was in elementary school and sent her rare (at the time) presents from Europe.

Kitamura, Akagi, and her mother, Hideko, after a long talk together, created a letter with their joint names and sent it out to a select group of concerned individuals. It was labeled "The Handing-Over of the Wife Affair" and caused quite a stir. The brunt of the criticism was focused on Hideko. She was branded as a loose woman who had committed adultery, and Aiko herself had been expelled from Catholic school. She thought that was really the beginning of her drifting existence.

On the other hand, Kitamura, his wife having been "taken" from him, received a good deal of sympathy, and Akagi was held up as a chivalrous man. Kitamura's plan to be rid of his wife and daughter in one go worked well—almost terrifyingly so. Akagi and Hideko's platonic romance, the long friction between Kitamura and Hideko, Aiko's misfortune, Kitamura's cheating which had started the whole thing—like a dime novel they all became the hushed topic of public discussion among people who had no connection with the events, sometimes specially taken up as a feature story, and it became impossible to know what was the truth and what was rumor. The only thing that was clear was that Kitamura threw from him all his inconveniences and, lifted of them, became single and free. But, there is no doubt that Kitamura, too, hadn't assumed that it would lead to Aiko's expulsion. Remembering his panic at hearing of it,

Aiko instinctively stifled a laugh. When was it that she realized that she, too, had that evil streak passed down from Kitamura?

Ishinabe, who'd been searching Aiko's countenance, asked again.

"What do you think about it?"

"My sincerest apologies, but I must refuse."

Appearing to have anticipated this response, Ishinabe, showing no signs of surprise, turned tough.

"Why is that? Would you please tell me the reason? If I'm satisfied, I'll pull back. You may think my words to be considerably self-centered, but I'm interested in the girl known as Aiko Kitamura, the child who was handed over with her mother. I'm interested in the fate of that child. Is that wrong?"

"There is nothing particularly wrong with it. Both my mother and I are quite used to people being interested in us. But, why should I have to provide stories to satisfy the curiosity of other people? And on top of that, I was never 'handed over.' I was not adopted into the Akagi family. The whole time I was still in the Kitamura family register."

Aiko smiled as she spoke, so as not to be harsh. This technique, too, she had learned over a long period of time.

"That was probably because there would've been no successor to the Kitamura family if you were given away. Kitamura thought this through well. He gave complete control over your up-bringing to your mother and Akagi, while he himself was left carefree."

"That's true. But until I got married, my father sent me money for my living expenses and any other necessities."

The truth of the matter was, immediately after Aiko and her mother had gone over to Akagi, Kitamura fell into bankruptcy. Living life day by day, hounded by taxes, he had to produce manuscripts in order to survive. One reason why Kitamura had so many more works to his name than other people was because of this. Kitamura, who spent every yen that he got his hands on (though not to the extent of being completely wild), could not even stay in possession of a residence. Even the estate that he was finally able to obtain with the enormous amount of money he came across during the one-yen book craze, that, too, he had to put on the market almost immediately because he became unable to pay the taxes, and from one to the next he changed houses at a dizzying pace. Since he left all the furniture when he moved, you could say his lifestyle was like that of a migratory bird. Even if Aiko sent him a letter asking for money for a school field trip or to pay the doctor, he would unabashedly write her back, saying, "Why don't you call off the trip?" or, "This month I don't have any money either."

Meanwhile, Akagi built a Western-style house in a quiet residential area in Yarai-cho. After passing through the chic, ivy-covered archway, a Western-style house appeared, the outer walls painted pink like a house from a fairytale. A sunroom, a mantelpiece, niches. The floor was inlaid with white and black tiles, with a cast-iron spiral staircase of incredible workmanship. How many architects must have come to observe its construction? Akagi's aesthetic sense far surpassed others. However, she felt as if Kitamura had scorned Akagi's taste itself as being a sign of weakness. In that point, too, there may be a similarity between the two of them. Aiko realized that she sometimes sneered at Ryūhei's particularity over certain things, and she felt a shiver run up her spine.

Aiko thought that while Kitamura was her father, he was certainly cold. After the "incident," Kitamura didn't try to understand what she went through at all, simply leaving her to live with Akagi. "I understand that you've done nothing wrong. However, no matter how famous a writer your father may be, we cannot have a girl from a family that has strayed so far from regular society here at our school." These were the words of the British sister who expelled Aiko from the Catholic girl's school. Aiko still remembered clearly the intonation and sound of the sister's voice when she pronounced the word *"writer."*

Kitamura always said that just the fact that a man is a writer means that he must walk a path few go down, that he has to live life a villain. Perhaps at some point both she and her mother had started living life infused with that sense of values. At the time when Aiko entered the Catholic school where girls from good families went, her father, too, was doing well economically, and he had bought a mansion in Osaka where they were living in triumph. Rich people and playboys, movie directors and actresses were constantly in and out. They gave Aiko expensive presents for no reason, and took her to see movies or Takarazuka Theater, where they sat and watched from the box seats. However, the world does not allow for the conceit of *writers*. Aiko was taught that the world she lived in was a special place. In the end, having been expelled from the Catholic girl's school, Aiko found herself with no other options, and for the rest of that year was forced to stay at home. The following year she finally found a school she could attend in Tokyo, but students throughout the school would constantly come to have a look at her. Even as she grew older, once they found out that Aiko's father was Kitamura they'd inevitably be surprised, and she always had the feeling that she could hear whispers around her. The steel protecting her body and heart became thicker and thicker. That being the case, wasn't this way of life the same as that of a writer who walks down the path different from others? Aiko felt that since being separated from her father, she was actually getting closer to him.

"Forgive me for my choice of words, but, Miss Aiko, I believe you have an obligation to write."

Ishinabe said, a cigarette in his mouth.

"And what obligation might that be?"

Aiko slid an ashtray in Ishinabe's direction and looked at his face. His eyes were tinged with fervor.

"To speak about your father, as the child of a great writer. And to talk about how you felt growing up. I believe these are both things you can give to the world of literature."

Aiko laughed involuntarily.

"Mr. Ishinabe, my apologies, but you're overestimating me a bit, aren't you? Literature is nothing. Everything was nothing more than a delusion my father thought up in his head. I have no such obligation."

A flash of anger appeared to cross Ishinabe's face upon hearing Aiko's words. That expression reminded her of what happened the first time they met.

"Why do you hide yourself so much like that? Truth be told, I have no interest in reading the memoirs of the lady Sachiko. That's because even before I read it I know the general contents. It's not as if it's because she won't give it to our company. At this point, Kitamura himself has written a frank account and his wife as well. The one you write would be far more interesting. I want to know how you feel."

Aiko pressed her cheeks, which had become hot from the gas stove directly in front of her, with her hands. Ishinabe continued.

"You should write it for your children, too. You have three, correct? Your children must always be wondering what their mother felt growing up. Why not try writing it for them?"

Aiko shook her head.

"I don't want to write it, and I can't."

"You *can* write it. That day I was amazed at how much you really are Kitamura's daughter."

Ishinabe suddenly stuck out his right hand. The burn mark. It happened at Shingū. The month was the same, February.

That winter, about half a year after the incident, Akagi brought Hideko and Aiko back to his hometown of Shingū City. It was so that they could see the Otō Matsuri, the epic fire festival that takes place at Kamikura Shrine. Akagi's father, who ran the hospital, always extended a warm welcome to his new daughter- and granddaughter-in-law. Akagi also went with the intent of begging money from his father, so he was constantly bringing them both back home with him. Even for Aiko, this was the third time she had visited Shingū. Fresh-caught fish, citrus fruits, fresh vegetables. City goods quickly arrived by ship. Being a collection point for lumber, Shingū City was a wealthy area where both people and money gathered, and Akagi's home was particularly well off. Since Hideko was originally from rural Gunma, she soon adapted herself to this new place. In addition, Akagi's parents liked her, so she became much livelier than when she was living with Kitamura. Akagi invited Kitamura to the festival as well and was looking forward to having everyone involved gather together. Akagi had his good points, which showed at times like these.

However, Aiko felt depressed. She was tired of having to watch what she said and did around Akagi and her mother as they started their new life together, and she also wearied of the consideration she received from those around her. Bereft of school as a place to go, Aiko was more alone than she'd ever been before. In addition, a letter came from Kitamura, who had promised her he would definitely go see the festival in February, saying he couldn't make it. As soon as she fully understood that her father wasn't coming, she realized just how much she was looking forward to seeing him, and she felt as if the sadness suddenly took shape and emerged from within her. Moreover, written in the letter were also his intentions to remarry.

Ms. Aiko,

How is Uncle Akagi? Owing to the fact that my writing is not progressing, I have become unable to go to Wakayama. Please give my regards to everyone.

I have an announcement. I will be marrying in April.

My fiancée is Ms. Tamie Yoshino. She works for the Bungeijin Publishing Company. I will introduce you to Ms. Tamie the next time we meet.

Due to the chaotic preparations my manuscript is late, which has resulted in me being unable to go to Nanki.

I will do my best to make it to Tokyo.

Your father

It was an extremely blunt letter. One of the distinctions of Kitamura's letters was that he never addressed the recipient using their proper name within the text. Even when he had spoken to Aiko's mother at home, he never called her anything but "you," or "hey." She didn't know if it was because he was embarrassed or because he was just lazy, but when this kind of one-sided letter came, in which he only wrote about himself, even

Aiko was saddened. Furthermore, hearing that he was to remarry so soon, didn't this mean that Aiko no longer had a home to go back to? Even if she stayed with her mother, whom she loved, she could never call Akagi her father, so she couldn't call their house her home. Besides, watching from the sidelines as day by day her mother's attitude and way of talking changed ever-so-slightly when she was with Akagi, Aiko couldn't deny her feelings of alienation.

It was an overcast afternoon, rare for Shingū in the winter. From the second floor she could see white smoke. Close-by there was construction going on, so perhaps they were burning wood chips? Aiko slipped on some *geta* and went out front. In the pocket of her knit-wool jacket was the letter she had recently received from her father. She was planning to burn it. But her mother was always telling her sharply to be careful with the handling of letters.

"No matter how insignificant a postcard, save every piece of mail you receive from your father. They say it'll provide material for posterity. And take care in the letters you write to other people as well. Examine the contents, for you must never reveal your true feelings. Things may happen and it's not safe to assume that the letters will never be made public. Write in ink, and make your characters beautiful. The only one you'll be humiliating is yourself."

Up to this point Aiko had followed her mother's wisdom, carefully putting the letters she received in a letter box, but she'd suddenly become crazy. As Aiko got closer to the fire, the carpenters who'd been circling it silently disappeared and she found herself alone in front of the raging flames. The hospital director's son, a writer, had received his wife from another writer—the rumors had spread throughout this little town as well. The people of the town had decided on their own to be nice to her, thinking the poor girl had been thrown away by her father. Aiko was very upset about that as well, and she took the letter out of her pocket.

"You're Aiko Kitamura, correct? I'm right, aren't I?"

Addressed so suddenly by a young man, Aiko turned around. A thin, young man was standing there in a black overcoat and round-framed glasses.

"You're the spitting image of him, so I figured it out instantly. Am I right?"

Aiko was often told that her facial features were similar to those of Kitamura. The arc of her eyebrows, the size of her eyes, and some other aspects of her face were the very image of him. The young man seemed overly thrilled at the fact that he'd run into Aiko, and it looked as if he couldn't stop himself from talking.

"I heard that you were kicked out of school and now you aren't attending anywhere. That's too bad. Even though you did nothing wrong."

Aiko shot him a sharp look at the words, the same words the nun had used.

"Who are you?"

"Sorry for being rude. I'm Ishinabe from the *Daily Times*. You must be tired of newspaper reporters, huh? Or maybe you've been told by your mother not to talk with any of us? By the way, have you decided on a new school?"

"Not yet."

"I see. But why not just think of it as a long vacation? That's one way to look at it, right?"

After the young man laughed cheerfully, he noticed the letter Aiko was clenching. The clear characters with traces of ink seemingly drew his eyes.

"Did that letter come from Mr. Kitamura?"

"That's right."

"Ah, as I expected, neat handwriting."

Baring his curiosity, Ishinabe leaned forward for a glimpse.

"Would you like to read it?"

Aiko asked. Ishinabe nodded his head over and over, like a child.

"Ah, I wanna, I want to read it. May I?"

Aiko pretended to hand it over to the young man, then threw the letter into the fire. The envelope appeared to be taken and pushed up by the force of the flames, and for a moment it blazed brightly. Ishinabe caught the burning letter, but quickly let it go. While Ishinabe howled "Hot, hot!" in pain, the letter burned to a crisp in mere seconds. Although she didn't realize it herself, Aiko had apparently been laughing. Ishinabe looked back at her with a shocked expression, so she hurriedly averted her gaze.

"I'm sorry."

"No, it's okay. I was soft. After all, you are Mr. Kitamura's daughter. It could never be that easy. By the way, is Mr. Akagi at home?"

Ishinabe seemed to be trying to endure the pain, his face twisting as he asked.

"He just went out for a walk with my mother."

"No, I mean the doctor."

Perhaps he was thinking to have Akagi's father treat the burn. She nodded, and then Ishinabe took a bundle of papers out of the black bag slung over his shoulder.

"Would you like to read this?"

The pages had been cut out from a magazine and bound, with a fake cover attached. With a glance Aiko knew it was from the literary magazine *Kaizo*, because when Kitamura had a publication running he had commanded her mother to arrange the printing. When Aiko hesitated, unable to reach out her hand, Ishinabe said, "Take it, it's yours," and forced it into her hands. Then holding his burned right hand as if to protect it, he went off in the direction of the hospital. With a nasty taste lingering in her mouth, Aiko read over the fake cover in front of the fire. It read "The Treasure: Shōkichi Akagi." It had run in 1922, so it was a work from about eight years earlier.

Aiko went back to her room and opened up "The Treasure." While reading she became so absorbed that she forgot about the passing time. "The Treasure" was based on the true story of how Akagi looked upon the friction between Kitamura and Hideko as their friend, and at some point while lending his ear to Hideko he began to fall in love with her. "My marriage was a mistake. That woman is stupid," spat Kitamura in reference to Hideko, and about Aiko he went as far as to say, "I never needed any children. I wouldn't care if she got sick and died." Furthermore, it also said that the source of the friction was due to a love affair between Aiko's aunt Mitsuko and Kitamura. It was a record of the selfish conflicts of adults who had just found out the whole truth for the first time. Partway through reading, Aiko's mother came to announce "dinner's ready," but Aiko declined, saying she wasn't hungry, and continued reading.

At one part, Aiko thought she was going to scream out loud and covered her mouth with both hands. It was the scene where even though Kitamura wanted to go out with Mitsuko alone, Hideko said she was going as well, and since she wouldn't listen to what he said, he got angry and gave her a sound thrashing with a cane. Aiko was only five years old at the time, but she had witnessed that moment. Although the event had at some point slipped from her memory, the shock she felt then was awakened once more. When little Aiko, scared by the yelling between her parents, went out the front door, her father ran through the house after her, shoes still on, and raised the cane at her mother. He hit her across the back two, three times, and she fell to her knees in the hallway and started sobbing.

Aiko decided not to turn the page. That wasn't just a bad dream, it was a real incident. Once again reminding her that yes, this wisp of a memory truly happened, was horrible beyond reason. She threw "The Treasure" into her desk drawer, sprawled herself out on the tatami floor, and ate a tangerine. Juice from the fruit splashed down and stung her eyes. Although her mother and Akagi had finished dinner and come upstairs, she continued to cram her mouth full of tangerines, still laid out on her side. Her mother was stupefied to open the sliding door and see Aiko lying there.

"Where are your manners? Sit up and eat."

She was most likely embarrassed in front of Akagi, but he let out a low, muffled laugh. Akagi's countenance was opposite that of round-faced, short Kitamura. He was tall like a Westerner, and his upper body had the perfect amount of flesh. And he had an oval face. However, the distance between his eyes was short and his jaw was drawn back, so he resembled a fish. Akagi was popular because he murmured funny things without breaking a smile, all the while with a face like a fish.

"Hey, maybe your uncle should take a nap, too." Akagi flopped himself down next to Aiko and called to her mother. "Come on and lie down, too, Hide."

Stuck between her mother, who had reluctantly lied down, and Akagi, Aiko, rigid, gazed up at the ceiling. Unexpectedly, Akagi recited an impromptu poem:

"Eating tangerines, the tears that appear from you, in one eye only."

She knew her mother had gone numb as if startled, but Akagi was wiping the lenses of his glasses with the sleeve of his kimono in a leisurely manner. Aiko said to her mother, lying next to her, "Mom, father said he can't come to Shingū. It was in his letter."

"He wrote it in my letter, too. Aiko, you must be very disappointed."

Her mother mentioned nothing of Kitamura's remarriage. She might've been thinking that if it wasn't written in Aiko's letter, then there was no point in telling her yet. When there was no reply, her mother propped herself up on one elbow, raising her upper body off the floor, and looked into Aiko's face worriedly.

"Aiko, show me the letter your father sent you."

"I burned it in the fire outside."

"Why did you do that?"

Akagi halted her mother from adding a reprimand with a motion of his hand, as if to say "Now, now." After putting his glasses back on, Akagi, to no one in particular, said, "I'm sure Kitamura's letter went something like this," and then mumbled like a bad actor speaking his lines in a monotonous voice.

"Since I haven't seen you in a long time
The hair on your head, too,
Must have gotten long.
I think I want to go and see that,
But your uncle can't go because he's too poor."

Aiko, still looking at the ceiling, protested.

"That was the letter you sent me two years ago. I remember it well, because I thought you were treating me like a child."

Akagi laughed, showing a snaggletooth from his mouth.

"That was rude of me. Aiko, the truth is your father, Kitamura, is also too poor to come. That man likes to impress to the point of hiding the truth, and it's not good. He can't write honestly. Don't worry yourself about it."

Kitamura didn't hide the truth. Rather, he was sickeningly truthful. Far from hiding his feelings, he said things with indifference that hurt the people around him, and he wrote the same things in essays, to the point of showing his own wickedness, his superficiality. *However,* Aiko thought, *Isn't Akagi, who's consoling me now, the same man who wrote "The Treasure?" Disclosing something that everyone wants to forget ever happened, hurting my mother, hurting me, and hurting Kitamura as well. Writing a novel exactly as it happened, painfully truthful, doesn't this do more to break the heart?*

"Aiko, it said in the letter that your father's going to get remarried, didn't it?"

Her mother was already speaking in a tear-filled voice. She had assumed that Aiko was hurt at her father's remarriage and had been crying alone, and now she was distraught. Aiko spoke to no one in particular, and without answering the question that had been put to her.

"I hate writers."

Akagi looked over at Aiko as if surprised.

"Why would that be? Does that include me as well?"

"It does."

"So you hate your uncle . . . That's too bad. What do you suppose I should do?"

Akagi spoke in an easy-going way and scratched his head. Aiko stared at the lamp shade hanging from the ceiling and whispered.

"I read the story you wrote. Because of your story, my mother and father split up. When you wrote that, you must've hated my father. So everything became a mess. Everything's your fault."

At long last her mother started sobbing. Akagi held his head in both hands.

"I know. That's why I swore never to write realistic fiction again. I have no intentions of putting that story in a book, and I stopped writing it half-way through. I swear, I'll never write one again. I promise you, Aiko. I'll never make the two of you unhappy. I'll never write another story like that ever again. I promise."

Akagi repeated the words "I promise, I promise," tears in his voice. Akagi always wept profusely when he became emotional. Suddenly the room was quiet. From far away the sound of waves could be heard. The humming sound of small waves, coming to shore. Or so she thought—it was actually the sound of Akagi and her mother sobbing.

Aiko was thinking back to the night when she heard about her parents' divorce from Kitamura. Akagi and her mother were holding their breath in another room, so she was prepared for the fact that she was probably about to hear something of great importance. Kitamura came into Aiko's room and made a bitter face. For a while Kitamura stood gazing at somewhere around Aiko's hair with large eyes, not saying a word.

"Um, your mother and I have decided to get divorced. It seems like your mother will get remarried with Uncle Akagi. So, Aiko, you'll go live with her."

Aiko sensed this was not a joke.

"What are you gonna do?"

Kitamura ducked his head.

"I'll be alone, but the fact that I'm your father is biologically the truth, so I don't think it'll be any different from now."

"But we can't live together, right?"

As soon as she said the words, the tears came. Kitamura saw Aiko's tears and turned his eyes away.

"Um, why not think about becoming a bride a little early?"

Kitamura was good at making you believe that what he said made sense. The fact was, if she thought as he suggested, things became a lot easier to envision. Aiko gave in and nodded her head. But, upon leaving the room with Kitamura, her mother and Akagi searched her face anxiously, and once they found evidence that she'd cried, their tears fell in torrents.

And now Akagi and her mother were crying again. Even though he was the one who wrote "The Treasure." And even though he was the one who sent her that letter which read, *"your uncle can't go because he's too poor,"* playing dumb even though she'd already turned thirteen. Wasn't the blunt Kitamura still better than this Akagi? Because Kitamura hated realistic fiction. He would rather be the "villainous" author than the "pure" poet. However, she was driven away by her father, to these people. Just like at the Christian academy, she was thrown out. *What kind of world is this?* Aiko fixed her eyes to the four corners of the room, to see if something wasn't lurking there.

"I was very much a child back then. Please forgive me."

Aiko apologized to Ishinabe, but just like the time they were in front of the fire, Ishinabe's presence was becoming more and more unpleasant. Still, Ishinabe brightened his expression.

"Your facial expression, it's exactly like Mr. Kitamura. He often laughed in that high-pitched voice, but sometimes his brow clouded over and he wore an unpleasant expression. You look exactly like him when he did that."

"Mr. Ishinabe, I cannot do it, and I don't want to."

"If that's the case, allow me to ask you one thing. Why do you think people write novels?"

Aiko pretended to be thinking deeply, but she already knew the answer. *After all, he's a poet, and poets are pure, see? You have to be a villain to write novels!* Ishinabe was waiting for Aiko's response, but since Aiko was never going to say it, he apparently became impatient and answered himself.

"Aren't authors people who couldn't live if they couldn't write novels?"

Just as he'd promised Aiko, Akagi never wrote another realistic novel. Perhaps that had weakened him as a writer. Aiko glanced at the bookshelf. Akagi tried out children's books and detective fiction, and many other forms of writing, but no matter what he wrote, it seemed his writing had lost that sparkle of his early masterpieces, or even of "The Treasure." On the other hand, simply by looking at the title written on the spine of any of Kitamura's works, there hung an air of rich fiction that seemed almost to encroach on reality.

Suddenly Aiko was worried about the time, and she glanced at the clock above the fireplace. *I have to get ready.* Although it was time for Ryūhei to be coming back with his students, she hadn't finished making the preparations. Aiko became anxious.

"I'm sorry, but we'll be having guests tonight."

"I understand. My apologies for taking up so much of your time. Today I'll take my leave here, but may I call on you again?"

Ishinabe implored her, getting up onto his feet. Aiko shook her head.

"Please don't come here anymore. You're not welcome."

"You're honest."

Ishinabe gave a wry smile, then took up his coat which had been left on the sofa.

🍃 🍃 🍃

Shortly after five o'clock in the evening there were signs that Ryūhei had come home with his students. Aiko met them at the door, still wearing her apron. Talking with Ishinabe had made her late to boil the rice, but preparations for the stew were complete. When she saw Ryūhei's figure, the first to open and come through the door, for a single moment Aiko thought it was Akagi. Tall and lanky with a face like a fish, both eyes close together. His glasses were the same shape, and the fedoras they wore were the same color. The calico scarf he wore in the collar of his coat was a memento of Akagi. The scarab ring he wore on his left hand, too, was one he had made to look like the one Akagi wore. The real one was bequeathed to Hideko, so he couldn't get his hands on it.

"Please pardon the intrusion."

"Good evening. Thank you for having us over tonight."

The young people piled in, full of liveliness. There were some who were lightly dressed in a sweater and windbreaker, and there were also some who were in their school uniforms or who were dressed in the popular "ivy look." The narrow hallway was immediately filled with the oily smell of young men. Among them there was a new face. He was a serious-looking youth in a school uniform. The uniform-clad boy stared at Aiko's face, and when she smiled at him he dropped his gaze to the floor, abashed.

"That one, he heard you were Kitamura's daughter and got all worked up."

Ryūhei whispered into Aiko's ear. The majority of the students who came over knew about Aiko; at first they were reserved, but still they shot her glances which showed their curiosity. And Ryūhei was amused observing his students' reactions.

"I just saw someone from The Literary World Press."

Aiko informed Ryūhei while taking the coat and scarf he handed her. He looked back at her.

"For me?"

"No, he asked if I'd write a memoir."

"Oh, that's too bad," joked Ryūhei, making a funny face. "So, are you going to do it?"

"I won't write it."

"Why?"

Ryūhei turned around. His face was like a cold fish, but the inside was different. He inherited his good-natured quality and cheerfulness from Akagi. Ryūhei was the kind of man who wanted to be a high school teacher more than a scholar.

"Because I can't."

"But the information would be very valuable, since there're things only you can testify to."

He said the same thing as Ishinabe. Ryūhei was a good-natured person, but he likely didn't know her true feelings. Aiko dodged the issue with a smile and hung Ryūhei's coat, still smelling of the winter air, on a hanger. In the bedroom Ryūhei took his casual kimono from its place on the rack and was changing. Aiko knelt on the tatami mats and folded his clothes. They could hear cheerful laughter coming from the dining room, likely Naoko come down from the study room greeting the students.

"About what you were saying before, when people see someone involved in something keep quiet, they assume that they actually have something they want to say."

Ryūhei spoke while tying an *obi* around his thin frame, raising a spirited, zipping sound. Aiko nodded vaguely, but in her heart she thought, *you're exactly right.* Perhaps in keeping her silence she was going against her destiny. Ryūhei put his scarab ring away carefully in a small box in his dresser and headed toward the dining room where his students awaited him.

Once Ryūhei and the students had finished their dinner they moved to the study, where they were apparently holding a debate while drinking. Every once in a while she could hear a youngish voice raised in drunkenness or the sound of something being knocked over. But Aiko didn't worry about the details and, sitting under the warm *kotatsu* in the living room, the television left on, she nodded off. She was exhausted from the preparations for dinner and Ishinabe's visit. The phone rang. She was reluctant to raise herself out of the *kotatsu*, so she let the phone ring several times before she finally took it. Her feet were chilly.

"Aiko? It's me."

It was from Hideko. Hideko was sixty-nine years old. According to Aiko's younger brother, Kazuo, who lived with their mother, it seemed she had suddenly succumbed to old age after Akagi's death. Indeed, her voice sounded as though it had weakened. Kazuo was Akagi and Hideko's child, Aiko's half-brother fifteen years her younger.

"Mother, are you doing okay?"

"I think I have a bit of a cold, but I'm fine. And Yōhei always tells me, 'Granny, get better!' I'll do my best somehow. Even so, it's frustrating that your father died before Kitamura, even though he was six years younger."

Even though Kitamura was Aiko's real father, Hideko spoke with regret from deep within her heart. After marrying Akagi she suddenly started to show her strength. It was said that the one Kitamura originally liked was Hideko's older sister, Yaeko. Yaeko was famous as a fiery, strong-willed geisha. Hideko's younger sister, Mitsuko, who Kitamura was enamored with, was also strong-willed, and she became an actress. Only Hideko alone was said to be plain and of a reserved nature, but perhaps she and her sisters shared a common character that Hideko simply kept hidden from the world. Aiko had heard that she was really in charge at the literary salon which Akagi had presided over. Even if her voice sounded weak she was still full of life, and that made Aiko break into a wry smile. It was because she realized that, ironically, her knowledge of Yaeko and Mitsuko, too, was gained through Akagi's story, "The Treasure."

"So, here's the real reason I called: you know that next month is the second anniversary of your father's death, right?"

She hadn't forgotten, but on hearing the words "next month," Aiko instinctively turned her eyes to the calendar on the wall.

"That's right. Time flies."

"As you get older, time seems to pass more quickly. 'Time flies like an arrow' is an expression reserved for the old," said Hideko with a sigh, and then she broke off. Maybe she was recollecting something. "Kitamura went to the other side, everybody's dying off. Maybe I'm next."

"Don't say such things."

Aiko laughed. However, she'd be turning fifty next year herself. Her mother and Akagi, who'd laid down beside her in Shingū and cried with her between them, at the time must've been in their late thirties. Perhaps it was perfectly natural that they cried. Aiko thought about her heartlessness when she was younger.

"So, I'm torn as to whether we should invite Sachiko to the second-year memorial service. She has also had a death in the family, so I was wondering what to do. Could I get you to call Sachiko and ask her for me?"

She would most likely not come even if invited, and probably her mother was concerned about it being rude if she didn't say something. That her mother felt distant from Sachiko was certain. Aiko replied that she'd take on the responsibility and then hung up the phone.

As for the person Kitamura spoke of when he wrote, "I will be marrying in April. My fiancée is Ms. Tamie Yoshino who works for the Bungeijin Publishing Company," they got divorced after only a single year together. Behind the early divorce was Sachiko's presence. Sachiko was a daughter from a long-standing, high-class Japanese restaurant proprietor in Kyoto, the oldest of three sisters. The sisters were famous throughout the Kansai region for their beauty and wit, but Sachiko in particular had a reputation as being brilliant in all things. Before she kept company with Kitamura, Sachiko's husband, who had married into the family, was swindled, the restaurant fell into other hands, and the three sisters spiraled into ruin, to the extent that they were living in a beachside changing room. However, they were nevertheless a well-known presence among high society in the Kansai region. Sachiko was well out of Hideko's league. Kitamura preferred arrogant, luxurious women to reserved women who didn't try to make themselves noticed, like Hideko. No, it was that he liked himself prostrated before such women.

Kitamura liked to move, yet he never tried to create a new environment on his own. He preferred to be entranced by something and, while being taken of his soul, immerse himself in that scene. Once Kitamura had established a new household with Sachiko, he enjoyed the frequent comings and goings of Sachiko's sisters and her children from her former marriage. He enjoyed being infused with the atmosphere of Kansai upper-crust society which Sachiko and her sisters produced, and he searched for the seed of creativity there. When Aiko heard the name of her father's third wife she felt more distant from him than ever. It wasn't as if she hadn't known a small taste of Kansai's high society herself. When her father bought the mansion in Osaka, many people like Sachiko were constantly in and out of her house. The girls at the Catholic school were also of the same social stratum. People who had many servants and lived as lords and ladies. Hideko was different. Akagi, the local intellect, was different as well, in another way altogether. The bridge between the two houses was her role, pleasant or not, she thought as she picked up the telephone.

"This is Kitamura."

Sachiko answered the phone with a soft Kyoto accent. Aiko was surprised simply because she thought Sachiko wouldn't answer the phone herself.

"This is Aiko. I'm sorry we haven't talked in a long time."

"Aiko? I'm delighted! How have you been?"

Sachiko spoke in an innocent way, like a young girl.

"I'm fine, thank you. How are you, auntie? Are you feeling a little better?"

Aiko addressed her as "auntie," but she and Sachiko were only thirteen years apart in age.

"No, I'm really lonely. This house in Atami is empty and it's so painful. But, nothing will come of me saying that. Kitamura is dead, after all."

Sachiko let out a great sigh. Her way of talking was such that her sadness could be felt. However, the voices of small children could be heard in the background.

"But it seems lively there."

"Yes, right now my daughter is over with Chō and them."

Chōko was the name of Yumiko's oldest daughter, Yumiko being Sachiko's daughter from her first marriage. Kitamura gave her the name. Even now, at sixty-two and with grandchildren, Sachiko was still like a well-bred young lady.

"Um, about Akagi's second-year rites, what are your plans? They're in March, but seeing as how it' still cold, my mother thought it might be inconvenient for you."

"Oh, it's already been that long? That's right . . ." It seemed like Sachiko was thinking. "If I didn't go, it would be rude now, wouldn't it? But I'm still down and sadder than anything. You understand me, don't you Aiko? That's why I can talk with you, but even if I keep pressing the point, nobody understands me, deep down inside. That makes me feel lonely, too . . ."

It seemed she might continue for a long while. She hadn't given a definite answer, but when she wouldn't give a quick answer, it meant "no."

"That's true. I understand. I'll let my mother know nicely, so please don't worry about a thing."

"I'm sorry . . ."

Sachiko quietly hung up the phone. Kitamura had found this person interesting and had attended to her wants. Aiko turned her thoughts to Kitamura's decision to abandon another dependent after having met Sachiko.

Aiko's partner in marriage was arranged for her by Akagi. He was Akagi's older sister's son, Ryūhei. She had met Ryūhei once before when she was still attending the Catholic girl's school. Once, Aiko called the thin, oval-faced Ryūhei "Little Akagi," to the amusement of Kitamura. When Akagi asked her if she would mind marrying that same "Little Akagi," Aiko was hesitant. She didn't like him, but it wasn't as if she hated him either. However, there was no real alternative. Whichever way she chose, having turned twenty-two Aiko had no choice but to leave the Akagi household. Kitamura had married Sachiko, and Akagi and Hideko had strengthened their trust with the birth of Kazuo. Kazuo would be the one to take over the Akagi house. And if that were the case, there was no other way for her to live except to become a bride and establish a new household of her own. Currently her oldest daughter Kyōko was attending a foreign language institute, on the path to becoming an interpreter. But, before the war, being a career woman was a unique way of life. Aiko decided to marry Ryūhei. Akagi was extremely pleased with the union.

"Aiko, thank you for choosing Ryūhei. I've lived my life thinking that I have wronged you more than anyone else. So I wish for your happiness. By marrying Ryūhei, the bond between the Kitamura house and the Akagi house will become even stronger. If that's the case, I can continue to watch over you. That would make me happy."

Looking up suddenly she saw Akagi, standing tall, tearing up yet again. They were tears she hadn't seen in some time.

Upon receiving notice of their betrothal, a letter came from Kitamura saying: "Since you should come as a bride from the Kitamura house, you must return to Kyoto." She was going to live with her father again for the first time in many years. However, by her father's side was Sachiko.

"Thank you for coming, Aiko. You don't have to call me mother . . . but I guess that's what I am in this situation."

Sachiko covered Aiko's hand firmly with both of hers. They were very hot. No matter where Kitamura went he was accompanied by Sachiko, so needless to say Aiko had met her many times before. On the surface Sachiko appeared beautiful and graceful, but she had plenty of self-confidence and a strong will. She was definitely the Kitamura type.

Aiko was to stay in the Kitamura house for two months. During that time, Sachiko selected the belongings Aiko would take with her when she married. Whatever connections she had, if Sachiko went there, any kimono or accessory store sold her the best merchandise at a discount. Kitamura seemed pleased that Sachiko was tending to Aiko. He wanted both himself and his daughter to be enveloped by her.

One night, with a week before the wedding, Aiko was called into Sachiko's room. Kitamura was out due to a meeting. Sachiko showed Aiko a "visiting" kimono, worn by married women when they leave the house, with a fan pattern on Tyrian purple fabric. Aiko knew it was an irreplaceable kimono, one which was made for Sachiko when she married. Aiko had heard Sachiko speak about how even when she had fallen into

ruin and was forced to sell off her valuable gems and other kimono, she absolutely refused to part with this one.

"Aiko, take this."

Sachiko pushed the kimono in Aiko's direction, still wrapped in carefully folded, thick Japanese paper.

"But this is your most precious kimono, isn't it?"

"It's alright. It's alright because you're Kitamura's one and only precious daughter," Sachiko said slowly. "I have a favor to ask of you. It's okay if you don't want to do it. But, I'm speaking honestly, so please don't laugh."

"What is it?"

"I really love Kitamura. Maybe you're wondering what this old woman is saying, but you're smart so you probably understand. Before you get married, I'm thinking of asking Kitamura to marry me officially. So, would it be alright if we remove you from the family register?"

She spoke in soft tones, but the end was resolute. Aiko was going to marry into the Itō house, leaving the Kitamura household, so the Kitamura heir would disappear. She'd been wondering what they were going to do, but she hadn't expected removal from the family.

"Then, what's going to happen to the Kitamura family?"

"We'll have Kitamura's youngest brother, Junzō, join for a time, and then remove him soon after."

The ending was ambiguous. In other words, Aiko takes steps to remove herself from the family register and Kitamura's youngest brother, Junzō, enters the family temporarily. She wondered if this was the result of Kitamura and Sachiko thinking through the problem. Or just Sachiko.

"I don't mind either way, since . . ."

She didn't say she was being driven out of the family, but it looked as though Sachiko understood, for the tears rolled down her cheeks and she bowed her head low.

"I'm sorry, Aiko. Thank you."

Three days before the wedding of Aiko and Ryūhei, Kitamura officially brought Sachiko into his family. Aiko was to open a new register with Ryūhei so she didn't mind, but she couldn't figure out why Sachiko had gone as far as to say, "I really love Kitamura." By marrying Ryūhei, Aiko had effectively left both the Kitamura and Akagi households.

However, two years before Kitamura died Aiko was shocked at an essay she read in a literary magazine. It said that when Sachiko had become pregnant, although she entreated him to let her have the child, Kitamura ordered her to have an abortion. Furthermore, it read that he said—although she knew it wasn't from the heart—that the reason was because he felt pity for Aiko, who was born first. The real reason was an extremely selfish one: if Sachiko started a family and the house started to feel like a home, it might affect his creations. But Kitamura wrote that knowing Sachiko had been upset over this for a long time, he felt regret, and became inclined to do anything she asked of him. It was a naked confession from her aging father. The two events, Aiko's removal from the family and, after the war, his alliance with Sachiko's other children, were joined together in a common thread. Aiko would no longer inherit the rights to Kitamura's works. More than Sachiko's expectations, there was Kitamura's even stronger will. By abandoning Aiko and giving Sachiko's dependents their own legitimacy, perhaps he was apologizing to Sachiko for the deep hurt he made her bare. Yet again, the writer truthful. It was impossible to be a novelist if you weren't a villain. And there is also the woman who lives beside the villain, accompanying him until the end. That woman's preparation of heart, too, is not lacking. Aiko remembered the warmth of Sachiko's hands enfolding her own.

One morning a few days later, Aiko had a small argument with Ryūhei before he went to work, because he said that he was going to bring home students again that night.

"It was just a few days ago. Try standing in my shoes for a minute. And Naoko is studying for her exams, too. I feel bad for her."

After the students went home, drunken Ryūhei would snore himself to sleep, but Aiko would be busy washing the dishes and cups and cleaning up.

"Sorry, this is the last time," Ryūhei said, without any hint of remorse. "These kids are about to graduate, so I'd like to treat them once."

"How many people do you see coming?"

Aiko asked, handing over a calico scarf. The scarf that Akagi loved to wear was infused with the smell of the tobacco he used to smoke. On the one hand feeling a sense of nostalgia, a feeling of shame also welled up inside her that, after all, she was going to end her life still caught up in the destiny fixed for her by Kitamura and Akagi. Her life was going smoothly: she had three children, and Ryūhei was gentle. Yet, it was times like these when it showed itself—the fear that perhaps her true self, which had been hidden away, was made of the same stuff as Kitamura. Perhaps as Hideko had married the gentle Akagi and her true nature had come forth, had Aiko married anyone but Ryūhei, a nature exactly like Kitamura's may have shown itself. As long as she didn't live the life of a writer, it could become a burden in her daily life, such a troublesome aspect of herself.

Ryūhei said something, but Aiko, lost in thought, didn't hear him. He said it again, his face very similar to Akagi.

"Hey, hey, are you listening? I said five people. You can make a stew like the last time. What, you don't even have to put any meat in it. Boiled tofu'll be enough."

"Buying a lot of tofu is heavy and hard work, too, you know."

Recalling the iciness of cutting the tofu in cold water, a chill ran up her body. That morning was particularly cold.

"I'm going."

Disregarding her parents' words to each other in the doorway, Naoko went out. She left the image of a red scarf.

"And making a lot of rice balls burns the palms of my hands."

Aiko was still scolding him. Why couldn't she just take it easy like her mother? Sometimes when she went to Akagi's house in Yarai there was some guest or another, and Hideko mingled with them, chatting pleasantly. The peaceful expression that was on that face was something she never saw when they lived with Kitamura.

"Please, I've already promised the students."

"Okay. I'll throw something together."

Aiko decided to stop troubling Ryūhei.

"Ah, I owe you one."

Ryūhei did his best imitation of Akagi's voice, then went out. She remembered Akagi and Kitamura miming someone—she didn't know who—playing around, talking in that kind of voice, and Aiko laughed. She went out the front in order to clean the entrance and the garden. There she saw that one letter was in the mailbox. It was to "Mrs. Aiko Itō." On the back was "Kaname Ishinabe." This time he was requesting a draft by letter, was he? After Aiko finished all of the cleaning throughout the house, she opened the letter while warming up under the *kotatsu* in the living room.

Mrs. Aiko Itō,

Thank you for sharing your time with me the other day. I would like to voice my appreciation at your willingness to hear my selfish request, even though I came into your house unannounced.

About our discussion the other day, I am writing this letter in the hope that you have had a change of heart. I can picture your disgust at my persistence. However, editing being my occupation, my skin, too, has gradually become thicker. Please forgive me.

I know very well that being a child of a noted author does not necessarily mean that the person can become a good author themselves. Rather, I have seen the exact opposite case repeatedly. However, I have a strong desire to read what you have written. That is probably because I have a vivid memory of that winter day, when I went all the way to Shingū City and encountered you.

At that time I was with the Wakayama branch office. I went to Shingū because I was told by my superiors that the Akagi family had gone back there and I was to get some kind of story from the wife or daughter. As I was walking toward Mr. Akagi's house, I saw you in front of the bonfire lost in thought. I knew who you were immediately because I had often seen how your face looked the same as Mr. Kitamura in some ways in newspapers and literary magazines. I was excited because I could talk with you. It was not only my ambition, but also because I was interested in you as a person. Think of it as a journalist's intuition. So, even this burn, for me, was wonderful material which showed who this person called Aiko was.

I believe you read "The Treasure" which I gave to you. How was that? Now, after thirty-four years have passed, this is what I want to ask you. I wanted to know what the daughter of an author who lays anything and everything bare thinks about as she lives her life. The truth is, that is the heart of what I want you to write.

You grew up quickly in the Akagi household, married Akagi's nephew, and your connection with the Kitamura household was broken. What lies in your heart? Please write—no, just hearing it would be enough. If you would but tell me, I would not even mind death. For I most likely only have about ten years left anyway, and for the past thirty-four years I have been possessed with what lies in the heart of Aiko Kitamura. The reason I moved from a newspaper company to a publishing company was simply because I wanted to know exactly what a writer is.

Recently I revisited Shingū City. Are you familiar with "The Floating Forest"? From what I know of Akagi, he must have gone to see it, likely accompanied by you and your mother.

Suspended above a bottomless pond, it is a floating body of peat which has formed into a mat. A rare floating island, carrying a forest with a mix of both cold and warm weather vegetation. If a heavy wind blows the island moves, and they say the height changes depending on the amount of water. Would I be overstepping my bounds to say that I have a feeling that you and this "Floating Forest" are similar?

Surely you are an island floating above the bottomless pond of society, created from the peculiar circumstances of Kitamura and Akagi. For that very reason, please let me read it. Please speak what is in your heart.

Sincerely,
Kaname Ishinabe

Aiko reread the letter twice, and then placed it back in the envelope. She had continued her habit of saving letters in a letterbox, but she suddenly had wild thoughts of tearing up Ishinabe's letter and throwing it away. The way she felt was physically impossible to express in words. She detested those who, even though she felt this way, asked her to "simply write it down." The source of her rage was in being likened to "The Floating

Forest." Just as Ishinabe had guessed, Aiko had gone with Akagi to "The Floating Forest" numerous times. You walk along a narrow bridge and cross over to the island. Once you step on the surface of the island, your feet sink and become stuck—something that had scared her. For Aiko, a "floating island" was synonymous with instability and uncertainty. Was Ishinabe saying that she was unstable, uncertain, or somehow unsteady? Aiko was flush with anger, and furiously thought she would write down all of her thoughts and send it off to him. How refreshing it would be to scribble down everything she felt, everything she had tried to forget, without thinking for one minute about whom she might hurt. For a split second she thought, *Is it not these very kinds of extreme emotions that are "The Floating Forest?"* recalling that unusual island. Both cold and warm weather vegetation. If a heavy wind blows the island moves. The height changes depending on the amount of water. There was a "floating forest" in both Kitamura and Akagi. And in herself as well. If that were the case, then perhaps Ishinabe wasn't mistaken in his words. Although it was midwinter, sweat was gushing from Aiko's brow.

"Mother, what're you doing?"

Aiko was startled, because Naoko was standing directly in front of her.

"What's wrong?"

"What do you mean, 'what's wrong?' Today's Saturday. I'm hungry. Don't we have anything?"

Accusation showed in Naoko's eyes. Perhaps she saw her mother as lazy, sitting in the *kotatsu*, making no move to prepare for lunch. Naoko glanced sourly at the letter that'd been thrown haphazardly on top of the *kotatsu*. The childishness in that expression. She was still a child. Suddenly Aiko realized that she would've been the same age as Naoko when she left Kitamura and started to live with Akagi. Aiko felt as if she finally understood what the adults in her life had seen in her.

Toshiyuki Horie

Toshiyuki Horie was born in Gifu Prefecture, studied at Waseda University, lived in Paris for three years during graduate school, and received his doctorate from the University of Tokyo with a major in French Literature. He now teaches Creative Writing at Waseda University. He is a critic and translator of authors including Michel Foucault, Hervé Guibert, Michel Rio, and Jacques Réda. His many awards include the Mishima Prize for *Oparavan,* and the Akutagawa Prize in 2001. In addition, he has received the Kawabata Prize, the Tanizaki Prize, the Kiyama Shohei Prize and the Yomiuri Literary Prize. Since 2008 he has served as a member of the selection committee for the Noma Literary Prize for New Authors.

The Bonfire

Translated by Tyran Grillo

I KNEW, YOU WOULD BRING, ANOTHER ONE BACK, said Yōhei in his hoarse, methodical voice. He spoke to the rhythm of his own pulse. It was, he believed, the best way to express oneself. Though slender and frail, years of long-distance running as a young man had left his heart as fit as that of someone half his age. In his idle daily life, his heart rate dropped far below average, much to the surprise of the family doctor. *Just one beat, of my heart, carries more oxygen, than most people's.* Yōhei maintained perfect posture and spoke with a halting cadence, pausing between every phrase in a way that made people of any age shut up and listen. Kinuyo had just come back from a pleasure trip with some old high school friends to a hot springs resort, where she bought an oil lamp as a souvenir. Yōhei touched the kerosene lamp, honed in fine brass. *Why not just enjoy, the sights and sounds, like everyone else? It would be one thing, if you actually used them, but don't you have enough already? Anyway,*

I've said my piece. Just do, as you wish. He spoke calmly, wondering whether he should even bother anymore.

"But they're not safe to light. The soot would ruin all the work I put into repainting them, and all that paper on top would flare up in an instant."

"But you used to . . ."

"You've always gotten along just fine reading and writing by candle-light, haven't you? It's because you're such an old man now. The past is the past. I had the children's eyesight to think of."

Kinuyo wasn't exaggerating about Yōhei's age. He was twice hers and would be turning 72 this fall. Kinuyo had been collecting kerosene lamps since before they'd become an item. She bemused her friends—who collected everything from triangular souvenir pennants to travel passes—by insisting on buying one to commemorate every trip. It was one of her few passions. Why not, they told her, just go to a camping supply store? If she really wanted to satisfy her collecting bug that badly, she was better off checking with local wholesalers.

Yet these lamps were Kuniyo's postcards. Souvenir shops in the countryside were inundated with dead stock, and department store display models were often blemished in a way that just didn't sit well with her. And so, whenever she did come across a lamp during her travels, she snatched it up at once, not caring that she'd have to lug it all the way back home. While some were gold-plated with perfectly fluted glass, usually they were of cheaper tin, and in no time lamps of many shapes and sizes were hanging in rows from the blackened beams of her living room, ever unlit.

"What about typhoon season? The children would love it, if you used them, during a blackout. It wouldn't have to be, all of them. Only one, or two, would do. It's just a thought."

The children of which Yōhei spoke were not their own, but local grade schoolers who attended his calligraphy classes. That summer marked the twelfth anniversary of their son's passing.

Early in the fall, two years after the death of her father, life on a big farmstead had grown lonely for Kinuyo with only an aging mother to keep her company. She put out a picture ad through a local real estate agency, in search of a single female to rent out the upstairs room. The old farmhouse was located in a ravine just off the main road, where buses ran to the city only twice an hour. The room had a low ceiling, bare crooked beams, and a wooden floor generously estimated at 300 square feet. While it did have some storage space, all kitchen, washing, and bathroom privileges would be shared in the main house. Meals were included, but were a small compensation for the lack of amenities. The young manager who had since then taken over the agency jokingly told her that the rental was thirty years ahead of its time. According to him, quite a number of young people were on the lookout for places just like it nowadays: open storehouse-like rooms with wide jet-black floorboards. Kinuyo didn't quite understand it, but indeed many of the trendier cafes along the main road were made to look that way.

Six months went by without a single prospective tenant. Thinking that "single female" might have been too vague, they were about to change tactics when a new face wandered aimlessly into town. Yōhei had never been too keen on apartments, and gave up on living with his mother one cold Sunday at the end of February. Yōhei asked Mr. Broker—or so he called the real estate agent—if he might have, a vacant room, with hardwood floors. He was in his mid-forties, but spoke in that same gravelly aged voice as he did now. Needless to say, Kinuyo and her mother were surprised when he showed up at their doorstep. They told him they weren't renting out to men. *Yes, I was already, informed of that, but I came anyway.* Kinuyo was still in her twenties at the time and Yōhei couldn't seem to keep his eyes off her. Oblivious to her discomfort, he went on to plead his case. For as long as he could remember, he'd dreamed of opening a calligraphy studio, and had quit his corporate job to do just that. Setting up shop in a respectable and convenient location was far too expensive, and none of the urban properties he'd seen were big enough to accommodate his vision to begin with. He'd also considered renting out local community center assembly halls, but the tables and chairs clashed with the linoleum flooring. That, and the town clerk wouldn't allow him to charge for meetings held in a public facility. Because this little town was out of the way, had public transportation, and was close to the elementary school district, he figured he could drum up enough interest among the locals. He insisted that he wouldn't be living here, but only wanted the space as a classroom for a few hours in the evenings—and all this without ever having seen the room.

Mother and daughter exchanged confused looks. Not only because of his gender, but also because they never would have guessed his reasons for wanting the place. In any case, considering all the trouble he'd gone through, they saw no harm in filling him in on the details. Yōhei offered them some red bean mochi, which the three of them shared over tea. As they chatted, Kinuyo couldn't help but think that his reasons for leaving the corporate world had less to do with his pedagogical aspirations and more to do with the fact that he didn't belong there. Neither was he an outcast, but had the air of one who simply wished to forge his own path in life. Even his age was a mystery to her. Yet something in Kuniyo told her she could depend on him, and to her mother's bewilderment she responded favorably. Having the children around, she said, would liven things up. Her mother, as mothers so often did, seemed to be looking at Yōhei from an altogether different set of criteria, but his slowness of speech had convinced her of his sincerity.

They agreed on a rent and made quick work of the lease. Within ten days, five long narrow folding tables, dozens of flat floor cushions, and a host of attendant supplies—paper, ink, brushes, and bunches of old newspapers used as blotting mats—had transformed the space into a respectable classroom. Once things had settled into the new school year, fliers and word of mouth had brought Yōhei five pupils from different grades. It hardly seemed like enough to get by on, but by summer vacation that number had grown to twenty. The house was never the same.

Students from the lower grades would just be finishing their lessons whenever Kinuyo biked home from work. They never spent much time in the main house, only rushing through it on their way to the stairs in the corner of the living room. Those creaky steps provided them with plenty of amusement, and they delighted in the cacophony they could produce by stomping down them. The constant comings and goings became a regular part of Kinuyo and her mother's lives, making them feel like a much larger family than they actually were. Before long, the children never left without shouting farewell to their new "auntie" and "granny." One day, Kinuyo insisted they call her "big sister" instead. For some reason, this filled her with joy.

Because Kinuyo had been a late child, her mother was now already in her sixties. Even so, at nighttime, when the children grew hungry and restless from their long study sessions, she would forget all about the worrisome pain in her knees and improvise a light meal of rice and vegetables, flavored to their taste. She even prepared rice balls as mid-afternoon snacks, always making extras for Kinuyo and Yōhei. Although she wasn't getting any younger, she seemed to find a forgotten joy in cooking family-sized portions. Kinuyo felt this maternal pride keenly, and even forwent socializing after work to rush home and interact with the children. Word of the meal-inclusive calligraphy classes spread like wildfire among parents, some of whom went so far as to request field trips and longer stays. Once the children completed their lessons to Yōhei's satisfaction, they ate in the downstairs living room beneath a hanging gallery of immaculate lamps. They did their homework at the dinner table and watched TV in the next room. Since her mother couldn't follow their conversations, Kinuyo had to be there no matter what. If anyone had asked, she would have said she had two jobs.

At first, Kinuyo was hesitant to look in on the classroom, but with all the calls she fielded from parents and all the afternoon refreshments to be fixed, it became an integral part of her life. Yōhei had set up his desk right at the top of the stairs, giving him quick access to the only shelves in the room. As a result, the first thing any of his students saw when they came running up was his back, straight as if held up by a wire, and his thin, chicken-like neck. While the children busied themselves with writing up their copybooks, Yōhei's head remained perfectly perpendicular to the floor cushion, like a traditional storyteller who only told the beginning without launching into the tale proper, and from that position he rarely budged, regardless of whether he was talking with his students, correcting their penmanship, or grinding away on his inkstone. It was the same during meals, and when he occasionally did lean to get something with his chopsticks, he looked all the more unnatural. *Let a ghoul grind your ink, and a demon hold your brush.* This was Yōhei's personal motto, his way of saying that, no matter how much power you possessed, when you were here you had to restrain yourself. For him, it was a way of life.

Yet what won Kinuyo over was the smell of learning that began to permeate the classroom. The children used readymade India ink, and only their teacher took the time to grind his own. Seven or eight of his students did one page after another, setting the good ones to dry on the newspaper spread out next to them. During the winter months, when the windows were closed, the scents of dried and wet ink delicately mingled. The combination, though sweet, somehow reminded her of dead animals, and it brought Kinuyo back to a time when the house was overrun with crawling things. When she was little, her grandparents raised silkworms on the second floor. "Kinu" meant silk, hence the name they'd given her. Putting all their love and energy into those precious creatures that granted their livelihood, her grandparents referred to them as their "pride and joy." Because their son and his wife both helped out from home, there was no chance of their granddaughter inheriting the family business. Many of the locals dabbled in sericulture at that time, and with names like Kinuko, Kinue, and of course Kinuyo, it wasn't uncommon for daughters to bear the stamp of their family trade. Even so, Kinuyo was never pleased with the thought that her name had anything to do with the caterpillars squirming around contentedly in their rows of shallow boxes above her head.

When bid to touch them, she found them to be extremely supple yet resilient. It seemed like so long ago, but the moment she set foot inside this classroom she could almost smell the pale, ragged deerskin gloves used in handling the worms and the rough sounds they made. She remembered with striking clarity the grotesque skin of the silkworm and the fine thread spun from within it. She also remembered her friend Kinue, with whom she shared half a name, and what she once told her: *It's because your skin's as smooth as silk, not because you raise silkworms, that you were named "Kinuyo."* Anyone not from her hometown would have thought it an unbefitting association for a girl. Still, the moment she smelled that ink, that eerie memory blended into an undeniable nostalgia.

When she said as much to Yōhei, he told her with his usual gravity: *Ink is made from, the ash of burnt pine, mixed with oil and glue. Glue is actually extracted from, animal bones and skins, so it's only natural, you would feel that way.* Like crude oil, it was the product of a deep, morbid, and relentless chain.

It was then that Kinuyo began to develop an interest in his life. Seeing each other and sharing meals as they did almost every day, her desire to know about the past, and the future, of this enigmatic man mounted steadily, and it was all she could do to stop herself from finding out all she could. When was he born? Where was he raised? What kind of childhood did he have? What had he been like as a young man? At one point, she boldly requested to see his old family album. As they flipped through it in the living room, she plied him with questions and unwavering interest, hardly believing the things she didn't know about him. As he stole an occasional glance at Kinuyo's profile, Yōhei offered such polite explanations to every question, by turns too serious or seemingly evasive, that it made her anxious. Now it was her turn to stare at him.

Kinuyo's feelings were confirmed when, the following year, her mother, who'd had such a fondness the children, died from a sudden heart attack, made all the worse for being at New Year's. A meeting was held in the classroom, where everyone was to calligraph their favorite things and share their New Year's resolutions with the group. Yōhei stood up last, surveyed the room, and held up what he had written: "Silk Road," the name of wildly popular TV show at the time. *My resolution, for this year, is to walk the Silk Road,* he said, eliciting a smattering of laughter. The children merely thought he was joking, not realizing what he was really trying to say. But to Kinuyo (who'd made do with *New Year's First Sunrise*) the message was clear. Her cheeks flushed a little. In that one gesture Yōhei had taken a name she'd always hated, despite the praises it had earned from adults who associated it with a famous actress of the same, and turned it into a sensual metaphor.

That fall, Yōhei took Kinuyo as his wife. She quit her job at the appliance store behind the train station to help out with classes, collected money in advance for meals, and reopened for business. She even got her driver's license and convinced Yōhei to let her attend an eccentric Western cooking school on a hill by a snowy pond, in the hopes of making better food. As a reward for her efforts, the local parents joined her. Her son Yui was born three years later. Kinuyo was 28, Yōhei 50. They doted on their first and only child. Yōhei maintained his rigid posture, even as he held the baby in his arms. The sight of it never failed to make Kinuyo laugh.

Yui loved bicycles. By grade school he was able to ride without training wheels, and often played outside with his neighborhood friends. Only after the fact would Kinuyo find out just how far they ventured. Yui went through wheels like shirt sizes: from twelve-inch to sixteen-inch, and soon to twenty-inch. Recently, during the twelfth anniversary of his death, they had met up with Tomita from the bicycle shop for the first time in years. After the incense offering, Kinuyo listened gratefully to Tomita's stories over drinks. He told the same one at every memorial, always forgetting he'd told it before. *Yui was one of our best customers*, he began. *He always did whatever was asked of him.* He faced Yōhei with the utmost sincerity when he spoke. And who could blame him? There was no better time or place to rehash old memories.

"Family businesses like ours had their fair share of trendy things. One day he came to me wanting to outfit his bike like our latest competition racing model, so he just pulled the grips right off and wrapped the bare handles with cloth tape. I told him the rain would discolor it, but all his friends had red and blue and he wanted black. He spoke with the conviction of an adult. Just like you, Yōhei . . ."

One day, during his second year of grade school, Yui came home bragging that he'd learned how to fix a flat tire from Tomita. Kinuyo was amazed to discover he'd accomplished this through verbal instructions alone, more so when he vowed to save up for a water bottle of his own. He'd even offered Tomita collateral to seal the deal. Where on earth had he learned a word like "collateral?" That was pretty big talk, she said, for someone his age, and chided him for intruding upon Tomita's time. *But Tomita is the nicest person*, he said in all seriousness. *He knows everything about bikes! How's he going to stay in business if we don't buy something from him?* At this, Kinuyo burst into laughter. He was right, in a way. How were local shops supposed to compete with the larger department store chains? Every time she saw Tomita's face, Kinuyo remembered proudly the way Yui made her laugh, and that way he had of looking at her like a puppy being praised by its owner.

Noticing Kinuyo was feeling lonely, Yōhei asked her if they might get a dog or some such pet. She refused, saying she thought of his students as her own children. As a girl, she'd had a Shiba Inu named Kouta who did everything he was told. One summer, she took him to the Ona River and released him into the cold shallow waters. Before letting him go, she kicked the sand at the bottom of the river, afraid it might get in the way of his paws, but Kouta navigated the water with his stumpy little legs as if it were the most natural thing in the world. Everyone said he was okay swimming on his own, and that he could keep his head above water just fine. Kouta reached the riverbank in no time. The expression on his face was almost too human, something of a smile, but now Yui's face was forever superimposed over it. Both had become indistinct, like some distant memory. As she took out a towel to dry him, Kouta evaded it deftly. He shook his shivering body, sneezed once, and began cavorting along the bank. When she went back home and told her parents about it, they said it was his instinct to swim near shore, and that if by some small chance he were to be swept away by the current, there was nothing she could do to save him. What if she jumped in after him and drowned? From now on, she was to take a friend with her. Just in case.

Just in case? Kinuyo muttered to herself. What did that mean, exactly? It had been eating at her mind ever since. Because there was always that small chance of error, even in the most foolproof situations she always made sure to cover her bases, "just in case." *It's as if I've lived my whole life "just in case." People always tell me it's better to be safe than sorry, and I've done my best to follow that rule. God knows I'd have done anything to ensure his safety. If only I'd told him not to go out on that one fatal day, just in case.*

A midnight storm had flooded the streets. The muddy current roared in search of low land, leaving only cars and telephone poles visible. Despite the official flood warning and school cancellation, Yui went out after eating breakfast, took one look at the torrent, and boasted to his mother that the *real* river must be even more exciting. When she wasn't looking, he put on his big rubber boots, slipped on a raincoat, and went out to see the Ona River nearly a quarter of a mile away, hauling his bike all the while. Since the path to the bridge was on an incline, he was able to coast through the last half of the journey. He'd planned on coming back right away after seeing the river, but his boots were weighed down with water and hindered his step. To make matters worse, the sewers were overflowing. The high water pressure lifted a manhole cover, leaving a gaping hole unseen in the sullied waters. Yui got sucked into it and carried along a dark tunnel all the way to the river, where Kinuyo had once let Kouta swim so many years before.

The body appeared a few days after the rain had stopped, in a rocky stretch three miles downstream. Although she'd expected the worst when they found his abandoned bicycle, Kinuyo was now beside herself, wailing frantically: "I want to die, too! Just let me die!" It took Yōhei, who'd put on some brawn since his arrival, to hold her down until she was calm. *You're always so absentminded!* she screamed. *We were all home, but you didn't pay attention!* Yōhei could only stand there and take it. Even after her anger passed, Kinuyo couldn't bear the sight of his students, brimming with life. She felt utterly useless, wondering why these children were unharmed and hers was gone. Hardest of all was that Yōhei never forgave himself. Even when he reached his sixties, by which time one would think he might have come to terms, his regret grew all the more.

On the surface, nothing had changed in him. He didn't spring back, but neither did he age. He simply focused on his breathing and swept his brush across the paper, committing himself fully to teaching, for which his lung capacity and concentration were vital. During his off time, he continued to show his face at dinner parties and let his wife take small pleasure trips with old friends. That was when the lamps began to multiply. Still, Kinuyo never lit them. No matter how much Yōhei teased her about it, she never went near a match.

"I knew, you would bring, another one back." Yōhei's comment prompted a memory from the funeral. She heard Tomita's voice. *I need to tell you something, but don't be angry with me,* he said. She felt his eyes peering into her. *Long after Yui bought his last bicycle, he removed the front wheel generator. He wanted one of those clip-on lights—like a lantern, only battery operated. This was before halogen lights were all the rage, so I suggested attaching it to the handle shaft and switching it on and off manually. The light wasn't as strong, but at least he could pedal more easily uphill at night due to the lack of wheel resistance. And as long as he had a battery, he would have a steady light no matter what the speed. The only problem was they were heavy and broke easily, so I told him to stick with the generator. If only I'd just put it on for him, he would have had light even as he was pulling his bike through the rainstorm. Someone surely would have spotted him and sent him home . . .*

As she listened, Kinuyo had stared at the kerosene lamps hanging from the rafters, possessed by a sudden urge to give him one. And when she offered it, she felt a fresh wave of grief pass over her. Tomita politely, and tearfully, refused. Yōhei only muttered, *Is that so? It can't be. Is that so?* He didn't even cry. As far as Kinuyo knew, the only time Yōhei ever had cried was during the futile search for his missing son. Even during the funeral, and every memorial service thereafter, he only lifted his chin slightly, ever the stoic picture. His back was as straight as it had been on the first day they'd met. *The children would love it, if you used them, during a blackout. It wouldn't have to be, all of them. Only one, or two, would do. It's just a thought.* The moment she heard those words, she responded in an unexpectedly clear tone:

"Let's do it, then. Right now."

"But wait, we don't have, anything to light them with."

"How about we do it in the garden?"

"You are really, serious about this? Then why don't we wait, until the children come, tomorrow?"

"No, I'd rather we did it now. Help me, will you?"

Kinuyo quickly changed her clothes, then hauled out a stepladder and a red kerosene tank from the shed. Unscrewing the burners one by one, she instructed Yōhei to pour in the kerosene. By the time she had them all lined up in the garden, there were over forty in all.

"We'll light them all and watch from Mount Gongen."

"This isn't like you, at all. What if, there's a fire?"

"There's nothing flammable in the garden. If things get out of hand, we'll just come running back down. What did they used to call those people who sounded alarms on land?"

After a long silence, Yōhei agreed, but couldn't bring himself to look her in the eye. *Even if we, climb the mountain,* he muttered, *we'll get a chill, without a jacket.*

"Don't worry. The climb will warm you up."

"Well . . . if you say so . . . but I am, a little cold."

Surprised, Kinuyo stared fixedly at Yōhei's profile. In the decade she'd known him, he'd never once gotten sick. Only now did she notice that his hair was falling out like a well-worn calligraphy brush, and that his head was reeling. *What is it, are you okay?* she said. As Kinuyo put her palm on his small prune of a forehead, she could have sworn the lamps were already glowing. Sweat seeped through his pores like diluted ink.

Ira Ishida

Ishida was born in Kyoto. He studied economics and worked in advertising before turning to writing. He graduated from Seika University in 1983 and won the Naoki Prize in 2003 for *4TEEN*. Ira Ishida writes about various topics, but he is famous for writing about Japan's underground teenagers and slum dwellers.

Ikebukuro West Gate Park, usually referred to by its initials, *IWGP,* is a series of urban novels. It was adapted into a very successful TV series directed by Tsutsumi Yukihiko, and then a manga which has been published to worldwide acclaim. *IWGP* explores topics relevant in Japan today such as drug dealers, drug addicts, computer hackers, gangsters and Yakuzas, NEETs, prostitution, and "compensated dating" for underage girls. Ishida investigates and clearly explains the dark side of Japan's younger generation.

Ikebukuro West Gate Park

Translated by Jonathan W. Lawless

THERE IS ONE *PURIKURA* STUCK TO THE BACK SIDE of my PHS. A faded sticker with the five members of my team bursting from a tight frame. The picture on the frame is of a green jungle. A bunch of indecent monkeys are swinging around after bananas. It's no different from the real world. In the *purikura* we're pressed together cheek to cheek, and with our faces lined up in a row we look like we've just heard the funniest joke ever. Naturally, Hikaru and Rika are there, too. I can't remember what we thought was so funny. Some people ask me how long I plan on keeping that sticker there. Every time I make up some answer like, "It's a memory of summer," or, "It's the glory of the past." But the truth is, I'm not really sure why I leave it there either.

My name is Makoto Majima. Last year I graduated from the local technical high school here in Ikebukuro. Very impressive. At my school, by the time graduation rolls around about a third of the students have dropped out. A certain Youth Division officer I know, Yoshioka, once told me that my school was a farm for *yakuza*. Stealing, drugs, fighting. Any punk with a strong arm was immediately scouted from above. There were even some among them that were too dangerous to become *yakuza*. Yamai for example. I just couldn't get away from him since elementary school. He was huge, square, got angry easily, and for some reason the hair on his head was hard as a rock. Try to imagine a hundred and eighty-five-centimeter-tall refrigerator with about ten thousand golden wires sticking straight up off the top. And don't forget the chain, the kind usually reserved for vicious dogs, that connects the piercings in his ear and nose. As far as I know, his fight record is at four hundred ninety-nine wins, one loss, out of five hundred fights. I'll tell you all about that one loss later.

The incident that gave him his nickname was in the summer of our second year of junior high. Yamai and some other member of our class made some stupid bet. Whether or not he could beat the Doberman that we always saw at the General Ward Gymnasium outside the station's east gate. Yamai said that he could beat it, someone said he couldn't, and then we all bet our snack money one way or the other. The next Saturday Yamai and a crowd of other people filtered out of the gate of the junior high school and we all made our way to the gym. The dog was there. The old man who owned the dog was sitting far across the open space in front of the gym. The Doberman was wandering around, sniffing the stink under the bench. Yamai had a chunk of lean beef in his left hand and he held it out for the dog. The dog wagged its tail in delight and came running toward him. Yamai sunk his favorite weapon deep into his right hand. A wooden pole with a fifteen centimeter nail shoved through it. T-shaped, like a corkscrew for cheap wine. I had seen him sharpen the point of the weapon during shop class. Sparks flying from the tip of a fifteen centimeter nail. When the Doberman jumped for the meat, mouth drooling, Yamai pulled the meat back, and thrust his right hand straight out. Fifteen centimeters of nail being absorbed by the dog's narrow forehead. Watching from way back, I couldn't even hear the sound. Yamai scooped it up once in a swinging motion, then yanked the spike out. The dog fell at his feet. Almost no blood spilled from the dog's forehead. The Doberman blew foam from its mouth and its whole body was convulsing. I heard someone throw up. We all disappeared from the place fast.

Starting the following Monday, his nickname became "Doberman-killer Yamai."

Since graduating high school I haven't done anything. I couldn't get a proper job, and I didn't feel like it either. Part-time jobs are boring and I can't motivate myself. When I run out of money, I help out at the fruit shop my mom runs to get some pocket change.

When I say fruit shop, I'm not talking about the tidy little fruit parlors like the ones in Ginza. Our store is in the Ikebukuro West Old Shopping District. People from around here would understand just from that. The street is a string of fashion massage parlors, adult video stores, and barbecue restaurants. It's my mom that watches over the street stall my old man left behind when he died, a store with nothing very special about it. Displayed at the front of the shop are melons or watermelons, new loquats or peaches or cherries—only the more expensive things are on display there. So to nab drunks whose purse strings have loosened a bit, the store is open until the last train has gone; there's sure to be at least one like it around any other station, that kind of shop. Then there's my house. It's only five minutes on foot to West Gate Park from the shop. Half of that is waiting for the streetlight.

Last summer, whenever I had some spare change or one of my friends had some cash, we spent most of our time on a bench in Ikebukuro West Gate Park. Just sitting there idly, waiting for something to happen. There's nothing for us to do today, and no plans for tomorrow either. The same monotonous twenty-four hours, over and over. But even with that kind of day-to-day life it's possible to make friends.

Around that time my best friend was Masa. Masa is short for Masahiro Mori. A genius who by some miracle managed to slide his way into the worst of colleges after graduating from the same high school as me. But he hardly ever got near the campus, and always hung out with me at West Gate Park. He said that when he was with me he had good luck picking up girls. He bared his chest openly, black from the tanning salon, and in his left ear he had three piercings. On a rainy day last June, we were in the Marui near the west gate. Cover from the rain. When you have no money, rainy days are always trouble. There's no place to go. Since neither of us had a cent, we just walked around the inside of the store aimlessly, unable to buy anything. Bored, we went to check out the underground Virgin Megastore's bookstore, and there we saw something interesting. Photographic collections, art books—the corner of the store where they keep expensive things. A short guy wearing glasses, a little on the skinny side, was stuffing his shoulder bag with an oversized book. The little guy, acting all nonchalant, made it safely past the register with book in hand. He went up the escalator to the first floor and left from Marui's main entrance. We followed after the little squirt. We crossed the intersection and caught up with him in the open area in front of the Tokyo Metropolitan Art Space building, where we called out to the runt from behind. He leapt about a meter into the air. Nice. I wonder how much he's worth? The three of us went into a nearby coffee shop.

In the end, we didn't make a cent. We only got free iced coffees out of it. The little guy's name was Shunji Mizuno. He told us that the book he stole was a collection of artwork by some French animator. At first Shun hardly said anything, but at some point he started speaking fast and then we couldn't make him stop. He came to Tokyo from the countryside, and had been going to design school for three months. He talked with almost no one. He had no friends. Only idiots at the school. Class was boring.

Even when talking fast, there was no emotion in his eyes. A little dangerous. Masa and I made eye contact. This was going nowhere. Even if we tried to rob him there was nothing to gain. Shun took a sketchbook from his bag and showed us some illustrations he had drawn himself. Really good. But what good is that? It's just a picture, nothing more. We left the shop and went our separate ways.

The next day Masa and I were sitting on a bench in West Gate Park when Shun came over and sat down next to us without saying a word. He pulled out his sketchbook and started drawing illustrations. The next day was the same. And so Shun became our friend.

The true face of Ikebukuro West Gate Park (when we're trying to be cool we always call it "West Gate Park" in English) shows itself in the middle of the night on weekends. The circular area around the fountain becomes a hook-up coliseum. The girls sit on the benches and the boys circle around and talk to them all in turn. If they hit it off, they leave. Bars, karaoke, and love hotels are all right there next to the park. Several huge CD players the size of dressers are set up in front of the fountain, and the dancer teams practice their choreography in time with the bass, the kind that reverberates in your stomach. On the other side of the fountain the singers sit on the ground holding onto their guitars and sing/ shout something. After the last bus of the day has left, gang members from Saitama line their cars up in the terminal and cruise around slowly, coaxing girls over from behind smoked-glass windows. Hey, you wanna get with us? The Tokyo Metropolitan Art Space, which is parallel with the park, closes its shutters at night, but the area in front of it is a play-ground for style. The boarder and BMX teams compete with each other, performing acrobatics on their skateboards and mountain bikes. Each team has their own invisible territory in West Gate Park and the warriors among the G-boys prowl the borders like sharks searching for the smell of blood. The public restroom in the corner of the park is a market. All night long they're all buying and selling stuff. Every five minutes a seller goes into the bathroom and a schoolgirl wearing loose socks disappears into the men's bathroom with him.

And every time Saturday came around, as if immersing ourselves in boiling water, we spent the whole night killing time at West Gate Park.

Sometimes we picked up girls, and sometimes we were picked up. We picked fights and took them up. But usually nothing happened at night, and while we were waiting for something to happen, the sky in the east would become clear, the summer night would brighten, and the first train of the day would start to move. Even so, we went to "West Gate Park."

Because there was nothing else to do.

It was just such a night when we met Hikaru and Rika, too. That particular night we had money—rare for us—and Masa's attempts to get girls were also coming up with nothing—rare in itself. It looked like the sun was going to come up at any minute, so Masa started to panic and talk to girls one after another. If they looked up for it, that was good enough. I gazed absently at the water in the fountain as it sprang up into the air, then came tumbling down. Shun was under a streetlamp drawing in his sketchbook as always. That's when four legs appeared in front of us. Both of them in the popular white leather sandals. The ones with fifteen centimeter heels. One pair of legs were perfectly shaped, white and naturally long. The other pair were short, but well-tanned, and with plenty of flesh.

"Watcha doin'?" the black one asked us after taking a peek at Shun's sketchbook. A slip dress the color of pearl. Big eyes and a face that looked a little bit like a monkey. Her hair was cut short, and she was short and cute. Maybe sixteen-ish?

"Oh my god, like, that's so good!" Why do young girls always have such loud voices? Their laughter is like a siren.

"Tone it down," I said without thinking, and then the white one responded, "What's wrong with that? We're just looking at his picture."

The white one was tall, with a teeny black midriff-baring mini-T and miniskirt. Her breasts were huge, and they were thrust up at an angle. She looked like one of the pin-up girls from *Young Magazine*. When I met her eyes they shone a bright brown. What is she, only half-Japanese?

"Hey hey, relax you two. Shun, draw a picture of these two lovely ladies in your notebook there. Seeing as how your drawings aren't useful any other time than this," said Masa, having come back quickly once he realized that we were talking with girls. It looked like he was interested in them. Especially the white one. He was doing his best to put the moves on her. After a while, Shun finished the drawing. Toward the bottom of the page the black girl was on the pavement of West Gate Park. With cat ears and a tail. Her legs were flung out to the sides in a sexy, inviting pose and she had a fawning slight smile on her lips. The other girl was at the top of the picture. Pure white, she had large angel wings and was floating in the air. A far-away gaze and a sad profile. The first time I noticed it was when I saw Shun's illustration. The fact that the white girl was extremely beautiful. The girls loved the picture. After that the five of us went to a nearby karaoke box. Because it was dawn, and our stomachs were empty. And we sang many of the same kind of songs. The tall, white girl introduced herself as Hikariko Shibuzawa, and the short, black girl introduced herself as Rika Nakamura. Hikaru told us, "Never call me by my real name, Hikariko, okay?" I thought it was a little strange, but then again, I've had an ugly girl from Saitama tell me to call her Jennifer before. Whatever. It wasn't until much later that I learned the reason why Hikaru hated her name so much.

After it was already too late.

From then on, Hikaru and Rika began coming to "West Gate Park" every day. The upper-class high school they both went to was also in summer vacation. The five of us ended up always hanging out and having fun together. In the beginning, every time we met, Hikaru would always come with a present for somebody. The first time was German-made watercolor colored pencils for Shun, as thanks for the drawing the other day. Sixty-four colors neatly arranged in a wooden box, dazzling. Until then I had never even seen such a thing. Next, she gave Masa sapphire earrings. The holdings were twenty-two karats. She said they were worthless stones she bought from her friend, a jeweler's daughter. Last was me. Nike Air Jordan's. The '95 Michael Jordan model. I thought they'd suit you Mako. After all, I want the head of our team to be cool, right? Don't worry, I have a relative that runs an imported goods sports shop, so I got them cheap. Angelic smile. I took them reluctantly.

Later I called Rika over and asked her.

"Is Hikaru always like this?"

"Yea, most of the time. If it's a person she likes."

"Is her family rich?"

"Seems so, rumor has it her family's been rich for generations."

"What does her father do?"

"I heard he's an important person in the Ministry of Finance."

The next day I called up just Hikaru on my PHS. Our meeting place was the east gate's P' PARCO. I sat on the shrubs near the entrance and waited. In the small sky above Ikebukuro I could see thunderheads. Hikaru came right at the agreed time. A white, sleeveless one-piece dress with white, high boots. She looked like Amuro given a little more height, made a little whiter, and with a little extra glamour. That just about covers it. I could feel the gazes of all the men in the vicinity tracing the line of Hikaru's body from top to bottom. She sat down next to me and the men all suddenly looked aside.

"This is the first time I've seen you when it's just the two of us, Mako."

"True."

"You have something to talk to me about, right? It's hot here, so let's go to a café or something. I'll pay for it."

"No, that's okay. I was the one who called you, so I'll pay."

We went to a nearby McDonald's. Two iced coffees. We got seats near the window on the second floor. From the window we could see the waves of people in front of Ikebukuro Station.

"So, what did you want to tell me?"

"It's about the presents."

A strange expression. Hikaru was silent.

"You gave presents to everyone, right? So that's it with the presents. You understand?"

"What, I don't get it."

Suddenly she pouted. Her eyes glistened as she gave me an upward glance. What, is she going to cry?

"See, Hikaru, when a person receives something they have to give something back in return. And if a person always just gets things, they start to expect it."

"What's wrong with that? So I'll just keep giving presents."

Big teardrops spilled from the corners of her eyes. The man sitting next to our table glared at me. I glared back at him. He lowered his gaze.

"Listen, Hikaru, we're not hosts. Even if a girl doesn't spend money on us, if we like her, then we'll hang out together. So, no more presents. Got it?"

Hikaru's expression suddenly brightened and she smiled through her tears. Intense girl.

"Hey, could you say that last part again?"

"So, no more pres—"

"Not that part, what you said before that."

There was nothing I could do so I repeated myself.

"If we like her, then we'll hang out together. So stop crying."

A smile like the summer sky after a rainstorm returned to her face.

We left Mickey D's. While waiting for the light to change at the diagonal crossing in front of the station, Hikaru, standing at my side, all the while looking straight down, said, "Mako? Even if it's somebody's birthday, or something special happens, or something like that, I still can't give anyone a present?"

"Hmm . . . Oh well. I guess in those cases it'd be okay."

When the light turned green Hikaru suddenly ran forward. Both arms flung outward, posed like an airplane. Dodging through the crowd, she whirled about right and left. I watched her in surprise. When she reached the far side of the street she turned back to me and, making a megaphone with her hands, shouted.

"You're the best, Mako! Let's get together again tomorrow!"

Going to karaoke, clubs, or arcades, fighting, stealing CDs or clothes, calling random international phone numbers on stolen cell phones, calling out and laughing at men using telephone club dating services.

Our fun was senseless. Why did we think it was so fun at the time? It still seems a little strange to me. But good times never last.

In the first week of August, that infamous series of attempted strangulations of high school girls took place. The magazines and TV called it the Ikebukuro Strangler (using the word "Strangler" in English) or something like that and it was a really popular story, so you probably all still remember it. The first victim was a second year student from a Tokyo metropolitan high school. She was found unconscious at the love hotel "Espers" in Ikebukuro's second block. The girl was forced to drink some kind of drug, was choked with a rope, then raped. The next incident was about two weeks later, a girl who had just quit high school, found in the same way, unconscious, at the east gate hotel "2200" on the other side of the station. Both of them regained consciousness soon after reaching the hospital, but they both adamantly refused to say anything about the perpetrator. It seems they were badly threatened by the Strangler. The streets of Ikebukuro were flowing with uniformed patrols and ugly street clothes. Quite the nuisance for us.

Meanwhile, some weekly magazine did an investigation into the school girls' behavior and exposed what they found. The title was "The Pitfalls of Schoolgirl Prostitution." Their classmates talked about rumors of them selling themselves, people who knew them from around town disclosed the girls' prices, and neighborhood housewives happily discussed the girls' broken homes. The list of brand-name goods the two bought with the money they had saved from hooking was that issue's top feature. After that it appeared that any form of mass communication was free to write whatever they wanted, and thus began the horrendous slander. For a special fee they would let their sadistic clients choke them. The reasonable price for necrophilia play. On television S&M commentators explained about S&M play that could be practiced safely in the home.

Around the time the Strangler was causing a stir, Rika and Hikaru also started acting weird. Although they had been arguing about something, as soon as we got there suddenly they pretended to be the best of friends or they left the karaoke box in the middle of the night and never came back. I thought it was something between girls so I just left it alone.

One Sunday afternoon the four of us, minus Hikaru, gathered together as always at a bench in West Gate Park. Hikaru was at a classical concert at the Art Space that she had promised to go to with her father several months earlier. We were going to meet up with her later.

Masa painstakingly checked his hairstyle and Shun quietly drew in his sketchbook. Just like any other Sunday. After fixing her make-up Rika came over to where I was sitting.

"Hey Mako, I need to talk to you about something . . ."

"Sure, what's up?"

"Here's kinda . . ."

"What, something you can only talk about with Makoto?" cut in Masa from the side.

"That's right. It's important, so I won't let you in on it."

"Fine, fine, whatever. Everyone's always like 'Mako! Mako!' I'm just about sick of it."

Shun apparently saw something and stood up, waving his hand.

"Hey! Over here! Over here!"

We could make out Hikaru in the middle of the long line of people coming down the escalator from the Tokyo Metropolitan Art Space building. A deep blue bare-shouldered dress. The kind of thing you'd wear to a party after a wedding. It sparkled like the sapphire piercing in Masa's ear. Hikaru was beautiful with her hair up, but something was strange about her. She was walking stilted, like a puppet. Hikaru cut her way unsteadily through the throng of dressed-up people in front of the theater and came straight toward us. Without a word, she squatted down in front of the bench. She looked pale. The blood had left her bare shoulders, leaving them a bluish gray. Hikaru threw up a little right there. The clear spittle traced lines on the pavement.

"Hikaru, you okay?"

We sat Hikaru down on the bench. Rika rubbed her back.

"Hey Shun, go buy some warm coffee for her."

"What's wrong? Are you okay, Hikaru?" Rika looked helpless.

Hikaru was breathing raggedly, but after a while she spoke.

"I'm okay now. During the encore, they played a song I hate. It made me feel sick."

"What song was it?" Shun asked as he handed over a paper cup filled with coffee.

"Thanks. Tchaikovsky's *Serenade for Strings.*"

It was then that I realized Hikaru was truly born among the elite. She lived in a completely different world.

"Ah! Hikaru's father!"

We all turned to look at what Rika was looking at. There stood a tall man. A dark suit with a silver tie. Frameless glasses. His hair was half white. I thought he looked like a newscaster from some show. The area around his eyes looked strikingly like Hikaru. Her father nodded to us with his chin, then disappeared in the direction of Theater Street.

Once Hikaru had calmed down I asked Rika, "Oh, Rika, what'd you wanna talk to me about?"

"Ah, well, Hikaru doesn't seem to be doing so well, so let's just talk next time."

"Is that alright?"

"Yea, it's fine, it's fine," Rika said, laughing. But it wasn't fine. I remember that smile clearly. I should have forced her to tell me then. Because after that, what she wanted to tell me was lost forever.

One night the following week as I was watching over the store, my PHS rang.

"Hello, Makoto? This is Masa. Something really bad has happened—" Masa's voice cut out partway, then there was the sound of people noisily struggling with each other for the phone.

"Hey, this is Yoshioka. This evening the body of Rika Nakamura was found. Can you come to the Ikebukuro Police Station immediately? I need to ask you some things."

"Alright, I'll be there in a minute."

"By the way, what were you doing all day today?"

"I was watching the store all day. Am I a suspect?"

"No, but I just thought 'what if.'" That's right. That "what if" just happened to Rika. Anything is possible.

"And don't go telling anybody about this incident."

"Got it. Be there in five."

"I'll be waiting."

I hung up the phone. I went up to the second floor and called out to my mom who was watching TV. I'm going out for a bit. As I jumped down the stairs my mom's voice followed after me. Are you staying out all night tonight, too? On the news show a female reporter was walking fearfully about the love hotel area around Ikebukuro's west gate. The area directly behind our house.

The Ikebukuro Police Station is behind the Art Space, next to the Hotel Metropolitan. I ran through the streets of Ikebukuro's night, filled with drunks and couples. Ignoring the light, I ran straight across the main road, three lanes going each way. I didn't think about Rika. This was the first time I had run since gym class. Still, the muscles in my legs moved with ease. The night wind caressed the front of my body.

Upon reaching the Ikebukuro Police Station I ran up the stairs to the side of the entrance. I gave them Yoshioka's name at the reception desk for the Youth Division. That night the floor was packed. Most likely it was because of the incident with Rika. Toward the back, Yoshioka stood up from behind a desk near the window and raised his hand to me. Next to the desk was a folding chair, and sitting in it was Masa. When his eyes met mine it looked like he was about to cry.

Yoshioka walked up to me slowly. He didn't take his eyes off me.

"Hey, sorry to spring this on you so suddenly, Makoto."

"Whatever. What happened to Rika?"

"Come with me."

Yoshioka started walking ahead of me. He was short. Thin, greasy hair and tanned skin. Dandruff covered the shoulders of his cheap-looking suit. I followed him silently. A row of interrogation room doors was in one corner of the same floor and I was directed into the farthest room in the back. The interrogation room that the G-boys call "Big Booth." You can't see the inside of Big Booth unless you do something pretty bad. That's what they said. I sat down across the desk from Yoshioka, the wall in front of me being a mirror from waist-up.

"Starting right now everything you say will be recorded as evidence. Remember as best you can and tell it to me straight, got it, Makoto?"

It wasn't his normal voice. He wasn't talking to me, but to someone behind the mirror. He asked me everything I did all day. When did you wake up in the morning? What did you have for lunch? What did you watch on TV while you were eating lunch? What did Tamori do on TV? From when to when were you watching the store? Did anybody you know come to the store? How many melons did you sell today? I told him honestly as much as I could remember. The Yoshioka that night wasn't the Yoshioka I knew. It had been five years since, at thirteen, I crushed in a classmate's cheekbone. I was used to Yoshioka's interrogations. He knew that I was used to them, too. The guys behind the mirror didn't know that.

"When was the last time you met Rika Nakamura?"

"This past Sunday."

"Did you notice anything different about her?"

"No, nothing." I'm not sure why, but I left out the part about Rika wanting to talk to me about something. That was like stepping on a landmine.

"Isn't it true that Rika said she had something in particular to discuss with only you?"

"Yea, now that you mention it, she did." Masa. Oh well. I said that Hikaru was feeling sick so I never got a chance to hear it. It was as if Yoshioka didn't believe me. For almost the next hour, our conversation danced around what Rika wanted to say. I repeated the same story forty or fifty times. When he saw that my story didn't change no matter how many times I repeated myself, Yoshioka got up from his chair and left the room. Two hours had passed since the interrogation started. Yoshioka came back into the room soon.

"I guess that's all. You can go."

"Wait a second. I answered everything you asked me. But I still haven't heard anything about Rika. You could do your part and tell me a little, too."

Yoshioka made a sour face. He grabbed me by the front of my shirt and yelled, "You little shit! Don't let yourself get carried away! This is murder! Like I'd tell anything to a punk like you!"

His spit and cigarette-smelling breath flew into my face. Suddenly he lowered his voice so only I could hear him.

"Idiot, are you trying to spoil my act? Play along for a little longer. I'll tell you later."

"I'm really sorry, detective," I said in the loudest voice I could manage.

"I guess I'll let it slide. Wait for me at my desk."

When I left Big Booth, Yoshioka patted me on the shoulder. It was a little stronger than usual, but I apologized, saying I'm sorry one more time in a loud voice.

When I got to Yoshioka's desk, Masa was already gone. It was past midnight and people were sparse. Yoshioka came about fifteen minutes later.

"Makoto, what am I going to do with you? Did you want to hear the whole story right there in front of headquarters' entire investigation team? Since this case is going to be plastered all over tomorrow's paper, they're handling it with the utmost secrecy, friggin' amateur."

"I'm really sorry, detective," I said again in a loud voice.

Yoshioka gave a wry smile.

"Well, I guess as long as you keep up that attitude. I'll bet you're hungry. I'll buy you ramen or something. Come on."

We left the police station and went to a Hakata ramen shop behind West Gate Park. Even after the last train the shop was still full of people. Greasy tables, greasy chairs, greasy air. We ordered ramen, dumplings, and beer. There were two cups.

"Want a drink?" he asked me. I shook my head and he filled his own cup and drank it down in one gulp.

"Instead, tell me about Rika."

"Just hold your horses."

Yoshioka pulled out a black notebook and, flipping the cover up so I couldn't see in it, he began reading: "Today, 6:20 PM, Ikebukuro's second block area, the hotel 'Knocking On Heaven's Door'—how come these sex hotels always use that kind of swanky name recently?—room number 602, Rika Nakamura of Kawaguchi City, Saitama Prefecture, sixteen, was found dead. She was discovered by a part-time cleaning lady at the hotel. The exact details will have to wait for the official autopsy, but the cause of death was most likely strangulation. Marks from what looked like a rope were left on her neck. The police are currently making every effort to find the whereabouts of the young man Rika Nakamura went into the hotel with at 4:03 PM."

The ramen arrived. Yoshioka slurped the cloudy white soup as if it were tasty. I broke my chopsticks apart, but I had absolutely no appetite and couldn't eat a single bite.

"So, the murderer was the Strangler?"

"We don't know that, but there is a fairly good chance."

"There's no video or anything?"

"If we could catch criminals easily with cameras, we'd have them plastered all over the city. It'd sure make our job easier. But the Strangler makes sure that he himself is in the camera's blind spot when he passes through the front of the hotel. I can't help thinking about how many times he must have gone over all these dirty hotels. He knows the love hotels in Ikebukuro and he thinks fast."

I watched Yoshioka stuff ramen and dumplings into his stomach. It was around then that I remembered Rika's smile. The inviting pose.

"Well, don't think too hard about it. But if you happen to remember anything else, contact me anytime. You have my cell phone number, right?"

"Yeah."

Yoshioka drank what was left of the last glass of beer.

"I have to go spend the rest of the night writing the report. Unbelievable."

I was staring hard at the empty cup in front of me.

"Oh, and Makoto, don't you guys even think about doing something on your own. This pervert is the police's prey."

The next day the four of us gathered together at the bench in West Gate Park. To go to Rika's funeral. We went by JR from Ikebukuro to Kawaguchi. From the station at Kawaguchi we took a taxi. This was the first time for any of us to go to Rika's house. As the taxi approached her house we started seeing people in black clothes. The area was made up of laid-back subdivided houses. We got out of the taxi at the entrance to a dead end street. Both sides of the street were lined with white matchbox houses. Every house had the same kind of red flower. But the front of Rika's house was jammed with police, TV cameras, and reporters. The people in mourning dress were waiting, turning their faces away from the spotlights. We went to the end of the line. It was my first funeral. I was too small when my dad died, so I don't remember a thing. Next to the front door we wrote our names and handed over our condolence money, and copying the actions of the people in front of us, we were back outside again before we knew it. It was all too fast. All I could remember was Rika's father, mother, and little sister huddled together, looking small. In just one night they had black circles under their eyes and their faces looked as if they had lost weight. The kind of faces found on people whose shock was so great that they didn't even cry. And the photograph of Rika (which she never would have picked out for herself), surrounded floor to ceiling in white flowers. It might have been a picture from when she first entered high school. She was smiling innocently, her white face yet to be darkened at the tanning salon. What was Rika like at home? I couldn't even imagine.

The summer afternoon sun was blinding when we got outside. We left Rika's house among the crying from her classmates. Hikaru cried silently while walking. We stopped a taxi and took it back to Kawaguchi Station. As we came up the overpass, the windows of the air-conditioned taxi were filled with thunderheads. The upper parts shone white where the sun was hitting them. Rika would never see storm clouds again. One question kept spinning around and around in my head.

What can I do for Rika . . . what can I do for Rika . . . what can I do for Rika . . .

We split up at Kawaguchi Station in front of the ticket gate. All of us had little to say. Masa and Shun passed through the gate and went down to the platform. Hikaru was dragging. I wanted to be alone.

"You too, go on."

"I have something I want to talk about though . . ."

"I don't want to hear it."

"Even if it's about Rika?"

I couldn't say no if it was about Rika. Hikaru and I went to a family restaurant near the station. We sat in hard vinyl chairs. Hikaru said: "At some point it will probably come out on TV or in some magazine, so I'll tell you first, okay. You see . . . Rika . . . sometimes she had a kinda part-time job. I want Masa and Shun to hear about it from you, Mako, 'k?"

"You mean hooking?"

"But she said she didn't go all the way. She found customers using like telephone clubs and stuff and went to karaoke or couples cafes with them, but she said she only went as far as second base."

"But this time . . ."

"Maybe she needed the money, so she went all the way."

The cup of iced coffee that I hadn't touched was heavy with sweat.

"Hikaru, did you hear about anything that was bothering Rika? She told me last Sunday that she had something to talk to me about, but that's where it stopped."

"Maybe it was about . . ." Hikaru furrowed her eyebrows.

"It's okay, tell me."

"Well, it might sound a little strange, but Rika said she had this customer who was really loose with his money. She called him 'sensei.' Because she said she was scared, I walked with her to the place they were going to meet sometimes."

"Do you remember his face?"

"Yes."

I called Shun on my PHS. He was still in Ikebukuro. I told him to bring his sketchbook and pencils and come back to Kawaguchi.

I had an idea of something I could do for Rika.

Shun said that this was the first time he'd ever drawn a likeness by description only. I asked Hikaru about the sensei's features, and Shun drew a little, then showed it to Hikaru to confirm. The whole process moved along a little bit at a time. At some point it had become night outside the windows of the family restaurant. It took three hours to somehow finish a picture that Hikaru was satisfied with. In the drawing was a man with his hair parted down the middle. A spoiled rich boy. Sharp-jawed, slim and handsome. I thought he probably got good grades in school.

"Sorry to ask this, Shun, but could you make about a hundred copies of this at the convenience store over there?"

As Shun dashed out of the family restaurant, I called up the GK on my PHS.

GK doesn't stand for goalkeeper. It means the G-boys' king. His name is Takashi Yasufuji. Takashi is the head that binds all the gang boys in Ikebukuro together, and the king of all the teams. How did he do it, you ask? With fist and brain. The two most famous kids at the high school I went to were "Doberman-killer Yamai" and "Carl Yasufuji." Carl is Carl Lewis's Carl. Yamai was strong because he was huge, physically strong, and tough. Takashi was strong because he was lithe, fast, and precise. He was about 175 centimeters tall. He was about ten centimeters shorter than Yamai, and he was a lightweight. But his arms and legs were knit like a tightly wound wire rope. I once saw Takashi catch a glass with the sleeve of his jacket and knock it from the table at a club in Ikebukuro. He noticed it while he was talking about something with one of his friends and instantly his hand was there under the table. When his hand appeared back on top of the table, he was gripping the glass. Not one drop of his drink had spilled. Not only that, but the hand that held the glass was the same one that had knocked over the drink. His speed was like sorcery. After that I went over to him and started a conversation. He said that since he was born he had never let anything fall on the ground. He said he could catch anything before it got that far.

Yamai and Takashi's man-to-man was in the summer of our third year of high school. Everyone around who knew they were the strongest of the strong wanted to find out which one was stronger before we graduated, so we encouraged them. In so doing, oddly enough, little by little the two of them began feeling that this was something they had to do. It was a lot of trouble for the two of them. One day Yamai came to me requesting I set up a meeting. He said he had no other friends that he could trust to ask. I didn't think of myself as one of his friends, but since it's hard for me to say no to a guy who shyly begs a favor, I did as asked.

The following Sunday, the showdown of the century began in the gym, locked up tight. The spectator seats were full, even the guys that had dropped out of school came to see the show. Betting odds were sixty-forty, in Yamai's favor. Takashi was moving left around Yamai, drawing a circle within the center circle of the wood plank basketball court, while taking small rapid punches. The muscles in his back stretched cleanly and, like some spring-loaded device, only his arms thrust outward then bounced back. Three sharp punches, four sharp punches, in the same way, in the same spot. Yamai tried hard to somehow grab a hold of Takashi, but there were wings on Takashi's legs. Every once in a while one of Yamai's whirling rain of fists grazed him. But even then, without changing his expression and without overcompensating in the least, he constantly hit Yamai in the same way, with precise, fast punches. When I saw that, I knew how the fight was going to end.

Takashi's punches shaved off a bit more of Yamai's power and stamina each time they landed. Yamai was a monster, tough. Even suffering a hail of punches he kept going forward, forward. But the one standing after fifteen minutes was Takashi. Although Takashi's last line was: "I never want to fight you ever again."

"Hello?" Takashi's leisurely voice flowed from my PHS.

"It's me, Makoto. Can you get the heads of all the teams together for me tonight?"

"Is this about that girl who was with you?" As always, right to the punch.

"That's right, I wanna do what I can for her. I have a good lead."

"The Strangler . . ."

There was a short pause. I listened to the noise from the street coming through the PHS.

"Sure, let's meet tonight at 9:00 in the lobby of the Hotel Metropolitan. I'll assemble the rest of them."

The phone hung up on Takashi's end. I nodded at Hikaru, who was looking in my direction with concern.

The lobby of the Hotel Metropolitan was empty at night. All of the hotel workers' eyes were fixed on one corner of a couch in the lobby. Four were heads of the G-boys, one more leader each for the boarders, the BMX teams, the singers, and the dancers, and me and Takashi. Once we were all there we took the elevator up to a conference room that Takashi had reserved.

Ten punks all with their own unique and flashy style, sitting back in black leather chairs, the kind that executives use. Quite a sight. Nobody spoke a word. Takashi opened the meeting.

"We just had a regular meeting last week, so sorry for calling all of you together so suddenly. I had you all come today to discuss the Strangler. The one who summoned you all here was Makoto Majima over there. I believe you are all familiar with him. Also with the fact that a girl in his team was killed yesterday. Okay Makoto, you take it from here."

I talked about Rika. About Yoshioka's information and Rika's part-time job. And about the sensei that Hikaru saw. I took out the stack of copied drawings and passed them out to the members.

"With this meeting I want you to start up a guard system. A twenty-four hour patrol and hotel and telephone club stakeout. And I want all the various Boys & Girls in Ikebukuro to carry a copy of this picture. Two girls almost dead, one girl killed. I think it's about time that we started getting serious, for these streets and for ourselves."

"What's the guarantee that the Strangler's gonna strike again?" said one of the skinhead G-boys.

"I don't know. But in the last month there have been three incidents. I'm certain that he'll move again in the near future."

"Do you have any proof that this 'sensei' is the Strangler? He might just be some old lech," said the singers' leader, his long hair braided up like an Indian.

"There is that chance. But this is the only thread of information I've managed to pull in. It's worth a try. Besides, we're not the police. We can use any means we want to make him talk. There's no way even the Strangler can get past us by pretending not to know anything."

One by one they gave their opinions in order. The rule for these meetings was that each person absolutely must speak. Takashi spoke last.

"Alright, I've heard what you have to say. We will enter preparations for an A-class guard for the next month. I'd like each team to produce guardians for four rotations over twenty-four hours. Love hotel districts, telephone clubs, and couples cafes. Make sure there are guardians watching over all these places. And make every kid in Ikebukuro walk around with three of these pictures. Tell them to keep special watch for couples far apart in age, with this 'sensei' as the prime target. Got it? This time it's our turn to hunt the Strangler."

Starting the day after Rika's funeral, the streets of Ikebukuro became a combat zone. The police and G-boys were bloodthirsty. The newspapers and television caused a sensation by reporting that the criminal series of attempted strangulations had given rise to the first victim. It looked like they were having a field day with the story. Good for business. I became the coordinator for the Strangler hunt. I gave out assignments to the people on patrol and received communications from each team. Also, once every three days I'd do the rounds of Ikebukuro's jungle for six hours with Masa and Shun, and when it was convenient for her, Hikaru. I carried around five untraceable cell phones that I got from Takashi, and they were constantly ringing. That was the first time in my life I had experienced exhaustion from just thinking.

After that a week passed quickly. We continued to strike out with little strong information. Only a few couples made up of schoolgirls and old men fueling the sugar daddy business got caught in our net. However, not one of Ikebukuro's Boys & Girls-turned-guardian complained. I started seeing young kids around town wearing T-shirts with a black and white print of Rika. Below Rika's aggressive face, glaring straight ahead, piercing the hair that fell in her eyes from the explosive wave-perm on her head, the words "REMEMBER R" in red letters like blood. I bought the same T-shirt from a Colombian working a street stall on Sunshine Avenue and put it on.

During a break from our patrol, when me, Masa, and Shun were resting on a bench in West Gate Park, two guys came up to us. One had a notepad and a tasteless black shoulder bag. The other one had a camera with a huge flash attached to it and a camera bag. Wiping the dripping sweat from the nape of his neck, the fat notepad spoke up.

"Hello, you guys wouldn't happen to know the Rika Nakamura that was killed, would you?"

We exchanged glances amongst ourselves. Masa's eyes got narrow. Dangerous.

"Nah, who's that?"

I played along.

"That girl that was murdered by the Strangler. You know her, right? She was selling herself or whatever. Sucks to be her, getting killed and all because she sold her body just to get money for brand name clothes or bags or something."

"Oh, that's right. Did you guys figure anything out?"

"No, this girl is different than the last two because her friends aren't saying anything. Well, there has been some questioning about her involvement in organized prostitution . . ."

Rika? Organized prostitution? I didn't know what to think. Right as I was about to ask him a little more, Masa abruptly punched Notepad.

Shun spit on the camera then sprayed tear gas at the cameraman.

"Screw you! If you write a bunch of lies about Rika I'll kill you!" screamed Masa.

We ran out of West Gate Park before people had a chance to start gathering.

After that another two weeks. Since no one had seen the Strangler, the jumpier of the G-boys couldn't contain themselves any longer, and they turned to hunting older men. Aiming at couples with vastly different ages. Well, I guess it couldn't be helped. You reap what you sow. Yoshioka put a call in to my PHS. You're not up to something are you? The streets are dangerous. I said I know nothing, I'm doing nothing. Yoshioka told me to hand the prey over to the police, without fail, then hung up.

It was around that time, during a late-night patrol. The three of us were just blowing around the love hotel district. A G-boy was sitting on the guardrail in front of a convenience store talking with someone on a cell phone. A guardian. He confirmed it with eye contact and I nodded back slightly. Just like that, we turned down a narrow street lined on both sides with love hotels. Dimly lit. Everywhere a green vacancy sign. Two women were standing in the circle of light from a streetlamp. Almost-illegal miniskirts. From far away they looked like young girls, but close up, make-up hiding deep lines. The kind of faces you usually see on women in their late thirties through to fifty. Both of them saw the Rika T-shirt I was wearing.

"Good luck, you guys. Go get 'em for that girl."

I gave them a copy of the picture Shun drew. Since the happening with Rika, it seemed that subtle bonds were born on the streets of Ikebukuro between people who had had no ties at all till now.

It was nearing the end of the one month guardian operation, the fourth weekend. The patrols and watchdogs continued on like a machine. When the G-boys decide to do something, they do it. We were on duty that night until dawn, so the four of us had dinner a little after eight at the West Gate McDonald's. Lots of Big Macs, fries, and sodas. All the seats in the place were full, so the cigarette smoke made the far side of the room seem as if it were in a haze. It was Saturday night, and the mass of people we looked down on from the window looked like they were having a little more fun than usual. One of the cell phones rang inside my backpack. Hikaru sprang on the bag and got the phone out. Bingo on the second try. She handed it over to me.

"This is Makoto."

"Makoto, this is Killer Zoo's Yoshikazu. Right now I'm in front of the couples café 'Mezzo Piano,' behind Marui. A man that looked exactly like the sensei just went in with a young girl."

"Got it. Stay where you are. We'll be there in five." I hung up the phone, then said to everybody, "Let's get to the couples café 'Mezzo Piano.'"

From the McDonald's in front of the West Gate rotary to Marui at the West Gate five-way intersection, walking fast, three minutes. If you pass by Marui and turn at the second small alley, you'll see a group of pubs. The couples café 'Mezzo Piano' is in a building filled with various businesses, narrow like a pencil, on the left-hand side of that street. There's no sign or anything. If you didn't know about it, you'd probably walk right past it. In front of the slightly dirty elevator facing the street was a fourteen- or fifteen-year-old, short G-boy. Baggy jeans hung from his hips and he practically swam inside a huge Utah Jazz uniform. I gave him a thumbs-up and then greeted him: "Yo, good job. How long ago did he go in?"

"I think it's been less than ten minutes."

"How did you know he went to 'Mezzo Piano?'"

"The elevator went up to the sixth floor, then it came back empty."

"Are there any other exits besides the elevator in this building?"

"There are emergency stairs, but no matter how you get out, you have to pass in front of this entranceway," Yoshikazu answered spiritedly. Smart boy.

"You've done great. I'll be sure to tell both the head of Killer Zoo and Takashi about you."

What should I do? I looked at Hikaru. She nodded.

"Right now Hikaru and I are going to go into the café and make sure it's the sensei. Call Takashi and inform him that we're keeping a close eye on the guy. After that, just do whatever Takashi tells you to. Good?"

I looked Masa and Shun straight in the eyes. Shun nodded. Masa looked like he wasn't entirely satisfied, but in the end he nodded.

The elevator doors opened at the sixth floor to a tight hallway, and directly in front of us was a gray steel door with a plastic plate hanging from it that read "Mezzo Piano." The same kind of door you'd find to a regular apartment. Not much like a business. I pulled open the door.

Compared with the fluorescent lights in the hallway, the inside was dimly lit. A small space, maybe three tatami mats wide, cut into sections by curtains. To the right was a counter, and behind that a middle-aged man with a black bowtie and thin moustache. Our eyes met.

"Come in. Welcome."

A sickeningly smooth voice. Hikaru and I set foot in the store.

"This way, please."

Thin Moustache led the way. Passing through a black curtain, we headed for the back of the room; it was long and rectangular, and within the roughly eight mats of space there were six red velvet couches facing each other in pairs over small tables. Since my eyes had yet to grow accustomed to the dark, all I could see was the vague outline of people. When we entered the room, all the couples stopped moving. The last empty seats were in the corner in front of us. We sat down there. Thin Moustache lit up a menu with a pencil light and Hikaru ordered.

"Oolong tea."

"Make that two," I said.

"I'll bring them shortly. Thank you."

When Thin Moustache lifted up the curtain and left the room, the couple next to us, who looked like a businessman in his late-twenties and an OL, was the first to start moving. The girl got on her knees between the man's legs and put his penis in her mouth. She purposefully made noise. The man reached out to the tight skirt of the girl who was sticking her ass out and rolled it up. The OL wasn't wearing anything underneath. In order to show the middle-aged couple directly in front of them, she shook her hips up and down slightly. Hikaru put her arms around my shoulders and, after putting her tongue inside my ear, whispered to me. Goosebumps.

"Mako, it'll look even weirder if we don't do anything. I'm okay with it, so don't worry." After saying that, Hikaru took my right hand and pressed it into her breast through her halter top. No bra. Soft balloons filled with hot liquid, sticky like pulp. Grasping it felt like something was going to come spilling out between my fingers. I got hard.

I looked around the room while feeling up Hikaru's breasts. In front of us was a plain couple, an older man with thinning hair and what appeared to be his wife, eyes wide. Pass on that couple. Pass also to the businessman and OL, as well as the middle-aged couple across from them that looked like they knew what they were doing. That left the two couples in the back. At a couples café, as long as you don't make eye contact, it seems you can look at each other as much as you want (or at least that's what everyone was doing), so it was very convenient for me. The sofa in the farthest corner diagonally and across from us had two school kids in jeans, stuck together like clams. Before long they stripped off their jeans, then their underwear. Still wearing their white socks. Strange. And last, in the same line with us there was one sofa, and he was there. He had the girl up in a pose like she was pissing, and he was rubbing her clitoris from behind. She was young, maybe at the end of her teens. Ah, ah, ah! The man whipped his neck around like an owl, casting his eyes all about his surroundings. His hair was parted down the middle, he was thinner than Shun's picture, and he had a seemingly sharp face. He was the sensei. I put my lips up to Hikaru's ear and whispered. She let out a sigh.

"Look at the couple on the farthest couch on our side."

Hikaru nodded, still flushed. Without changing her position she bent forward and put her head on my thigh, and she looked at the far sofa as if leaning over. Her hand continued to stroke my bulging zipper. After a while Hikaru put her arms around my neck again and said into my ear: "No doubt about it, that man is the sensei."

After that we faked at playing with each other a little while more, then Hikaru and I left the shop. We paid at the counter. Three couples sat in chairs lined up in front of the counter waiting for the next available seat inside. In the elevator, Hikaru said that she could get into the habit of doing this. Let's come again. When we got off the elevator there was no one in front of the building. I couldn't even see anyone that looked like a guardian. I quickly called Takashi on my PHS.

"Takashi? It's definitely the sensei. We confirmed it. What do we do from here?"

"First, send the girl home. I've prepared several cars and scooters, and they currently have the building surrounded. Makoto, it's not 'what do we do from here.' What do you want to do?"

Takashi isn't called the king of the G-boys for show. He has the power to read a person's heart. That's the biggest difference between him and Yamai.

"I want to make sure whether he's the Strangler or not directly. It might get a little rough though. I'd like to ask for enough backup so that he can't get away."

"Alright, go on Makoto. Go bag yourself a Strangler."

I told her I'd call her later, then sent Hikaru home. Don't be reckless she told me worriedly, and she faded off in the direction of the Tokyo Metropolitan Art Space building. I crossed the street, sat on the guardrail opposite the building, and waited for the sensei. Waiting wasn't hard at all.

REMEMBER R.

Another thirty minutes, and it was past ten at night. The doors to the elevator opened yet again, and the sensei appeared in the entrance of the building with his arm around the shoulders of the young girl. A whitish suit with no tie. On his shoulder, a coach's bag. The girl's legs were very unsteady and he held her up while they walked. He checked behind him to make sure no one was following. I went into action too. I crossed the intersection in front of Marui, heading toward the Art Space. The boarders and BMX teams were performing impressive stunts as usual in the area in front of the Space, the same as any other Saturday night. The sensei was squeezing himself through the crowd and heading for the love hotels behind West Gate Park. The two of them passed out of the park, then went down a narrow alley beside the Art Space. The area was deserted. At the end of the alley were two love hotels. Service time starting at 4000 yen.

Speeding up, I walked past them and stood in front of the love hotel. The sensei's eyes and my eyes met. He had a handsome face, like an actor's. A young mid-thirties. Like a professor at some good women's college. He was surprisingly small. Maybe just about 170 centimeters.

"What are you supposed to be?"

"Nobody, I just want to find out if you're the Strangler or not," I said, and immediately he started panicking. Swimming eyes.

"What are you talking about. I'm just on a date with my girlfriend. I'll call out if you're trying to rob me."

The girl's eyes were watery and distant and her gaze was wandering around the night sky.

"Call out if you want. But if you're not going to, let me have a look in that bag."

He suddenly pushed the girl. She sank straight down to the asphalt and didn't come back up. The guy pulled something shiny out of the pocket of his bag and pointed it at me. A small blade. It was like a scalpel. The sensei was almost crying.

"Go on, quick, get out of here. If you don't move fast I'll stab you."

"If you want to do it, do it. But there's no way you can escape. This place is completely surrounded."

"You're lying."

Trembling scalpel in a back alley.

"Nope, even right behind you."

Keeping the scalpel on me, he took a quick glance behind him. I dropped my backpack from my shoulder and, grabbing the strap, I brought it down on his right hand. Small and quick. Inside the backpack were the five cell phones for communication with the G-boys and my PHS. With the first hit the scalpel went flying, and next I aimed for the head. Two times, three times, four times. I kept on whipping my back-pack around. He covered his head and fell to the ground.

"Nice work."

The voice came from behind me. I raised my backpack up and spun around. Takashi stood with his arms crossed. He was smiling slightly.

"Hunph–"

Facing back around on hearing the sensei's cry, the guys in Takashi's team had just finished up kicking him to the ground. The sensei was laid out face down, and around both wrists and ankles they were running a circular plastic cord. They pulled it tight and when it stopped with a snap, he couldn't move at all.

"Made in America. Works pretty well, huh?" said Takashi. I picked up the sensei's bag from the side of the road. I opened the flap. A hemp rope, surgical gloves, a small bottle with some thick, clear liquid, two vibrators, another scalpel, a Polaroid camera, a stopwatch. Takashi looked at me and shook his head.

"Stop, don't look through there! Those are my personal belongings! Who the hell are you people? You're not cops, right? Do you think you can do this to me and get away with it?" the man yelled from the ground, wriggling around restlessly like a caterpillar.

Takashi picked up the fallen scalpel from the ground. He walked toward the man. The boys in his team all stepped back.

"Are you familiar with the movie *Chinatown*? Jack Nicholson and Faye Dunaway. That was a great movie, wasn't it? I only saw it on video though."

Takashi squatted down next to the sensei, grabbed him by the hair, and pulled his head up. He looked hard into the sensei's eyes.

"Yeah, I know it. Directed by Roman Polanski. What the hell are you going to do?"

The sensei lost to the strength in Takashi's eyes and turned his gaze away.

"If you tell us everything, I won't do anything. You're the Ikebukuro Strangler, right? Well?"

Takashi put the tip of the scalpel into the sensei's left nostril.

"I don't know what you're talking about, I don't want to say anything about that. I ought to have the right to remain silent."

Takashi pulled the scalpel toward him. A *psht* sound, like cutting through thick plastic. The sensei's nostril was cut and blood flowed from the wound. Raising an incomprehensible cry, his teeth and gums were stained red. Red froth mixed with saliva fell on the asphalt.

"This scalpel cuts pretty well. You don't have the right to remain silent, or any rights. I'll ask you again. You're the Strangler?"

This time he put the scalpel in the right nostril. Tears came to the sensei's eyes.

"Okay, okay, don't cut anymore. That's right, I did it."

"Did you kill Rika, too?" I asked him.

"Answer him." Takashi pushed the scalpel another two millimeters into his nose.

"No, I didn't kill anyone. It's just a game. I measure out the drug precisely and I keep my eye on the stopwatch when I choke them. I wouldn't do anything as shameless as kill someone."

Takashi and I exchanged glances.

"Really? Is that the truth?" I squatted down next to him as well.

"That's right. No matter how much you accuse me, if I didn't do it, I didn't do it. More importantly, I need to be taken to a doctor. This's going to leave a scar on my nose."

"Can't do that. Pretty soon the police should be arriving. You can't run anymore." I thought about Rika while listening to Takashi's voice as he replied. I wonder if he really didn't do it? Or is he just gambling, hoping that he can get out of this somehow?

"Please stop, I can give you money. Ten million, twenty million, I can raise money like you've never seen. I didn't know the girl that died very well."

"You knew Rika?" I asked.

"Yeah, we had a few dates."

"Did you choke her, too?"

"Only once. I paid her exactly as promised and there was mutual consent."

I didn't know what to say to him. There was a strange glimmer in the man's eye.

"I won't let you get away with doing this to me. If I'm caught by the police I'll give testimony against you. I'll send you to jail along with me, on account of personal injury."

The man was drunk on himself. Forgetting even the position he was in. Takashi laughed heartily. As if he were truly enjoying himself.

"You think you're so smart, don't you? Just because you're good at studying. But your luck ran out when your lust tempted you into the jungle. No matter how brilliant your brain is, it's not going to help a pig like you here. Get what I'm saying?"

The only thing moving on Takashi's face was his mouth. He wasn't even looking at the man.

"Enough of this. I'll hire the best lawyer and be back here before you know it. Then I'll be sure to take my revenge on you. I'll hire some yakuza to atta–"

Takashi pulled the scalpel and cut the man's remaining nostril. He grabbed a hold of the sensei's hair, then smashed his face into the asphalt. It happened in a split second. Yank, smoosh. The sound of a nose disintegrating. The man was crying and screaming something at the same time.

"Let's go, the cops are coming," said Takashi, who then held up his right hand and made a small circle with his forefinger. The G-boys who had been holding back the passers-by on either side of the street all dispersed.

"Come on Makoto, let's go, too."

"Go where?"

I was looking down at the crying man.

"To the club."

"You guys are gonna go drink? Now?"

"You're pretty slow yourself, huh? Us, today we've been drinking at that club since this evening. Right?" Takashi grinned at me.

"Right . . . Even right now, we're not really here." I smiled back at Takashi.

And so we went back. To the place we naturally belonged, the place where our friends were waiting.

❦ ❦ ❦

The club's name was "Luster Love." A place with a heavy G-boys influence. A black concrete box plastered with spray-painted graffiti. That night almost the whole place was reserved. All of the heads that were at the meeting were there. The guard system that lasted for almost a month was finally lifted, so it was a celebration. Everybody was drinking rum and dancing to the rhythm of laid-back reggae. Masa and Shun were there as well. I could hear people giving toasts here and there. But no matter how much I drank, the important parts in my head remained clear. Stopping the Strangler was cause for celebration (we learned that he had been arrested in that alley when someone who had been left to watch what happened reported in to Takashi). However, I couldn't get Rika out of my head. I didn't think that the Strangler was lying. There might be another criminal out there that killed Rika. Could there be another pervert roaming the streets carefree? But if that was the case, it looked like there was nothing I could do about it. I killed time quietly drinking alcohol. I lifted myself up heavily a little past two in the morning, right as the club was just about to go crazy. When I opened the door and was about to step outside, a G-boy came up and told me that Takashi was calling for me. I went to the back of the club where Takashi was surrounded by his flunkies. Our eyes met and Takashi nodded. He beckoned me over with his hand. Deafeningly loud Sly & Robbie. Takashi spoke next to my ear.

"Good job today. Makoto, I'll take you in as one of my execs any time. And there's something else . . ."

It was unusual, but it looked like Takashi was having trouble saying what he wanted to.

"Watch out for that girl Hikaru. That's all."

I walked home, crawled under my blanket, and went to sleep. On my way home, this time it was Takashi's "that's all" about Hikaru that kept circling around in my head. I feel like I had a lot of bad dreams that night. Although I don't remember any of them.

The next day, Sunday, I woke up around noon. The front page of the Society section of the newspaper was an article that read: "Perpetrator of Attempted Strangulations Caught!" I read the newspaper from my bed. Since the thing with Rika, reading the newspaper had become a habit. If I could take a Japanese test now, maybe I could actually get a slightly good score.

It said the Strangler was an anesthesiologist at some university hospital. Thirty-seven years old, single. He was serious at work and one of the promising elite. How could it have been *him?* A conventional story. But it said that the police denied that he killed Rika. Hereafter they planned to take time and complete a thorough investigation.

I went to West Gate Park. I sat on the bench as always. Masa and Shun came, and in the evening Hikaru came as well. I talked about the night before. Everything, except the part about Takashi cutting the Strangler's nose. It seemed like none of us were satisfied with the way things had gone with Rika, but we were pleased with the fact that we had caught the Strangler ourselves. After that we spent a long time just shooting the shit. The first relaxed Sunday afternoon we had had in a while. No more patrolling.

The evening sun struck the buildings, whose shadows were lengthening. Summer would soon be over. I gazed absently at the round space of West Gate Park. Across the way from our bench was a face I hadn't seen in a while, "Doberman-killer Yamai." Yamai pulled out a cell phone and punched in a number. Hikaru was chatting with Masa when her phone rang. Hikaru fished her cell phone out of her black Prada bag.

"Hi, this is Hikaru . . . What? Hey, don't call me . . . If I need something, *I'll* call *you*. Hmph."

Hikaru hung up the phone immediately. At first she had a cute voice, but partway through it sounded like she suddenly lost her temper. While listening to Hikaru's voice, I idly watched Yamai. It looked like his phone call was over, too. It must be a coincidence, I thought. Until I remembered Takashi's "that's all."

That night, since Shun and Masa were going to the "Luster Love" to drink all night, among other things, we split up early. Saying she was bored, Hikaru went home as well. As she was about to leave Hikaru poked me in the chest with her forefinger and said let's go to that café again sometime.

Before I went home I stopped by the Virgin Megastore under Marui. The first time in my life to visit the classical section. I had never ever listened to classical music. I tried asking a young guy who had his long hair tied up with a rubber band and who was wearing the same polo shirt as the rest of the staff.

"You wouldn't happen to have Tchaikovsky's *Serenade for Strings,* would you?"

The salesman took me over to the "T" rack. There was tons of Tchaikovsky.

"Karajan, Davis, Barenboim, Mravinsky, which conductor would you like?"

When I told him I didn't care which one, he handed me the Davis, saying that it was the best deal for my money. I paid for it at the register, went home, then popped it in my CD player. I then listened to the song six times in a row that night.

Serenade for Strings was the kind of song that played during ballroom scenes in foreign flicks. A sweet, sad waltz. Young ladies of refined society with their puffy dresses forming a circle and dancing, dancing. The next day and the day after that, from morning until night I listened to that song and just kept on thinking. Rika, Hikaru, the Strangler, Yamai, organized prostitution. The same words ran circles inside my head a million times. But still, I didn't stop thinking. Rika couldn't think for herself anymore, so it should be okay for me to do it for her.

The third evening I called up Takashi on my PHS.

"I want to know Yamai's cell number, think you can find it for me?"

"Is the sky still blue today too? Don't ask stupid questions."

Takashi called me back in a second and told me Yamai's number. I dialed it right away.

"Hello?"

I heard Yamai's slow voice over the hum of the streets.

"Yo, this is Makoto. I have something to talk to you about. Do you have some time now?"

"Yea."

"Okay, West Gate Park in thirty minutes. See you there?"

"Yea."

The phone went quiet. Talkative guy.

I sat on a bench and waited for Yamai. It was starting to get dark around me. Businessmen on their way home cut hurriedly across the park, and since it was a weekday, there were only a few G-boys as well. A little after the agreed time I saw Yamai's golden head in the entranceway of the park's Tōbu department store. He found me and came straight over. Sturdy black engineering boots with camouflage pants and a gray T-shirt with the sleeves ripped off. Many slash marks ran across his wrists. The piercing connecting his nose and ear had changed to gold.

"Yo."

He sat down next to me.

"Hey."

"What do you want?"

Yamai's voice was low. Like a flat rock was rubbing against the back of his throat.

"I want to ask about Hikaru."

I said it without taking my eyes off him. His expression didn't change at all.

"You finally figured it out, huh?"

"Figured out what?"

"That that girl is mine."

"Are you two dating?"

I was surprised.

"No, we're not going out. But she's mine."

"Why?"

"Since I was born, this is the first time I've ever met the same kind of person as me. That's her. We're not going out like you're thinking. But that girl is mine. If you try to take her, I'll kill you Makoto."

The Doberman killer and the princess are the same kind of person. Maybe there's something wrong with his brain?

"I don't think anyone thinks that you and Hikaru are the same."

"You guys can't understand. She doesn't even see it herself yet. That girl thinks she's in love with you. Did you know that?"

"I guess," I answered reluctantly.

"You're sharp, but a good guy. I'll say one last thing. I'm not afraid of you, or Takashi, or anything else in this world. Because I found that girl."

Yamai stood up. He might have grown taller than before. I called out to his back, thick as a door, as he walked away.

"Hey, when you called Hikaru the other day, was it on purpose? So I'd notice?"

"Of course."

Yamai left. The businessmen in his way parted for him instinctively as he walked past.

The next Saturday, a little after noon, I met with Hikaru alone. The place was, of course, the bench in West Gate Park. The weather was good. Although it was already September, the summer sun was still shining. Hikaru was wearing the same clothes she had on when I first met her, a black mini-T and black miniskirt. Hikaru spoke as she practically jumped onto the bench next to me.

"I'm, like, really happy. We can be together, just the two of us. Maybe it's a little early, but wanna go to that couples café we went to last week?"

Hikaru was cheerful as always. Angelic smile. But it wasn't the smile that Yamai fell for.

"I think I pretty much figured it out."

Hikaru was quick to read a person. Her expression suddenly changed.

"What are you talking about?" she responded cautiously.

"About Rika."

"But the Strangler did that, right?"

"I'm thinking it was a little different."

"Well then, who was it?"

"You."

Hikaru froze. There was only a brief pause.

"What are you talking about? I wouldn't do something like that? Rika was my friend."

"I believe that, really. But you did it, right?"

Looking deep into my eyes she said, "It wasn't me."

I looked even deeper into her eyes. A strange light was wavering.

"That's why you made Yamai do it."

It seemed as though Hikaru couldn't stand it any longer. Her tears spilled out, falling from her large eyes, plop, plop. Still, I continued to stare into her eyes.

"But I only asked him to scare her to death."

I remembered Hikaru's tears on the day of Rika's funeral. Not yet, Hikaru wasn't showing me rock bottom.

"Is that true, Hikaru, really the truth?"

I never took my eyes off her. I stared with more intensity. Yamai said it, too. I'm a sharp guy.

"If I tell you the truth, I'll lose everything. You'll probably hate me, too."

"If you don't tell me the truth, I'll despise you. Talk, Hikaru."

Hikaru breathed a big sigh. The tears pulled back from both her eyes. She was like a wonderfully skilled actress hearing the word "Cut!" Even her voice changed.

"Okay. I'll tell you. Rika was unlucky. Around the beginning of summer vacation, she ran into the Strangler while working the streets. Do you remember the week or so when Rika wore a scarf, she was using it to hide the bruises on her neck. After that the Strangler messed up and caused a stir, and Rika got more and more scared. 'I know him. Maybe I should talk to Makoto?' she was saying."

"But you stopped her."

"Right, because if Rika told you, then you'd find out about me, too."

"About how you introduce old men to young girls?"

"Yes. I arranged things for all the girls. The school, my parents, the police, they're nothing. But I just didn't want you to find out."

"Why?"

"Because . . . I . . ."

Hikaru's face suddenly changed again. From an actress to a little girl. Her eyes became misty like she had just done drugs. She began to chew on her beautifully manicured thumbnail.

"What is it, what's wrong, Hikaru?"

"It's because you're the first person I ever liked who was younger than papa. I hated it, but I've only fallen for men older than him."

"What was the deal with Tchaikovsky?"

"Papa likes that song. He likes Tchaikovsky, and he would often lock the door and we would listen to it together. *Serenade for Strings: Larghetto elegiaco.* He always petted me and loved me so much. Sometimes it hurt, and sometimes I didn't like it, but papa said it's what people do when they love each other."

The same kind of person, just like Yamai said. Yamai's dad was notorious around our neighborhood for being an alcoholic, and with or without reason he would lay into Yamai and his mother. One time in winter Yamai spent the night under our store awning to get out of the rain. One morning on my way to elementary school I saw the two of them huddled together sleeping under a railroad bridge. The old man died of liver failure when Yamai was in junior high school. Yamai said it served him right. The time he killed the dog was right after that.

"Hikaru, how old were you the first time it happened?"

"My last year of kindergarten. There was a lot of blood, and mama slapped me for getting the couch dirty. That's why I hate mama and I like papa."

"That's enough. Hikaru, it's okay."

"It's not okay!" Hikaru screamed. She switched back to the strong actress voice. She wasn't biting her nails. A blaze in her fiery, seductive eyes.

"It's not okay! Because I told Yamai to kill Rika. Somehow he instinctively knew about me and he fell in love. He said he'd do anything for me. He said he'd do things for me that other people wouldn't do. That's why I asked him to do it. To kill Rika."

"For money?"

"He said he didn't want money."

"Hikaru, did you make some kind of promise to him?"

"That's right, I told him I'd give him my body. Sex, three times. But no kissing. I only kiss people I really like."

"When you told him that, what did his face look like?"

"I don't know, I've never looked very closely at his face. Maybe a little sad?"

I was quiet. No words would come to me. It was Saturday afternoon and the Boys & Girls were starting to gather at West Gate Park. The blending of guitar and the bubbling of the fountain. In the vast sky, thin autumn clouds.

"Hey, Mako, let's forget about this whole conversation. As long as you don't say anything, no one will know. Let's get away from this dump of a town together. I'll work a lot, and you'll always get to wear cool suits and I'll let you ride in a Porsche. For you I'd be willing to sell myself. Let's live together and have fun. You can do whatever you want with my body. You want me, don't you? All you have to do is say 'yeah' for me."

"And then . . . ?"

"And then we'll live happily ever after someplace where no one can reach us."

"Do you really believe that? Do you really think you can keep lying to people all your life?"

"I do. Because I've done it so far. And I have no choice but to keep doing it."

Hikaru stood up and started walking unsteadily away. Walking like a puppet after hearing some Tchaikovsky concert. She walked on like that, cutting across in front of the Art Space. I watched her back the whole way. At Theater Street she stopped a taxi and got in. I didn't follow her. The taxi disappeared into the flow of traffic. That was the last time I saw Hikaru.

After that, I sat on the bench until it got dark. I didn't do anything. Two hours passed and I got out my PHS and pressed the numbers for Yoshioka's cell.

"Hello."

"Ah, Makoto. You certainly did a job on this one. I hear his nose is never gonna be the same. You wrecked a perfectly handsome face."

There was some quiet laughter.

"Oh. I don't care about that guy. More importantly . . ."

"More importantly, what? Is this about Rika?"

"Yeah, how did you know? I have to tell you about Rika and Yamai."

"Hey, don't doubt the police. The scene of the first two incidents and that of Rika's murder looked completely different. I didn't tell you that though. They were about as different as a bacteria-free lab and a dumpster. We're doing a logical investigation here. How did you find out about Yamai?"

"I thought it through, about a million times."

"Stay away from him. Since it's going to be in the papers I guess it's okay, but right now he's here on charges of assault in a different case. The same afternoon of the day Rika was killed, an eye witness came to testify against him, so that puts an end to the case."

"So that's what happened. Then I guess I'll just leave it at that."

"You don't have anything else you want to tell me?"

"No, that's it."

"Alright. By the way, Makoto, if you're just going to waste away your days hanging around, you ever thought about becoming a cop? I think you're fit for the job. If you're up for it, I'll talk to the police academy for you. How about it?"

"Thanks, but it looks like I'm not cut out for it. If this kind of thing happened every day, I think I'd go insane. Later."

I hung up the phone. I went home. That night when Masa called me up to go hang out I told him I wasn't feeling well. I crawled under my blankets and thought.

This time about what I could do for Hikaru.

The following Monday evening I threw my bag over my shoulder and headed out of the house. From Ikebukuro, twenty minutes on the Marunouchi Line. I had checked a map, so I figured out the place right away. Kasumi-ga-seki 3-1-1. A gorgeous gray brick building. Ten guards in front of three white arches side-by-side. The people who entered had to show a pass. I sat on a guardrail about a hundred meters from the gate and waited.

My first manhunt. I did nothing but continue waiting there. Five hours later, around ten at night, a tall man I had seen before had a few words with a guard and then exited through the gate. I followed him. There was hardly a figure in sight in Kasumi-ga-seki at night. As if taking a shortcut to the subway station, the man went into a small park. I dashed up to him and, circling around, spoke straight to his face.

"You're Mr. Shibuzawa, right?"

"Who the hell are you?"

Silver hair in a huge wave. Frameless glasses. Eyes like Hikaru. The man was calm and collected.

"I'm a friend of Hikaru's. I've got something to return to you."

The man knit his brows, perplexed. This guy was like an actor, too.

I took a step forward and pulled back my right hand in a fist. Feint. I punched Hikaru's dad in the stomach with a short left hook. When he doubled over, I clasped my hands together and slammed them between his shoulders. He crumpled to the ground. I kicked him over and over in the shoulders and thigh, slow enough to count each kick. Seven, eight, nine, ten. I faced the man who was on the ground, covering his head.

"I know what you did to Hikaru while listening to Tchaikovsky. If you want to know why this had to happen to you, ask Hikaru. Ask her to tell you everything. After that, if you want to go to the police, be my guest. That's up to the two of you."

I took off the man's shiny black leather shoes and threw them in the bushes. In their place, I slipped the pair of Nike Air Jordans I took from my bag onto his feet. The first and last present I got from Hikaru. The yellow '95 model.

"If you show her these, she'll understand. Tell Hikaru to finish this herself."

Without even waiting for the guy to get up, I quickly made my way toward Kasumi-ga-seki Station. Well, I knew that Hikaru's father wouldn't call the cops. It was probably just that I hated breathing the same air as him.

A few days later there was a small article in the newspaper. "Deputy Director-General of Financial Bureau, Ministry of Finance, Stabbed!" It said he was stabbed by his daughter, Miss A, whose mental state was constantly unstable. Luckily, the wound was shallow and it appeared as if it posed no threat to his life.

Hikaru settled things in her own way. I don't know whether it was good or not. But that's the end of my part of the story. So the rest is just news about what happened to everybody.

Hikaru is now in long-term hospitalization in an institution in Nagano or somewhere. I got a postcard once.

Hikaru's dad resigned from the Ministry of Finance, and became re-employed by some leasing company.

Masa recently joined a club at school. Surfing in the summer, snowboarding in the winter, the kind of club you join to get girls. Perfect for him. He rarely shows his face around West Gate Park, but he's still a good friend.

Shun is working part-time at a computer game company. Since work drawing characters is more interesting than vocational school, he's been talking about maybe quitting school and working full-time in the near future.

In the end, Yamai went to the pen without saying a word about Hikaru. She persuaded him by saying she would marry him or whatever when he got out. How Hikaru plans on running from him in a few years might be a sight worth seeing, but I'll bet that, of anyone, Hikaru can ward him off successfully. Because, after all, Hikaru's acting is a cut above Yamai's. Although he might actually understand Hikaru's intentions and forgives her, and is pretending to be tricked. That I don't know.

Takashi is still head of the G-boys. He had a little trouble and I helped him out as thanks for this time, but since that's another long story, I'll tell you next time.

So, about me. I started seriously helping out with the shop. Waking up early to go to the market sucks. As for changes, recently I've become friends with the salesman in the classical music section. For some reason it seems he thinks I like Russian music and he keeps recommending things. Stravinsky, Prokofiev, Shostakovich. So now our fruit shop alternates between playing *The Rite of Spring* and Bob Marley. I like Stravinsky more than Tchaikovsky.

If you come to Ikebukuro and find a fruit shop playing strange music, stop in and say hi. If I'm around I'll give you twenty percent off a five-thousand-yen melon.

Although, even so, we'd still be ripping you off.

Yoko Tawada

Tawada was born in Tokyo and educated at Waseda University. Since 1982, she has been living in Germany. With her debut short story *Missing Heels* she was awarded the Gunzo Prize for New Writers in 1991. In 1993 she received the Akutagawa Prize for *The Bridegroom was a Dog,* and in 1996 she won the Adelbert von Chamisso Prize, a German award for foreign writers in recognition for their contributions to German culture. Most recently, in 2005, she was honored with the Goethe Medaille.

Having spent a good part of her adult life in Germany, she explores what it means to be a foreigner in another land, deeply delving into the themes of alienation and isolation.

To Khabarovsk

Translated by Jessiqa Greenblatt

IF YOU OPEN UP A MAP OF THE WORLD, YOU CAN see a rift running through the middle of Siberia. It makes you wonder whether the expansive continent of Eurasia might one day break in two. The rift seems too big to be a lake—about the size of the main island of Japan, maybe even bigger. But it's said that only saltwater fish live in those waters, which in other words means that it must've been an ocean in the primeval past. If that were the case, the continent of Eurasia was likely formed by two land masses crashing together. Lake Baikal looks like a gash in a wall. If you peek through that chink, you just might see an ancient world waiting on the other side.

Not far from the lake sits a town by the name of Irkutsk. That's where you'd been staying. You took a stroll through town during the day and noticed an unusually large number of people exchanging greetings at street corners, red or yellow flowers in their hands. Though your breath was still a frosty white, the March light carried a golden overtone which had an influence over their moods. Just because the temperature managed to break out of the minuses, everyone was acting as if it were a spring fair.

But you were already on an eastbound train away from said village. It felt like Moscow was a million miles away, each passing second increasing that inconceivable distance. Three more days of traveling and you'll arrive at the eastern reaches of the continent. There floats Sakhalin Island, its shape flitting in and out of your mind in the image of a fossilized leaf print.

Right after waking up in the wee hours of the second night, you feel an almost apologetic pressure in your bladder. You have to go to the bathroom, you think as if it were somebody else's problem. You really don't have any inclination to wake up right now. Oh, if only this were a dream. You take into account the person who needs to use the w/c, the person who woke up in the middle of the night and the person who hates getting up, but when you add them all together it's still only one person. You've never had to convince yourself that you were merely one person more than you did at this moment. Well, even if you were traveling with other people, you couldn't very well wake them up so you could all take a dump together. When people need to relieve themselves, they always do so alone. It's a fate you simply can't escape. You'll just have to peel your body out of bed and cut through the chilly night car all alone.

You exit your compartment and walk through the corridor, stuffy with the odors of coal, garlic and Soviet-made cigarettes. The hems of the sweats you wear as pajamas are weak and frayed. In a strange way, it feels like regressing back to childhood. The windows look out into pitch black, without even a house or streetlamp to mark the train's passage. Your own shadow floats up to meet the glass surface in the middle of the night. The air by the window was freezing, so you made sure to keep some distance between you and the window and continued forward. Enticed by drowsiness, you walk on. Your eyelids feel heavy. Maybe you could keep your eyes closed, grope your way to the toilet, do your business and return to bed.

You put your hand on the handle to the bathroom door and push with a forceful thrust. The unresisting hinges swing the door open, and you fall forward, your feet leaving the floor behind. Swallowed up by the vast darkness swooping in, your ears are assaulted by the sound of the wheels grinding against the track, like a wave crashing down on you. The undertow pulls you in, grabs you by the arms, and washes you back to the physical world outside. Then, with a thud, you fall onto a frozen field. The ear-splitting thunder of the train quickly rolls to your side. *This is the end—I'll be run over and crushed into a pulp!* Tucking your neck into your shoulders, you hold your breath and wait. But, the train is still chugging along at your side. Nothing happened. You slowly lift your head up and see the caboose kicking sparks up into the darkness.

That was when the real terror began to roil up in your chest. You fell off the train. Alone, stranded on a field in the middle of Siberia, you'll freeze in the dark! There's no doubt that no more trains will pass through this area until tomorrow. Even if a freight train were to come, how would you let them know you were lying there? Despite the thick sweatshirt you wore instead of pajamas, the cold was already creeping down your neck. Isn't there something you could use as a scarf? What a pain in the ass. This is the first time in your life you really thought you were going to die. You scan around the area, but you can't see anything, not even a shrub. Far in the distance, you can make out a slight change in color which is presumably the horizon. But you're night-blinded and near-sighted; you even left your glasses on the train. All you can rely on at this point are the train tracks. If you walk alongside them long enough, you might eventually reach a village. It may be a long way, but it's a hell of a lot better than sitting here freezing to death.

With that in mind, you headed off. There wasn't any wind, but the resistance of the air as you walked forward was like a wall of ice. You could hear something that sounded like a person playing the flute in the distance, but it was too far to tell whether it was man, beast or machine.

After a bit of walking, your body feels like it's warming up. Your pupils dilated to acclimate to the dark, and you can see five thick shrubs ahead on your right. It looked like a giant hand was stretching out from the depths of the earth. You speed up, hedge past the hedges and proceeded to parallel the tracks. Finally, you arrive at a group of houses huddling close together. *Thank goodness,* you think with a sob. Well, it was intended as a sob, but it came out, comically enough, sounding more like a hiccough or a sneeze. But this was hardly the time to be overwhelmed by emotion. Curtains covered the windows of all the houses, no lights inside to shine through the fabric. But looking hard at the fourth house, you could see a faint glow. You pressed your nose up against the window.

Through the narrow part between the curtains you saw what looked to be a living room. There were no lights on in that room, but a door towards the back was ajar, and light was spilling out from the other side. Must be a kitchen—steam was rising up, and a brawny man stood with his back to you. It looked like he was cooking something. You rush around to the front entrance and bang violently on the door with both hands. The sound of a deep, reverberating voice from inside reached your ears before the door gradually opened. One look at your face left the man flabbergasted. You started to worry that he'd close the door on you, but fortunately that didn't happen. With a baffled expression, the man circled a lamp around your face to shed some light, his feet planted in the doorway where he stood. Stringing together fractured Russian, you explained how you fell off the night train. You had no idea whether or not he understood, but either way he opened the door and cocked his chin upwards as a signal for you to come in.

Two threadbare rugs were strewn across the hardwood floor. A rough, humble table and a cupboard also furnished the room, but there were no electric appliances. One small mirror hung on the wall. A coal stove was burning, heating the hanging pot above it. Steam trailed up from the pot and filled the air with the sweet, tart smell of simmering apples. You asked what was cooking, and in place of an answer, the man served up a bowl full of whatever was in the pot and placed it in front of you on the table. It was a thick and sticky yellow mush, hot enough to burn your tongue. You scooped some up with a wooden spoon, and as soon as you gulped it down, you felt a pillar of heat growing in your chest. That old Russian fairytale comes to mind, the one with the three bears—this is just the type of wooden spoon they would have used. The man trickled some hot water from the samovar and put some tea in a now steaming cup. He set it down in front of you along with a huge sugar jar. After finishing the porridge, you took a deep breath and sipped the tea. It made you completely forget what it felt like to be cold.

The man took out an old book from the back of the room and opened it, whirling out a musty, dusty-scented breeze. Ah, so it was a world atlas! But it was bordering on ancient; not only were the pages yellowed like autumn birch leaves, but the British Empire covered quite a wide portion of the world. You point to Irkutsk saying, "This is where I was yesterday." You slide your finger a little to the east. "This is where I was riding the train when I had to go to the bathroom. I opened the bathroom door, and then . . ." you began, but you didn't know the verb "to fall" in Russian. Standing your fingers in the likeness of a person, you mimed falling off the edge of table. The man laughed and clapped you on the shoulder. He said, "Make yourself at home," or something to that extent. At least you could get that kind of meaning from it.

A feeling of uneasiness swept over you for some reason, and you let out a shudder. By chance, your eyes happened to fall on the mirror hanging on the wall. The mirror caught the nape of the man's neck in its reflection, but something was off. When the man turned his neck, the reflection in the mirror became that of a woman's profile. Shocked, you look back at the man's face. It was the face of an honest, reserved, lonely man in his fifties. He had soft-looking, milky-white skin and a bristling beard. Returning your gaze to the mirror, you see an urban intellectual woman in her forties, proud, slender and rigid. About the only common feature between the two was the lonely expression. You begin to feel dizzy, eyes spinning. You've already fallen off the train—there's no way you could still be falling. But that's when the sensation of dropping really hit you.

After downing the tea, the man slaps your shoulder, as if to say "Come with me." Around the other side of the kitchen wall behind the cupboard was a large tub, the hot water inside puffing out clouds of steam. "Wash yourself here." You had a bad feeling about this. The man authoritatively drew himself up to his full height next to you and folded his arms. You knew without a doubt that if you tried to resist, his arm would force you down into the water. If the figure reflected in the mirror was this man's true self, there'd be no need to be afraid. Well, even if the figure you see before you was the man's true self, there wouldn't really be much to fear anyway. It was just that their appearances were so incongruous with each other that it was unsettling.

There was a pelt laid out around the tub, a bear's pelt. The guy probably shot it himself. You look at it closely and see that the face is still attached. The bear's face really resembled somebody, but you can't recall who. You get nervous. Was it the conductor you saw in the train? No, that's not right. Then, could it be the face of the student in the compartment next to you? No, not that person either.

You shake your head from left to right. "Very well, then. My sincere thanks." The man nodded in satisfaction, but he didn't make to leave from where he stood. Not having much of a choice, you undress, and not at all surprised, gaze down at your body which has suddenly taken on hermaphroditic features. As strange as that was, you knew that it's always been that way—moreover, even though you knew about it beforehand, you'd only been feigning ignorance of the matter.

Compared to how furiously the water was letting out steam, it wasn't very hot. You dip your left foot in, then your right. Scrunching up your stomach, you squat down, pull your knees to your chest and watch as the water around you rises. From the space between your plump, buoyant breasts, you can see your male parts swaying. You truly are both man and woman, crouching there in the water. It was a strange posture to take. Wondering just what the master of the house might be thinking, you lift your eyes and see him, arms crossed, intensely observing you. You get the feeling that you'll be scolded if you don't wash yourself, so you splash some water over your shoulders with your right hand and rub as a token gesture. The man's stern expression suggested that he wouldn't be fooled by such a feeble attempt, and he continued to stare fixedly at you.

It isn't as if you don't know how to take a bath, you think, helpless in your current situation. But you just can't seem to remember the proper way to wash your body. You look at the hazy reflection of your face in the water and try to think of it as either masculine or feminine. It could be both or neither—it's hard to tell when it's wet. Maybe it would become a little more obvious if you wiped off the drops of water. You tighten your stomach and try to stand up, when the man's hand stretches forth and sends you back to the water. You cautiously look to his face. He purses his lips and shakes his head from left to right, supposedly meaning, "Don't you dare get out of the tub until you give yourself a proper scrub."

You wonder what you would see if your own face were reflected in that mirror in the other room. You'd probably be too afraid to peek and find out whether the reflection looked more masculine or feminine.

Instead of cooling down, it feels like the water in the tub was heating up little by little. At this rate, you'll end up a soupy broth! Was there a stove underneath the tub?

The sweet, tart apple porridge you had earlier started to fizz in your bowels and you can't seem to relax your lower half. The female half of you swells up, the male part does likewise and starts to rise upward. It had only just started, but it was already more than you could handle. What's more, a tail like a paintbrush was beginning to grow out of your coccyx, and armadillo-like scales surfaced on your inner thighs. Every time a pulse passed through your veins, the boundaries of your body would creak. You're growing. You feel like your pelvis is about to split in half. The fluids coursing through you fill your lower half—not just blood, but lymphatic fluid, sweat, saliva. When you try to stand up, a big hand stretches out and holds your head down. With a splash, you fall on your behind back into the tub. You can't tell if the tepid water is enveloping you, if it's flowing out of your body, or if the liquids inside and outside your body are dissolving together. *But this can't be happening. A voice somewhere is protesting, No, don't! Stop! Don't cross this line—no, don't! This is bad! Stop it! You can't let this happen! There's no turning back once you've done it . . . It may already be too late. Just hold out a little longer.* Opposing that voice of reason, the captivation of this strange fusion weakens your will. *It's all right now, it's okay,* the voice whispers. And so you surrender yourself to the surreal situation. *It's all right. Drift with the flow and let it take you to where you're going. Don't struggle against it—after all, you have no control of the situation anyway. As long as it feels good, refreshing; that's all that matters.*

You jolt awake with a gasp. The dark ceiling is just above your head. You hear the sound of the car's shaking and rattling, the sound of friction between the tracks and the wheels. You have to go to the bathroom. A look at your watch tells you it's 2:30 a.m.—quite a bit of time before morning. It may be a pain in the neck, but when you gotta go, you gotta go.

Aoki Jungo

Jungo was born in Saitama. He graduated from Waseda University's Department of Literature. His first novel, *A Fairy Tale of Forty Days and Forty Nights,* was awarded the Shincho Prize for New Writers in 2003, while he was attending university. The story is about a man who has a part-time job handing out fliers in his daily life, while writing a novel. One of the selection committee members praised Jungo's work and prized it highly for his fresh ideas and profound representations of a *freeter's* life. In 2005, his second novel, *Near the Crater,* was nominated for the Mishima Prize and an anthology of these two novels won the Noma Literary Prize.

As Told by a Nocturnal Witness

Translated by Tomoko Kozaki

THE YOUNG WOMAN IN QUESTION WAS ON THE verge of conception. No one had even considered that such a thing could happen to her, of all people.

At this point the fact remains unacknowledged by anyone including the woman herself. There is nothing to be said just now. At the earliest the news will come out after a missed period (she is bound to use one of those easy pregnancy tests) and in a month or two (after tests on her urine sample at some clinic) the pregnancy will be revealed post factum.

But she, of all people! Her family was bound to have mixed feelings of joy, an awkward sort of embarrassment, and the urge to blurt out, "Show me the punk responsible and I'll $#%3 him!"

Due to his responsibilities to the young woman, her father wasn't going to keep quiet about the whole thing—and in fact he was far from staying silent. He embodied what they call the psyche of a typical male parent. He went on forever with his moralizing lectures, kept coming back to a point he'd already made, even resorted to unbelievably foul language.

No matter how you look at it, the mother was the only one with enough patience to deal with such behavior. Thus they seemed to fall naturally into their respective familial roles—the outraged father concerned for his daughter's well-being, and the mother trying to console him.

Scene 1. The two happened to be talking about that daughter of theirs that night as well. Nothing has "happened" yet—this scene is taking place quite a while before the young woman makes her confession. Of course, they're talking in the same living room in their usual seats in the house in which they raised their daughter. Every night in the same way the cool white lights, whether they're fluorescent or incandescent, have made the room bright as day and the figures now stand out as clearly as ever.

That's Dad.

And that's Mom.

She, the young woman, is their only daughter. Since she doesn't live with her parents anymore they're perpetually worried for one reason or another. She is at that ever-so-precious premarital stage and noncommittal relationships cannot be allowed. As they say, it's too late by the time something has gone wrong. Apparently there is talk of her current relationship having irremediable results if she just lets it drag on. It might be a rule of kin or what's said of life in general but that's the way it goes.

Is the issue a matter of individual will or is it mere selfishness on the daughter's part? She heaves a sigh in response to her parents' usual complaints and admonitions. She is already painfully aware of the differences in their perceptions of the world. "I started dating someone, so what?" she thinks. "I mean, could they get any more old-fashioned?"

Scene 2.

"—I'm in my late twenties for crying out loud."

"Uh-huh. And what did your dad say?"

"The same thing he *always* does . . ."

There has been no overt proof of any pregnancy and the couple is not aware of it. In fact, it's beyond their imagination. All four of them had been deep asleep at the exact moment she conceived.

Her parents lived in the neighboring prefecture. There was a highway and a phone line that connected them. There might be a slight difference in the weather and in the way they'd feel an earthquake but for sure they were in the same time zone.

It was the dad in his pajamas who had the phone in his hand and a second later her cell went off.

"Hello . . . but do you know what time it is? [The clock indicated roughly half past midnight.] (Where are you?) Home of course, what'd you think? (What're you doing?) Huh, I can't say. (How are you feeling?)"

Scene 3. The phone rings eerily in the middle of the night. From the way she's speaking into the phone anyone would think she was defending herself against accusations by a jealous boyfriend.

"It's my dad," whispers his biological daughter quite unhappily. She sticks her tongue out at the phone. The dad on the other end is scratching his back.

"(Is anybody with you?) Oh Dad, I'm busy right now, I'm fine, no one's here!—So good night!"

The daughter did her best to sound upset but had been on the verge of giving herself away with a tell-tale laugh. She held her breath as she pressed the end-call button. She had told herself not to laugh and that had only intensified the urge. What a situation she was in, and the tension!

"Ha, ha-ha . . ."

She was finally letting it out. It was as if she had succumbed without rhyme or reason. A swoosh of air came out of her nostrils, the kind that feels cooler when it hits your skin. Have I been laughing, she had asked.

"(Well yeah.)"

But for me it seemed simply impossible to understand such behavior. I shrugged my shoulders to say I wasn't getting it. I felt lonely for there was really no place for me to be, what with her parents, the father-daughter conversation, and now with her like this.

"What'd your dad say?" I asked anxiously.

Dad's turn.

Mom's turn.

"The likes of him need a real good wake-up call."

"You're right, it can't be helped. Let's give him a good old punch in the head."

The clock indicated it was about two o'clock. This was the night on which the daughter was going to conceive, or was getting closer to her moment of destiny.

She was in the room all by herself. A pair of male shoes was missing from the entrance to her apartment. There was something to it that denied the implication of his having left altogether. Both of them had run out of cigarettes, and since they were also low on their stock of alcohol he had gone out to the nearest store.

Outdoors, Scene 4. I crossed the street in front of the apartment and made a left, away from the station. Right away the signal for pedestrians started to blink and turned red as the cars got their green light. I could hear several cars heading this way and they zoomed past the light from right to left. For a while now there had been no cars going in the opposite direction. For whatever reason that had caught my attention. Normally during the day this road had quite a bit of traffic. Sometimes there was more and sometimes less, but late at night you could go in either direction without being stopped all that much.

A while later, the hurried footsteps of a woman in high heels on the apartment side of the road echoed all around. It was after the last train for the night had left and there were bound to be even less people walking. The woman was wearing a light spring coat in some spring-appropriate color. She seemed to be somewhere between twenty and forty years old.

The clicking of her heels had retreated into the distance long ago, and a car heading this way had been stopped at a red light three lights down. The narrow street turning on to this road was just as empty. The air was indicative of the lateness of the night. It was as though one was suddenly being reminded again of just how quiet it was.

But neither of us had been particularly paying attention to that silence outside. At once a mysterious growling of what was for sure a cat echoed down the road and reached our ears amplified. "What was that? Oh, a cat." "Huh? What is this, it doesn't even sound like a cat."

"UREYYY!!" "AHYYY AHYYY AHY WHOOOHHHHHHH!!" The meowing was pretty powerful. It was almost like a grown man howling from the pit of his stomach. It was hard to tell where exactly the cat was although it had to be somewhere nearby. It was a few moments later that I got back to the apartment.

I still had my back to her since I was locking the door but she started talking right away.

"By the way did you get any gum?"

"G . . . gum?"

"Yeah, gum."

"You mean gum as in gum?"

That's when I realized what she meant.

"Oh, sorry, I forgot."

"What? D'you do that on purpose?"

"Of course n . . . huh?"

No gum. There's no need. Don't forget the gum that we need. We can still without the gum. But we need the gum. But I can't go out just to buy the gum.

"Damn!"

". . . . . . No way."

The minor argument (Scene 5) had no choice but to be interrupted by the howling cat.

"URRIIIII!!" "DI-OWO-OWOWO!!"

The couple looked at each other.

"Wasn't that two cats?"

"Yep, there's two."

By sunrise the following morning a fertilized egg had begun to float around. Technically this was the beginning of a life and in fact was the zero-th day, or perhaps the first day of her pregnancy, but since the counting of any pregnancy is based on when the first day of the last period was, hers was surprisingly already in its second week. And no one even had a clue.

From a medical perspective pregnancy is defined from the point when a fertilized egg is safely implanted on the lining of the uterus after having travelled for a week through the fallopian tube. Until implantation there's the risk of ectopic pregnancy, hydatidiform mole, chemical abortion and more. There's no knowing what will happen and it isn't until the middle of the second trimester that the pregnancy becomes more stable, and even then there's still a long road ahead. I balled my fingers into a tighter fist.

That week the two of them drank and smoked like they always did, and continued to do so into the third and fourth week as well. The fetus is susceptible to all kinds of things at the beginning of a pregnancy and yet the couple was doing what they wanted to like any other day. That was their style.

The first symptoms appeared in the form of preferences for particular food and drinks. She stopped drinking what she used to love, the *chu-hi* as well as liqueur-based cocktails and fruit liquor, now wanting only beer and the low-malt kind called *happoshu*. Quite a change. She said her mouth felt icky at times and puffed on menthol cigarettes. She kept on asking for ice cream. It had to be a particular flavor by a particular company. Now I want something rich like vanilla and chocolate, she would say, and other times ask for the lighter, crushed flavored ice. She suffered from unaccountable headaches, fever, exhaustion and other symptoms akin to morning sickness. In the end it was "Oh my gosh I didn't get it yet."

This implied the following:
- No need to use sanitary napkins or worry about staining underwear
- No monthly discomfort or pain
- No more anemic days from losing blood and iron
- No more "I can't today because it's you-know-what."

Or perhaps it was just a loss of cyclic regularity.

It's hard to forgo thinking about those mysterious cats. Like the mom and dad in the story the roles of the cats were merely a "Voice 3" and a "Voice 4," but for whatever reason their feline presence was such that they also came to be talked about by the descendants of the pregnant daughter.

The tiger-striped male and the white female never once showed themselves and yet would often appear as two individual cats in the stories shared in the family. In effect it was actually a story of some cats that had brought good fortune to the family at night.

The pregnant daughter had learned of the baby's gender in the beginning of her last trimester. It was a girl and was named Kirara soon after birth. It was decided that in Chinese characters the name would be written not as 雲母 (cloud—mother) nor 希羅ﾗ (hope—woven cloth) but as 稀星 (rare—star). Apparently the implication was that the baby was a gift from the heavens, and the fact that they were discussing names so extensively was proof that the baby had become the main topic in the family.

Before coming home from the hospital the baby had stayed in the mother's room, with the mother always sleeping next to her. The father hardly showed himself. Other members of the family kept on popping their heads in to peer into the newborn's face and talked about who she looked like. The cats were completely forgotten about at this point. When compared with animals the baby, like many other babies, resembled the monkey the most.

With her eyes shut most of the time the baby girl had been flitting in and out of sleep. Real kittens are like this, too, they keep their eyes shut when they're born, but when someone talked to the baby or tickled her feet there were some very subtle responses around her eyes that were indicative of her being a human baby. Perhaps she was the most expressive with her hands. The plump and tiny maple leaf look-alikes would immediately wrap their fingers around the mother's finger that had touched them ever so gently.

Addendum. Cats are known to expand their territory when it's that time of the year. Typically the territorial radius of a non-domesticated cat is about a kilometer, and it is rare for male cats to go beyond their territory to hunt for a partner. In some cases a map will be necessary to track down the paths that will explain how a pair of cats met.

One day a male cat that had been roaming around the area south of Nokata Station in Nakano, Tokyo was walking north along the No. 7 highway loop as if he were heading for the Toyotama-riku Bridge, going over the Seibu Shinjuku railroad tracks, over the Shin Ome Highway, across several wards, all the way into Nerima.

The other cat had made her claim: the main shopping arcade in Minami-nagasaki, Toshima was her territory.

"We haven't seen that kitty lately."

"I wonder what's happened to her?"

A local shopkeeper and a customer had been talking about her a few days after she had left. It was rare for a female cat to leave her territory but she had not been seen.

Urban cats often develop a preference for narrow alleys, in which case a wide-open highway would imply the edge or the end of their world. In order to cross such a road a cat would have to wait until it was late at night when there was less traffic. It was past one a.m. when the two cats set their feet in the North Toyotama area.

One of them had crossed the New Mejiro Dori and had headed south while the other had gone across Kanshichi Dori towards a quieter area where there were hardly any shops, wandering aimlessly around the North Toyotama area. Evidently a chain restaurant called Gusto was all there was and a map of the area showed nothing else in particular.

The cats had been walking around for an hour or so. They had been sniffing and investigating their feline markings and at some point had become the pursuer and the pursued. One purred passionately and approached. The other showed signs of a response but growled fiercely if he dared to come any closer. An even more desperate pass is made. Sulking, one then looks the other way. "O-WO-OO." "SHAAA." Glaring at each other they had begun to walk in a circle.

The male cat runs after her and puts his front paws on her body. She is writhing to get away. He has his teeth into her and has wrestled her down. She rolls right and left and pees several times over. He now has her tucked underneath with his back legs. She stops moving.

Their bodies remain folded on top of each other for a few seconds, perhaps thirty seconds or so—

The male cat lifts himself up and steps back. The female cat suddenly springs up. (There might be times when she'll let out a "GYA-WO" and turning around deliver a *true* cat-to-cat punch.)

Caught off guard he is stunned. She, on the other hand, has already left him in search of another male.

Haruki Murakami

Haruki Murakami was born in Kyoto and now lives near Tokyo. He is one of the most popular and controversial of today's Japanese authors. His genre-defying work has been described as postmodern, off-beat, and surrealist. His writing has been translated into thirty-eight languages, and the most recent of his many honors is the Yomiuri Literary Prize, whose previous recipients include Yukio Mishima, Kenzaburo Oe and Kobo Abe. His publications that have been translated into English include *After the Quake; Dance Dance Dance; The Elephant Vanishes; Hard-Boiled Wonderland and the End of the World; Kafka on the Shore; Norwegian Wood; South of the Border, West of the Sun; Sputnik Sweetheart; Underground: The Tokyo Gas Attacks and the Japanese Psyche; A Wild Sheep Chase;* and *The Wind-Up Bird Chronicle.*

Super-Frog Saves Tokyo

Translated by Jay Rubin

KATAGIRI FOUND A GIANT FROG WAITING FOR HIM in his apartment. It was powerfully built, standing over six feet tall on its hind legs. A skinny little man no more than five foot three, Katagiri was overwhelmed by the frog's imposing bulk.

"Call me 'Frog,'" said the frog in a clear, strong voice.

Katagiri stood rooted in the doorway, unable to speak.

"Don't be afraid. I'm not here to hurt you. Just come and close the door. Please."

Briefcase in his right hand, grocery bag with fresh vegetables and canned salmon cradled in his left arm, Katagiri didn't dare move.

"Please, Mr. Katagiri, hurry and close the door, and take off your shoes."

The sound of his own name helped Katagiri to snap out of it. He closed the door as ordered, set the grocery bag on the raised wooden floor, pinned the briefcase under one arm and untied his shoes. Frog gestured for him to take a seat at the kitchen table, which he did.

"I must apologize, Mr. Katagiri, for having barged in while you were out," Frog said. "I knew it would be a shock for you to find me here. But I had no choice. How about a cup of tea? I thought you would be coming home soon, so I boiled some water."

Katagiri still had his briefcase jammed under his arm. Somebody's playing a joke on me, he thought. Somebody's rigged himself up in this huge frog costume just to have fun with me. But he knew, as he watched Frog pour boiling water into the teapot, humming all the while, that these had to be the limbs and movements of a real frog. Frog set a cup of green tea in front of Katagiri and poured another one for himself.

Sipping his tea, Frog asked, "Calming down?"

But still Katagiri could not speak.

"I know I should have made an appointment to visit you, Mr. Katagiri. I am fully aware of the proprieties. Anyone would be shocked to find a big frog waiting for him at home. But an urgent matter brings me here. Please forgive me."

"Urgent matter?" Katagiri managed to produce words at last.

"Yes, indeed," Frog said. "Why else would I take the liberty of barging into a person's home? Such discourtesy is not my customary style."

"Does this 'matter' have something to do with me?"

"Yes and no," Frog said with a tilt of the head. "No and yes."

I've got to get a grip on myself, thought Katagiri. "Do you mind if I smoke?"

"Not at all, not at all," Frog said with a smile. "It's your home. You don't have to ask my permission. Smoke and drink as much as you like. I myself am not a smoker, but I can hardly impose my distaste for tobacco on others in their own homes."

Katagiri pulled a pack of cigarettes from his coat pocket and struck a match. He saw his hand trembling as he lit up. Seated opposite him, Frog seemed to be studying his every movement.

"You don't happen to be connected with some kind of gang by any chance?" Katagiri found the courage to ask.

"Ha ha ha ha ha ha! What a wonderful sense of humor you have, Mr. Katagiri!" Frog said, slapping his webbed hand against his thigh. "There may be a shortage of skilled labor, but what gang is going to hire a frog to do their dirty work? They'd be made a laughingstock."

"Well, if you're here to negotiate a repayment, you're wasting your time. I have no authority to make such decisions. Only my superiors can do that, I just follow orders. I can't do a thing for you."

"Please, Mr. Katagiri," Frog said, raising one webbed finger. "I have not come here on such petty business. I am fully aware that you are Assistant Chief of the lending division of the Shinjuku branch of the Tokyo Security Trust Bank. But my visit has nothing to do with the repayment of loans. I have come here to save Tokyo from destruction."

Katagiri scanned the room for a hidden TV camera in case he was being made the butt of some huge, terrible joke. But there was no camera. It was a small apartment. There was no place for anyone to hide.

"No," Frog said. "We are the only ones here. I know you are thinking that I must be mad or that you are having some kind of dream, but I am not crazy and you are not dreaming. This is absolutely, positively serious."

"To tell you the truth, Mr. Frog—"

"Please," Frog said, raising one finger again. "Call me 'Frog.'"

"To tell you the truth, Frog," Katagiri said, "I can't quite understand what is going on here. It's not that I don't trust you, but I don't seem to be able to grasp the situation exactly. Do you mind if I ask you a question or two?"

"Not at all, not at all," Frog said. "Mutual understanding is of critical importance. There are those who say that 'understanding' is merely the sum total of our misunderstandings, and while I do find this view interesting in its own way, I am afraid we have no time to spare on pleasant digressions. The best thing would be for us to achieve mutual understanding via the shortest possible route. Therefore, by all means, ask as many questions as you wish."

"Now; you are a real frog, am I right?"

"Yes, of course, as you can see. A real frog is exactly what I am. A product neither of metaphor nor allusion nor deconstruction nor sampling nor any other such complex process, I am a genuine frog. Shall I croak for you?"

Frog tilted back his head and flexed the muscles of his huge throat: Ribit, Ri-i-i-bit, Ribit ribit ribit Ribit Ribit Ri-i-i bit. His gigantic croaks rattled the pictures hanging on the walls.

"Fine, I see, I see!" Katagiri said, worried about the thin walls of the cheap apartment house in which he lived. "That's great. You are, without question, a real frog."

"One might also say that I am the sum total of all frogs. Nonetheless, this does nothing to change the fact that I am a frog. Anyone claiming that I am not a frog would be a dirty liar. I would smash such a person to bits!"

Katagiri nodded. Hoping to calm himself, he picked up his cup and swallowed a mouthful of tea. "You said before that you have come here to save Tokyo from destruction?"

"That is what I said."

"What kind of destruction?"

"Earthquake," Frog said with the utmost gravity.

Mouth dropping open, Katagiri looked at Frog. And Frog, saying nothing, looked at Katagiri. They went on staring at each other like this for some time. Next it was Frog's turn to open his mouth.

"A very, very big earthquake. It is set to strike Tokyo at 8:30 a.m. on February 18. Three days from now. A much bigger earthquake than the one that struck Kobe last month. The number of dead from such a quake would probably exceed 150,000—mostly from accidents involving the commuter system: derailments, falling vehicles, crashes, the collapse of elevated expressways and rail lines, the crushing of subways, the explosion of tanker trucks. Buildings will be transformed into piles of rubble, their inhabitants crushed to death. Fires everywhere, the road system in a state of collapse, ambulances and fire trucks useless, people just lying there, dying. One hundred and fifty thousand of them! Pure hell. People will be made to realize what a fragile condition the intensive collectivity known as 'city' really is." Frog said this with a gentle shake of the head. "The epicenter will be close to the Shinjuku ward office."

"Close to the Shinjuku ward office?"

"To be precise, it will hit directly beneath the Shinjuku branch of the Tokyo Security Trust Bank."

A heavy silence followed.

"And you," Katagiri said, "are planning to stop this earthquake?"

"Exactly," Frog said, nodding. "That is exactly what I propose to do. You and I will go underground beneath the Shinjuku branch of the Tokyo Security Trust Bank to do mortal combat with Worm."

As a member of the Trust Bank lending division, Katagiri had fought his way though many a battle. He had weathered sixteen years of daily combat since the day he graduated from the university and joined the bank's staff. He was, in a word, a collection officer—a post that won him little popularity. Everyone in his division preferred to make loans, especially at the time of the bubble. They had so much money in those days that almost any likely piece of collateral—be it land or stock—was enough to convince loan officers to give away whatever they were asked for, the bigger the loan the better their reputations in the company. Some loans, though, never made it back to the bank: they got "stuck to the bottom of the pan." It was Katagiri's job to take care of those. And when the bubble burst, the work piled on. First stock prices fell, and then land values, and collateral lost all significance. "Get out there," his boss commanded him, "and squeeze whatever you can out of them."

The Kabukicho neighborhood of Shinjuku was a labyrinth of violence: old-time gangsters, Korean mobsters, Chinese Mafia, guns and drugs, money flowing beneath the surface from one murky den to another, people vanishing every now and then like puffs of smoke. Plunging into Kabukicho to collect a bad debt, Katagiri had been surrounded more than once by mobsters threatening to kill him, but he had never been frightened. What good would it have done them to kill one man running around for the bank? They could stab him if they wanted to. They could beat him up. He was perfect for the job: no wife, no kids, both parents dead, a brother and sister he had put through college married off. So what if they killed him? It wouldn't change anything for anybody—least of all for Katagiri himself.

It was not Katagiri but the thugs surrounding him who got nervous when they saw him so calm and cool. He soon earned a kind of reputation in their world as a tough guy. Now, though, the tough Katagiri was at a total loss. What the hell was this frog talking about?

"Worm? Who is Worm?" he asked with some hesitation.

"Worm lives underground. He is a gigantic worm. When he gets angry, he causes earthquakes," Frog said. "And right now he is very, very angry."

"What is he angry about?" Katagiri asked.

"I have no idea," Frog said. "Nobody knows what Worm is thinking inside that murky head of his. Few have ever seen him. He is usually asleep. That's what he really likes to do: take long, long naps. He goes on sleeping for years—decades—in the warmth and darkness underground. His eyes, as you might imagine, have atrophied, his brain has turned to jelly as he sleeps. If you ask me, I'd guess he probably isn't thinking anything at all, just lying there and feeling every little rumble and reverberation that comes his way, absorbing them into his body and storing them up. And then, through some kind of chemical process, he replaces most of them with rage. Why this happens I have no idea. I could never explain it."

Frog fell silent watching Katagiri and waiting until his words had sunk in. Then he went on: "Please don't misunderstand me, though. I feel no personal animosity toward Worm. I don't see him as the embodiment of evil. Not that I would want to be his friend, either: I just think that as far as the world is concerned, it is, in a sense, all right for a being like him to exist. The world is like a great big overcoat, and it needs pockets of various shapes and sizes. But right at the moment, Worm has reached the point where he is too dangerous to ignore. With all the different kinds of hatred he has absorbed and stored inside himself over the years, his heart and body have swollen to gargantuan proportions—bigger than ever before. And to make matters worse, last month's Kobe earthquake shook him out of the deep sleep he was enjoying. He experienced a revelation inspired by his profound rage: It was time now for him, too, to cause a massive earthquake, and he'd do it here, in Tokyo. I know what I'm talking about, Mr. Katagiri: I have received reliable information on the timing and scale of the earthquake from some of my best bug friends."

Frog snapped his mouth shut and closed his round eyes in apparent fatigue.

"So what you're saying is," Katagiri said, "that you and I have to go underground together and fight Worm to stop the earthquake."

"Exactly."

Katagiri reached for his cup of tea, picked it up and put it back. "I still don't get it," he said. "Why did you choose me to go with you?"

Frog looked straight into Katagiri's eyes and said, "I have always had the profoundest respect for you, Mr. Katagiri. For sixteen long years, you have silently accepted the most dangerous, least glamorous assignments—the jobs that others have avoided—and you have carried them off beautifully. I know full well how difficult this has been for you, and I do not believe that either your superiors or your colleagues properly appreciate your accomplishments. They are blind, the whole lot of them. But you, unappreciated and unpromoted, have never once complained.

"Nor is it simply a matter of your work. After your parents died you raised your teenage brother and sister single-handedly, put them through college and even arranged for them to marry, all at great sacrifice of your time and income, and at the expense of your own marriage prospects. In spite of this, your brother and sister have never once expressed gratitude for your efforts on their behalf. Far from it. They have shown you no respect and acted with the most callous disregard for your loving kindness. In my opinion, their behavior is unconscionable. I almost wish I could beat them to a pulp on your behalf. But you, meanwhile, show no trace of anger.

"To be quite honest, Mr. Katagiri, you are nothing much to look at, and you are far from eloquent, so you tend to be looked down upon by those around you. I, however, can see what a sensible and courageous man you are. In all of Tokyo, with its teeming millions, there is no one else I could trust as much as you to fight by my side."

"Tell me, Mr. Frog," Katagiri said.

"Please," Frog said, raising one finger again. "Call me 'Frog.'"

"Tell me, Frog," Katagiri said, "how do you know so much about me?"

"Well, Mr. Katagiri, I have not been frogging all these years for nothing. I keep my eye on the important things in life."

"But still, Frog," Katagiri said, "I'm not particularly strong, and I don't know anything about what's happening underground. I don't have the kind of muscle it will take to fight Worm in the darkness. I'm sure you can find somebody a lot stronger than me—a man who does karate, say, or a Self-Defense Forces commando."

Frog rolled his large eyes. "Tell you the truth, Mr. Katagiri," he said, "I'm the one who will do all the fighting. But I can't do it alone. This is the key thing: I need your courage and your passion for justice. I need you to stand behind me and say, 'Way to go, Frog! You're doing great! I know you can win! You're fighting the good fight!'"

Frog opened his arms wide, then slapped his webbed hands down on his knees again.

"In all honesty, Mr. Katagiri, the thought of fighting Worm in the dark frightens me, too. For many years I lived as a pacifist, loving art, living with nature. Fighting is not something I like to do. I do it because I have to. And this particular fight will be a fierce one; that is certain. I may not return from it alive. I may lose a limb or two in the process. But I cannot—I will not—run away. As Nietzsche said, the highest wisdom is to have no fear. What I want from you, Mr. Katagiri, is for you to share your simple courage with me, to support me with your whole heart as a true friend. Do you understand what I am trying to tell you?"

None of this made any sense to Katagiri, but still he felt that—unreal as it sounded—he could believe whatever Frog said to him. Something about Frog—the look on his face, the way he spoke—had a simple honesty that appealed directly to the heart. After years of work in the toughest division of the Security Trust Bank, Katagiri possessed the ability to sense such things. It was all but second nature to him.

"I know this must be difficult for you, Mr. Katagiri. A huge frog comes barging into your place and asks you to believe all these outlandish things. Your reaction is perfectly natural. And so I intend to provide you with proof that I exist. Tell me, Mr. Katagiri: you have been having a great deal of trouble recovering a loan the bank made to Big Bear Trading, have you not?"

"That's true," Katagiri said.

"Well, they have a number of extortionists working behind the scenes, and those individuals are mixed up with the mobsters. They're scheming to make the company go bankrupt and get out of its debts. Your bank's loan officer shoved a pile of cash at them without a decent background check, and, as usual, the one who's left to clean up after him is you, Mr. Katagiri. But you're having a hard time sinking your teeth into these fellows: they're no pushovers. And there may be a powerful politician backing them up. They're into you for 700 million. That is the situation you are dealing with, am I right?"

"You certainly are."

Frog stretched his arms out wide, his big green webs opening like pale wings. "Don't worry, Mr. Katagiri. Leave everything to me. By tomorrow morning, old Frog will have your problems solved. Relax and have a good night's sleep."

With a big smile on his face, Frog stood up. Then, flattening himself like a dried squid, he slipped out through the gap at the side of the closed door, leaving Katagiri all alone. The two teacups on the kitchen table were the only indication that Frog had ever been in Katagiri's apartment.

The moment Katagiri arrived at work the next morning at nine, the phone on his desk rang.

"Mr. Katagiri," said a man's voice. It was cold and businesslike. "My name is Shiraoka. I'm an attorney with the Big Bear case. I received a call from my client this morning with regard to the pending loan matter. He wants you to know that he will take full responsibility for returning the entire amount requested, by the due date. He will also give you a signed memorandum to that effect. His only request is that you do not send Frog to his home again. I repeat: He wants you to ask Frog never to visit his home again. I'm not entirely sure what this is supposed to mean, but I believe it should be clear to you, Mr. Katagiri. Am I correct?"

"You are indeed," Katagiri said.

"You will be kind enough to convey my message to Frog, I trust."

"That I will do. Your client will never see Frog again."

"Thank you very much. I will prepare the memorandum for you by tomorrow."

"I appreciate it," Katagiri said.

The connection was cut.

Frog visited Katagiri in his Trust Bank office at lunchtime. "I assume that Big Bear case is working out well for you?"

Katagiri glanced around uneasily.

"Don't worry," Frog said. "You are the only one who can see me. But now I am sure you realize I actually exist. I am not a product of your imagination. I can take action and produce results. I am a living being."

"Tell me, Mr. Frog," Katagiri said.

"Please," Frog said, raising one finger, "call me 'Frog.'"

"Tell me, Frog," Katagiri said. "What did you do to them?"

"Oh, nothing much," Frog said. "Nothing much more complicated than boiling Brussels sprouts. I just gave them a little scare. A touch of psychological terror. As Joseph Conrad once wrote, true terror is the kind that men feel toward their imagination. But never mind that, Mr. Katagiri. Tell me about the Big Bear case. It is working out well, I assume?"

Katagiri nodded and lit a cigarette. "Seems to be."

"So, then, have I succeeded in gaining your trust with regard to the matter I broached to you last night? Will you join me to fight against Worm?"

Sighing, Katagiri removed his glasses and wiped them. "To tell you the truth, I am not too crazy about the idea, but I don't suppose that's enough to get me out of it."

"No," Frog said. "It is a matter of responsibility and honor. You may not be 'too crazy' about the idea, but we have no choice: you and I must go underground and face Worm. If we should happen to lose our lives in the process, we will gain no one's sympathy. And even if we manage to defeat Worm, no one will praise us. No one will ever know that such a battle even raged far beneath their feet. Only you and I will know, Mr. Katagiri. However it turns out, ours will be a lonely battle."

Katagiri looked at his own hand for a while, then watched the smoke rising from his cigarette. Finally, he spoke. "You know Mr. Frog, I'm just an ordinary person."

"Make that 'Frog,' please," Frog said, but Katagiri let it go.

"I'm an absolutely ordinary guy. Less than ordinary. I'm going bald, I'm getting a potbelly, I turned 40 last month. My feet are flat. The doctor told me recently that I have diabetic tendencies. It's been three months or more since I last slept with a woman—and I had to pay for it. I do get some recognition within the division for my ability to collect on loans, but no real respect. I don't have a single person who likes me, either at work or in my private life. I don't know how to talk to people, and I'm bad with strangers, so I never make friends. I have no athletic ability, I'm tone-deaf, short, phimotic, nearsighted—and astigmatic. I live a horrible life. All I do is eat, sleep and shit. I don't know why I'm even living. Why should a person like me have to be the one to save Tokyo?"

"Because, Mr. Katagiri, Tokyo can only be saved by a person like you. And it's for people like you that I am trying to save Tokyo."

Katagiri sighed again, more deeply this time. "All right, then, what do you want me to do?"

Frog told Katagiri his plan. They would go underground on the night of February 17 (one day before the earthquake was scheduled to happen). Their way in would be through the basement boiler room of the Shinjuku branch of the Tokyo Security Trust Bank. They would meet there late at night (Katagiri would stay in the building on the pretext of working overtime). Behind a section of wall was a vertical shaft, and they would find Worm at the bottom by climbing down a 150-foot rope ladder.

"Do you have a battle plan in mind?" Katagiri asked.

"Of course I do. We would have no hope of defeating an enemy like Worm without a battle plan. He is a slimy creature: You can't tell his mouth from his anus. And he is as big as a commuter train."

"What is your battle plan?"

After a thoughtful pause Frog answered, "Hmm, what is it they say— 'Silence is golden?'"

"You mean I shouldn't ask?"

"That's one way of putting it."

"What if I get scared at the last minute and run away? What would you do then, Mr. Frog?"

"Frog."

"Frog. What would you do then?"

Frog thought about this awhile and answered, "I would fight on alone. My chances of beating him by myself are perhaps just slightly better than Anna Karenina's chances of beating that speeding locomotive. Have you read *Anna Karenina*, Mr. Katagiri?"

When he heard that Katagiri had not read the novel, Frog gave him a look as if to say, "What a shame." Apparently, Frog was very fond of *Anna Karenina*.

"Still, Mr. Katagiri, I do not believe that you will leave me to fight alone. I can tell. It's a question of balls—which, unfortunately, I do not happen to possess. Ha ha ha ha." Frog laughed with his mouth wide open. Balls were not all that Frog lacked. He had no teeth either.

Unexpected things do happen, however.

Katagiri was shot on the evening of February 17. He had finished his rounds for the day and was walking down the street in Shinjuku on his way back to the Trust Bank when a young man in a leather jacket leaped in front of him. The man's face was a blank, and he gripped a small black gun in one hand. The gun was so small and so black that it hardly looked real. Katagiri stared at the object in the man's hand, not registering the fact that it was aimed at him and that the man was pulling the trigger. It all happened too quickly: it didn't make sense to him. But the gun, in fact, went off.

Katagiri saw the barrel jerk in the air and, at the same moment, felt an impact as though someone had struck his right shoulder with a sledgehammer. He felt no pain, but the blow sent him sprawling on the sidewalk. The leather briefcase in his right hand went flying in the other direction. The man aimed the gun at him again. A second shot rang out. A small eatery's sidewalk signboard exploded before his eyes. He heard people screaming. His glasses had flown off, and everything was a blur. He was vaguely aware that the man was approaching with the pistol pointed at him. I'm going to die, he thought. Frog had said that true terror is the kind men feel toward their imagination.

Katagiri cut the switch of his imagination and sank into a weightless silence.

When he woke up, he was in bed. He opened one eye, took a moment to survey his surroundings and then opened the other eye. The first thing that entered his field of vision was a metal stand by the head of the bed and an intravenous feeding tube that stretched from the stand to where he lay. Next he saw a nurse dressed in white. He realized he was lying on his back on a hard bed and wearing some strange piece of clothing under which he seemed to be naked.

Oh yeah, he thought, I was walking along the sidewalk when some guy shot me. Probably in the shoulder. The right one. He relived the scene in his mind. When he remembered the small black gun in the young man's hand, his heart made a disturbing thump. The sons of bitches were trying to kill me! he thought. But it looks as if I made it through OK. My memory is fine. I don't have any pain. And not just pain: I don't have any feeling at all. I can't lift my arm . . .

The hospital room had no windows. He could not tell whether it was day or night. He had been shot just before five in the evening. How much time had passed since then? Had the hour of his nighttime rendezvous with Frog gone by? Katagiri searched the room for a clock, but without his glasses he could see nothing at a distance.

"Excuse me," he called to the nurse.

"Oh, good. You're finally awake," the nurse said.

"What time is it?"

She glanced at her watch.

"Nine-fifteen."

"P.m.?"

"Don't be silly; it's morning!"

"Nine-fifteen a.m.?" Katagiri groaned, barely managing to lift his head from the pillow. The ragged noise that emerged from his throat sounded like someone else's voice. "Nine-fifteen a.m. on February 18?"

"Right," the nurse said, lifting her arm once more to check the date on her digital watch. "Today is February 18, 1995."

"Wasn't there a big earthquake in Tokyo this morning?"

"In Tokyo?"

"In Tokyo."

The nurse shook her head. "Not as far as I know."

He breathed a sigh of relief. Whatever had happened, the earthquake at least had been averted.

"How's my wound doing?"

"Your wound?" she asked. "What wound?"

"Where I was shot."

"Shot?"

"Yeah, near the entrance to the Trust Bank. Some young guy shot me. In the right shoulder, I think."

The nurse flashed a nervous smile in his direction. "I'm sorry, Mr. Katagiri, but you haven't been shot."

"I haven't? Are you sure?"

"As sure as I am that there was no earthquake this morning."

Katagiri was stunned. "Then what the hell am I doing in a hospital?"

"Somebody found you lying in the street, unconscious. In the Kabu-kicho neighborhood of Shinjuku. You didn't have any external wounds. You were just out cold. And we still haven't figured out why. The doctor's going to be here soon. You'd better talk to him."

Lying in the street unconscious? Katagiri was sure he had seen the pistol go off, aimed at him. He took a deep breath and tried to get his head straight. He would start by putting all the facts in order.

"What you're telling me is, I've been lying in this hospital bed, uncon-scious, since early evening yesterday, is that right?"

"Right," the nurse said. "And you had a really bad night, Mr. Katagiri. You must have had some awful nightmares. I heard you yelling, 'Frog! Hey, Frog!' You did it a lot. You have a friend nicknamed Frog?"

Katagiri closed his eyes and listened to the slow, rhythmic beating of his heart as it ticked off the minutes of his life. How much of what he remembered had actually happened and how much was hallucination? Did Frog really exist, and had Frog fought with Worm to put a stop to the earthquake? Or had that just been part of a long dream? Katagiri had no idea what was true anymore.

Frog came to his hospital room that night. Katagiri awoke to find him in the dim light, sitting on a steel folding chair, his back against the wall. Frog's big, bulging eyelids were closed in straight slits.

"Frog," Katagiri called out to him.

Frog slowly opened his eyes. His big white stomach swelled and shrank with his breathing. "I meant to meet you in the boiler room at night the way I promised," Katagiri said, "but I had an accident in the evening—something totally unexpected—and they brought me here."

Frog gave his head a slight shake. "I know. It's okay. Don't worry. You were a great help to me in my fight, Mr. Katagiri."

"I was?"

"Yes, you were. You did a great job in your dreams. That's what made it possible for me to fight Worm to the finish. I have you to thank for my victory."

"I don't get it," Katagiri said. "I was unconscious the whole time. They were feeding me intravenously. I don't remember doing anything in my dream."

"That's fine, Mr. Katagiri. It's better that you don't remember. The whole terrible fight occurred in the area of imagination. That is the precise location of our battlefield. It is there that we experience our victories and our defeats. Each and every one of us is a being of limited duration: all of us eventually go down to defeat. But as Ernest Hemingway saw so clearly, the ultimate value of our lives is decided not by how we win but by how we lose. You and I together, Mr. Katagiri, were able to prevent the annihilation of Tokyo. We saved 150,000 people from the jaws of death. No one realizes it, but that is what we accomplished."

"How did we manage to defeat Worm? And what did I do?"

"We gave everything we had in a fight to the bitter end. We—" Frog snapped his mouth shut and took one great breath. "We used every weapon we could get our hands on, Mr. Katagiri. We used all the courage we could muster. Darkness was our enemy's ally. You brought in a foot-powered generator and used every ounce of your strength to fill the place with light. Worm tried to frighten you away with phantoms of the darkness, but you stood your ground. Darkness vied with light in a horrific battle, and in the light I grappled with the monstrous Worm. He coiled himself around me and bathed me in his horrid slime. I tore him to shreds, but still he refused to die. All he did was divide into smaller pieces. And then . . ."

Frog fell silent, but soon, as if dredging up his last ounce of strength, he began to speak again. "Fyodor Dostoevsky, with unparalleled tenderness, depicted those who have been forsaken by God. He discovered the precious quality of human existence in the ghastly paradox whereby men who have invented God were forsaken by that very God. Fighting with Worm in the darkness, I found myself thinking of Dostoevsky's 'White Knights.' I . . ." Frog's words seemed to founder. "Mr. Katagiri, do you mind if I take a brief nap? I am utterly exhausted."

"Please," Katagiri said. "Take a good, deep sleep."

"I was finally unable to defeat Worm," Frog said, closing his eyes. "I did manage to stop the earthquake, but I was only able to carry our battle to a draw. I inflicted injury on him, and he on me. But to tell you the truth, Mr. Katagiri . . ."

"What is it, Frog?"

"I am, indeed, pure Frog, but at the same time I am a thing that stands for a world of un-Frog."

"Hmm, I don't get that at all."

"Neither do I," Frog said, his eyes still closed. "It's just a feeling I have. What you see with your eyes is not necessarily real. My enemy is, among other things, the me inside me. Inside me is the un-me. My brain is growing murky. The locomotive is coming. But I really want you to understand what I am saying, Mr. Katagiri."

"You're tired, Frog. Go to sleep. You'll get better."

"I am slowly returning to the murk, Mr. Katagiri. And yet . . . I . . ."

Frog lost his grasp on words and slipped into a coma. His arms hung down almost to the floor, and his big, wide mouth drooped open. Straining to focus his eyes, Katagiri was able to make out deep cuts covering Frog's entire body. Discolored streaks ran through his skin, and there was a sunken spot on his head where the flesh had been torn away.

Katagiri stared long and hard at Frog, who sat there now wrapped in the thick cloak of sleep. As soon as I get out of this hospital, he thought, I'll buy *Anna Karenina* and "White Nights" and read them both. Then I'll have a nice, long literary discussion about them with Frog.

Before long, Frog began to twitch all over. Katagiri assumed at first that these were just normal involuntary movements in sleep, but he soon realized his mistake. There was something unnatural about the way Frog's body went on jerking, like a big doll being shaken by someone from behind. Katagiri held his breath and watched. He wanted to run over to Frog, but his own body remained paralyzed.

After a while, a big lump formed over Frog's right eye. The same kind of huge, ugly boil broke out on Frog's shoulder and side and then over his whole body. Katagiri could not imagine what was happening to Frog. He stared at the spectacle, barely breathing.

Then, all of a sudden, one of the boils burst with a loud pop. The skin flew off, and a sticky liquid oozed out, sending a horrible smell across the room. The rest of the boils started popping, one after another, twenty or thirty in all, flinging skin and fluid onto the walls. The sickening, unbearable smell filled the hospital room. Big black holes were left on Frog's body where the boils had burst, and wriggling, maggot-like worms of all shapes and sizes came crawling out. Puffy white maggots. After them emerged some kind of small, centipede-like creatures, whose hundreds of legs made a creepy rustling sound. An endless stream of these things came crawling out of the holes. Frog's body—or the thing that had once been Frog's body—was totally covered by these creatures of the night. His two big eyeballs fell from their sockets onto the floor, where they were devoured by black bugs with strong jaws. Crowds of slimy worms raced each other up the walls to the ceiling, where they covered the fluorescent lights and burrowed into the smoke alarm.

The floor, too, was covered with worms and bugs. They climbed up the lamp and blocked the light, and, of course, they crept onto Katagiri's bed. Hundreds of them came burrowing under the covers. They crawled up his legs, under his bed gown, between his thighs. The smallest worms and maggots crawled inside his anus and ears and nostrils. Centipedes pried open his mouth and crawled inside, one after another. Filled with an intense despair, Katagiri screamed.

Someone snapped a switch and light filled the room.

"Mr. Katagiri!" called the nurse. Katagiri opened his eyes to the light. His body was soaked in sweat. The bugs were gone. All they had left behind in him was a horrible, slimy sensation.

"Another bad dream, eh? Poor dear." With quick, efficient movements, the nurse readied an injection and stabbed the needle into his arm.

He took a long, deep breath and let it out. His heart was expanding and contracting violently.

"What were you dreaming about?"

Katagiri was having trouble differentiating dream from reality. "What you see with your eyes is not necessarily real," he told himself aloud.

"That's so true," the nurse said with a smile. "Especially where those dreams are concerned."

"Frog," he murmured.

"Did something happen to Frog?" she asked.

"He saved Tokyo from being destroyed by an earthquake. All by himself."

"That's nice," the nurse said, replacing his near-empty intravenous-feeding bottle with a new one. "We don't need any more awful things happening in Tokyo. We have plenty already."

"But it cost him his life. He's gone. I think he went back to the murk. He'll never come here again."

Smiling, the nurse toweled the sweat from his forehead. "You were very fond of Frog, weren't you, Katagiri?"

"Locomotive," Katagiri mumbled. "More than anybody." Then he closed his eyes and sank into a restful, dreamless sleep.

Masahiko Shimada

Masahiko Shimada is one of the most visible authors and commentators in Japan today. During his studies in Russian and Eastern European languages at Tokyo University of Foreign Languages, he published the novella *A Tender Divertimento for Leftists* (1983), which was named runner-up for the prestigious Akutagawa Prize. He received the Noma Literary Prize for New Authors for *Music for a Somnambulant Kingdom*. His numerous literary awards include the 1992 Izumi Kyoka Library Prize, the 2006 Ito Sei Prize for Literature, and the prestigious 2008 Art Encouragement Prize awarded by the Minister of Education, Culture, Sports, Science and Technology. Several short stories and his 1989 novel *Dream Messenger* have been translated into English.

The Diary of a Mummy

Translated by Masahiko Shimada

AT ABOUT 2 P.M. ON THE 30TH OF JANUARY 1999 a meat industry worker was out hunting rabbits in the snow-covered wetlands of Kushiro in Hokkaido when he came across a dilapidated hut made of plastic. Thinking it the perfect spot to eat his lunch, he tentatively called out, "Is anyone there?" When he poked his head inside, he found an unexpected occupant had beaten him to it. Lying on a platform covered with straw was a mummy. Still bundled up against the cold, it was lightly coated in dust and frost. The exposed parts of its cracked skin were like a dark brown leather boot, its eyes had sunk deep in their sockets, and it was bone dry. The lower half of the face was covered in beard growth, there was a film of white mold on its bottom lip, and its abdomen had totally caved in. Evidently the corpse had somehow managed to avoid decomposition, becoming instead nicely desiccated. Perhaps it had lost weight while still alive, to make it easier to become mummified.

Scattered around the straw platform were a hatchet and nail clippers, some spent candles, a plastic container, and a washbasin holding the ashes of burnt paper, along with a suitcase and some clothing. A radio and a dozen or so books stood on a shelf made out of branches. There were no signs of dishes or food, nor the slightest hint of any cooking activity. Just what was he doing out here? Lodged between the corpse's legs was a notebook. This corpse was kind enough to come complete with an explanation of its own cause of death—the notebook contained a faithful record of the process leading up to that event.

The mummy was taken away the same day. The hunter returned home empty-handed, having found a mummy but no rabbits.

Based on the account in the notebook, the forensic specialists at a leading medical college and the investigating detectives who examined the body identified the cause of death as suicide by starvation. This must have called for enormous resolve and stoicism, but the motive remained unclear. The deceased was a male person estimated to be about 40 years of age, measuring 173 centimeters in height and weighing 35 kilograms. He had been dead for about 100 days. There were no indications of his name or occupation or what he had been like when alive, and attempts to identify him ran into difficulty. Despite various clues in the form of his skeletal characteristics, blood type, fingerprints and handwriting, nobody in the police databank of prior offenders or missing persons seemed to match the dead man's description. All that was certain was that he must have been someone out of the ordinary. Apparently nobody was looking for him and there were none to mourn his departure, so he was forgotten by the world. There were signs that he himself was well aware of this. Here is his complete diary.

Day One, 7th of August 1998

I've given up eating. Had my final meal at a sushi place in town. Although it was my last meal, I could only eat about the same as usual. It was cheap, so I had quite a lot of money left over. Everything I need for my suicide was in my suitcase, but I dropped in at a supermarket to buy various things just in case. Candles, a hose, a funnel, gum tape, *eau de cologne*, nail clippers, cotton buds, wet tissues, stomach medicine, a tin washbasin, plastic bags and so on. You need money for emergencies, but it seems this is one right now, so I blew the rest on playing pinball.

The spot I've chosen for carrying out my plan uninterrupted is the wetlands here in Kushiro. It's not that I have any particular ties or connections with Kushiro or Hokkaido—it's just that when I was a student I came here once and thought it would be a good place to die. After leaving the cycling track and walking for about an hour, I decided to set up my hut here. All I need is a tiny shelter, built using the existing trees. I hacked off some thick branches and positioned them across the trunks of four trees and placed three layers of vinyl over the top. The basic shape was ready by the time dusk fell. Then I hurriedly collected some straw and ditch reeds and spread them on the ground. There were lots of big mosquitoes, so I started a fire to get some smoke going. My clothes ended up reeking of smoke.

Day Two, 8th of August

No symptoms out of the ordinary. The floor is dampish with just a layer of straw, so I put some branches together to make a simple bed. While I was at it, I knocked together a shelf for my books and bits and pieces. Dug a ditch around the hut for drainage. Worked hard. At night I was dying for some food, and drank lots of water. I'd love something sweet to eat.

Day Three, 9th of August

When I became absorbed in Bach's music on the radio, my hunger just vanished. So perhaps music is edible. Had a bowel movement in the evening.

Day Four, 10th of August

Don't feel any hunger at all. They reckon you can last for a week without water, and for a month with water. It'd be nice if it was over in a week, but things would be tough without water, so I brought along one and a half liters of mineral water. Still had 500 cc left, but a while ago I accidentally spilled it. Does this mean I'll die sooner?

Day Five, 11th of August

Raining since morning. The heavens have ordered me not to die just yet. I used bent twigs to keep some plastic bags open, and collected drinking water by hanging them up where the rain was getting in or streaming down off the roof. When it rains, it sounds like I'm inside a drum. I can't even hear the radio. Once it clears up, I'm going to put some straw on the roof. Read all day.

Day Eight, 14th of August

Time is distorted, not moving. If I keep looking at my watch, the seconds feel like minutes. I wish I had a watch that would make time pass more quickly. I've decided on when I'll listen to the radio—from two to four in the afternoon. There's an FM program of classical music on then. The female announcer has a bell-like voice. She's the only person I have anything to do with. Even without eating a thing, you can still fall in love.

I'm sleeping for longer periods. While awake, I suffer from dizzy spells. I'm peeing more frequently. It's an effort to have to go outside to piss. Haven't had a crap since Day Six.

Day Ten, 16th of August

The sound of the rain is unsettling. When I close my eyes, it sounds like the footsteps of someone coming to visit me. I think it's still too soon to say it's the god of Death. I don't care who it is, as long as they'll talk with me.

Day Twelve, 18th of August

Blood in my urine. My head's clear, but my whole body is lethargic. I'm spending more time lying on my bed. Gave the radio a rest today.

Day Thirteen, 19th of August

I've lost quite a lot of weight. And my face looks like a dead person's. Slight improvement when I shaved. I'm hanging on to life by eating away at my own flesh.

Day Fourteen, 20th of August

Was that a typhoon? I thought my plastic hut would be blown away by the gale-force winds and rain. In the afternoon the wind died down for a while, so I went outside and used some branches to reinforce the hut. My body won't obey me anymore, so it was hard going.

Day Fifteen, 21st of August

Slept about 15 hours. When I turned on the radio, they were broadcasting a night game of baseball. Drank some fresh rainwater. Had a foresty smell about it. My body hurts all over. It seems as if my flesh is being whittled away from the inside.

Day Sixteen, 22nd of August

Another storm today. Lightning struck close by on several occasions, and each time it reverberated through my head. Why doesn't it strike my hut? I've decided to listen to the radio at night, because when I'm lying down in the darkness I lose track of where I am. If I respond to every single word coming from the radio I don't lose myself, and two hours pass in a flash. I keep my finger on the switch the whole time, and make a point of turning it off as soon as I get sleepy. Sometimes what they're carrying on about seems so ridiculous that I feel as if I'm already over there in the next world, listening to the broadcasts of this world.

Day Seventeen, 23rd of August

There was some blood in my urine. When I was at high school I was absolutely bushed when we went on a training camp for our handball club, and I had bloody urine then, but that was the last time. So perhaps fasting is a sport.

Day Eighteen, 24th of August

All the fat on my sides and back has completely disappeared. But my eyes glitter intensely. If anyone saw me now, they'd probably run away in fear. I'm gradually starting to look like bleached bones. No desire to eat. It seems as if my hunger nerves are no longer functioning. Once hunger goes beyond a certain point, the very thought of food makes your stomach hurt. By now my stomach would probably reject food as a foreign object, as if it were germs.

Tonight was a bright moonlit night. I'd like to die on a night like this. But I'd rather die in the daytime. They say life goes out on the ebb tide. Around midnight or noon. I'd like to die in the light.

Day Nineteen, 25th of August

During the day I had stomach pains and a headache. Received an unusual visitor in the afternoon. A centipede was crawling over my bed. No urge to eat it. I've heard that a child was locked in a tiny room by his parents and given nothing to eat, so he caught and ate insects and a mouse that came to nibble on his ears. Adults who abuse children should be sentenced to a fast.

Day Twenty, 26th of August

Felt like vomiting, even though there's nothing left to bring up.

There's still time. If I retraced the path I took to get here, I could return to life. I'd be bound to meet someone if I walked for just an hour. I'd have no feeling of shame. Fasting's no crime. In a week I'd be back to my old weight of 65 kilos, and no doubt I'd live for another 20 or 30 years. Rather, I would be forced to live. Just like in the past, still with no involvement in this world.

I believed I could reverse the insignificance of my life by the manner of my death. This is like the ritual of *seppuku* in the samurai world, which is a kind of corporate society, where those who could never become anything more than stepping-stones for others' success exalt a man in his final moments. For just once in their lives, let's give those dupes who could never have their own way except emotionally and who never had a single opportunity to express their own views the chance to be respected by others. Isn't that what *seppuku* is all about? This act erases all the humiliations suffered in this world.

I have already given notice of my death, but I think it will be a while yet before my turn comes round. I stopped eating on the 7th of August, so I reckon I'm about exactly halfway between life and death. I'm exactly half-dead.

Day Twenty-One, 27th of August

Yesterday I wrote my will, so there's nothing more to write.

What will I do if someone finds me before I die? Should I just quietly abandon my fast, or explain my decision and have them leave? There's absolutely no sign or sound of human life here.

In the evening I could hear the sound of insects. I'm not alone.

Day Twenty-Three, 29th of August

Couldn't bear the pain any longer, so took some stomach medicine. It's absurd to be taking medication when I'm trying to die.

Day Twenty-Four, 30th of August

The water tastes awful. Is water poisoning the cause of my stomach pains? I'm freezing, even though it's summer. I'm wearing a sweater, but I'm still shivering. My mind is the only thing that's clear. Today I read the Holy Bible. I've never been a believer, but I'd like to show respect to the many gods in the world, because a god somewhere might gather me up out of pity. Turned on the radio when I got sick of reading, to be greeted by a delightful female voice asking, "Did you have another fulfilling day today?" If only a woman like that would be at the reception desk at the entrance to the land of the dead.

Day Twenty-Six, 1st of September

My arms and legs are down to half their normal thickness. And my face is so tiny it could fit in the palm of a hand. There's just a covering of skin over my skull. If I'd seen myself a month ago as I am now, I wouldn't have recognized myself. Guess my weight is also down to about two-thirds. Yet my body feels heavy. My eyes are dim, making it difficult to read. When I happened to glance at the palm of my hand I noticed several horizontal indentations in my lifeline.

Day Twenty-Seven, 2nd of September

A mosquito stung me in the neck. Any mosquito that would suck the blood of such a bloodless person as me must be pretty hungry. I even feel a strange affection for it. My neck itches, but I murmured, "May God protect you" to the mosquito that sucked my blood. It seems I've become kind-hearted.

Day Twenty-Eight, 3rd of September

I feel pain, so I'm alive.

What you need in the next world is a hungry spirit. How can I put it ... dying takes guts too.

Day Thirty-Two, 7th of September

The radio is fading—my companion is weakening too. Just like my voice is getting croaky.

Despite wearing two pairs of socks and a sweater and a winter coat, I can't stop shivering. It seems winter has come to the wetlands. If things go on like this, I might freeze to death before I starve.

Day Thirty-Three, 8th of September

The pain in my stomach comes in cycles. It attacks like a geyser spouting hot water every few minutes. Perhaps my body is in sync with the rhythm of the earth. Priests who have attained Buddhahood in the flesh must have suffered from headaches and stomach pains and chills for some time too. No doubt their faith sustained them, but for an unbeliever like me, enduring it has no meaning. If I'd jumped off a cliff or hanged myself I would have died immediately, but instead I'm deliberately trying to experience every nuance of suffering for over a month before I die. I can't say it's ludicrous and stop now. Even if I wanted to jump off a cliff I don't have the strength to make it to the edge. And there's no rope handy to hang myself with.

Day Thirty-Four, 9th of September

Although I'm fasting because I wanted to observe the process of my own death, it's boring just thinking about death all day long. But while idly listening to the birds twittering, the thought came into my mind that I was already dead at the point when I started fasting, and that made me feel a lot easier. Death is just the remaining few percents.

Day Thirty-Five, 10th of September

The radio gave up the ghost before me, so I'm terrified of the nights. I disappear in the pitch darkness. If I stretch out my arms or poke out my tongue or blink, I'm not there. Perhaps someone else is there instead of me. When I wake in the night I think this here is the other world. In the darkness there are no subjects, no verbs, no adjectives. Nor any present, past or future tenses. Just thoughts going round and round in my head. Always half-formed, and with no beginning and no end.

When the darkness starts to lighten from my feet up, for a moment I can forget death. Light is a medicine, the dark a poison. But my joy in greeting the morning is short-lived, and then the suffering of being alive, that stabbing pain, is imposed on me in return for not having died. Of course, even at night my stomach hurts and my head too. Far more than in the daytime. Probably the night pain is the pain of death, and the day pain is the pain of life. Whatever the case, the pain is absolutely not worth it. There are many different ways to commit suicide, but fasting is a highly individual mode of death where you confront yourself and struggle with yourself over a long period. This manner of dying is truly not worth while. But I'm proud of having endured this suffering for as long as 35 days. I've done something that nobody would want to imitate.

Day Thirty-Six, 11th of September

When I flicked on the radio just for something to do, it was playing an opera I remember having heard before. The batteries have recovered a bit, so I was able to listen for about an hour. My whole body is revitalized. And I've plucked up the courage to die.

Day Thirty-Seven, 12th of September

Human beings can create diverse worlds in their minds. Even while still alive we can conceive of a world after death. But sometimes this ability is annoying. All I want now is simply to die.

Day Thirty-Eight, 13th of September

My handwriting has changed. And I'm having difficulty remembering how to write the characters. My batteries haven't run out yet. My breathing is a little uneven. I can feel death so close that I could touch it if I stretched out my hand. I guess the soul requires enormous energy to leave the body. The soul eats the flesh, storing up energy. Before long it should be able to depart my body. We're entering the countdown.

Day Forty, 15th of September

Today is the day I'm scheduled to die. I can't stand up any more. Come to think of it, by fasting, Buddha discovered how to live, and Moses likewise fasted for exactly 40 days and received the Commandments from God. Christ fasted for 40 days so as to be able to resist the temptations offered him by Satan. In terms of the number of days, I'm right up there with these holy people, but I haven't been enlightened in the slightest. But they must have been incredibly strong, since after fasting for 40 days they walked on their own two feet back to their people. I can't walk any more. All I can do is wait until I turn into a corpse.

Day Forty-One, 16th of September

Last night I lit a candle and paid tribute to the holy men who had endured a 40-day fast. Physically I was in pain, but mentally I felt great. I sensed these saints close to me, and Christ and Buddha both seemed to be my friends.

Day Forty-Three, 18th of September

My skin is now like a dried apricot. And it has an unpleasant smell. I guess this is the smell of death. I sprinkled on some *eau de cologne*.

Day Forty-Four, 19th of September

At night I lit the remaining part of the candle I used on the 15th. I watched the flame flicker in the draft. Tearing up Holy Bible page by page, I burnt the pages in the washbasin.

Day Forty-Six, 21st of September

I'm alive. What shall I do if there really is no afterworld? I don't want to die if after death the night terrors and pain all over are going to continue. Is death no release from suffering? No, that's not right. It's just that my mind is exhausted. These delusions occur because I'm not a believer.

Day Forty-Nine, 24th of September

My soul is weak, so it's finding it difficult to depart. Release me from my bodily suffering! My chest is being crushed. I feel like discarded socks. There's no body inside anymore.

Day Fifty, 25th of September

Where is the terminus of the Tokyo Loop Line? I've already been round dozens of times. This pain train stops at every single station. I want to hurry up and reach the depot.

Day Fifty-Two, 27th of September

I have to write a letter to the immigration officials in the other world: My soul will be arriving in two or three days. Please duly accept it.

Day Fifty-Three, 28th of September

I'm fed up with this. Goodbye.

Day Fifty-Four, 29th of September

The manager of the afterworld is not there anymore. Has that world turned into a desert? Even souls would get bored in a desert, so I want to get on the boat. But I don't have any money.

Day Fifty-Five, 30th of September

I feel like bursting out laughing when I think I'm still alive. I should get in the Guinness Book of Records.

Day Fifty-Six, 1st of October

Feel nauseous. My chest hurts. I think I'd feel better if I vomited. No doubt I'd vomit up my soul.

Day Fifty-Seven, 2nd of October

It hurts. I can't die.

Day Fifty-Eight, 3rd of October

Nausea. I want to get in the boat soon.

Day Fifty-Nine, 4th of October

I can hear laughter coming from the radio.

Day Sixty-One, 6th of October

There are lots of people. The river is flowing towards me.

Day Sixty-Two, 7th of October

There's a light.

Maki Kashimada

Kashimada was born in Tokyo. She is influenced by French literature and wrote many avant-garde works. While at the French Literature Department of Shirayuri Women's University, she published her novel *Two,* which was awarded the Bungei Prize in 1999. She married a clergyman of the Orthodox Church in 2003. Her novel, *A Case of Murder for White Rose's Four Sisters,* was nominated for the Mishima Prize in 2004. The next year, she won that prize for *Love at Six Thousand Degrees.* The story was based on French writer Marguerite Duras's "Hiroshima Mon Amour," about an inter-racial relationship at the time of the Hiroshima atomic bomb. In 2006, her *Number One Construction* was nominated for the Akutagawa Prize and in 2007 she won the Noma Literary Prize for New Authors for *Picardie Third.*

The Female Novelist

Translated by Tyler Tape

SHE HAD DOUBTS. WAS THERE REALLY ANY NEED TO wash your face in the morning when you couldn't sleep all night? She'd been performing this insignificant ritual for 20 years, so it was a little late for her to be questioning it. Your eyes can't get crusty if they aren't closed, and you don't feel the emotional rush of greeting a new day, so you're in no way bound to wash your face—she should have realized this on her first sleepless morning. With hardly a single satisfying night of sleep in the past two decades, there had been plenty of opportunities for her to consider the inevitability of face washing, but they all had been wiped out in the great current of habit. Without even realizing that she was under the influence of such a great current, she had been washing her face for 20 years. Even more, if you count her well-rested childhood.

She knew little of things invisible, no matter how large, but so long as they could be seen, even the smallest things held her attention. What fascinated her was not that great river of habit, but rather the droplets of water that trickled out one by one when she turned off the faucet. To put it precisely, it wasn't that they fascinated her, but because of her hypersensitivity, in short they simply "got to her."

From childhood, after washing her face she would space out for a moment, watching as the water formed droplets and fell from the tap. When the first droplet fell, she waited for the next. She knew they didn't fall with a constant rhythm. The rhythm of falling water droplets is by no means evenly spaced. It slows down with each drop, and this irritated her. It was a kind of masochistic pleasure that made her focus her nerves on the irregular and irritating, and that she still indulged in these games though she was nearly 40 was proof that her manner of perception hadn't developed since adolescence. That is to say, while young babies play games consisting of regular repetition and tend to enjoy the measured movements of a metronome, adults on the other hand have developed an immunity to boring cycles, and eventually lose their passion for spotting the randomly selected numbers on their bingo cards. In other words, you could say that her burning obsession toward irregularity put her senses somewhere between those of babies, who love periodic phenomena, and adults, who are neither upset nor excited by the irregular.

Thus this woman, having not matured past adolescence, was bound by habit and unaware of it, like a teenage girl who goes to school every day and practices spelling a given word over and over again in her notebook. Then a new boy, a transfer student suddenly shows up, and—though she hardly knows him—she falls in love. She loves the change in and of itself, ignorant of the true nature of the object of her affection. If you actually showed this woman a simple formula involving energy that would explain the irregular rhythm of water droplets, she would probably lose interest. It wasn't their mass she was interested in; it was their irregularity.

"Beneath no light, reflecting nothing, this drop will plummet meaninglessly," she murmured. She was convinced it was the true nature of the water droplet that interested her, and she tried to describe it faithfully. Then she rejected the words she had murmured a second earlier. "Doesn't work." She had been repeating this process of making observations and then rejecting them for 20 years.

She was a novelist. Of course, one would be hard pressed to find a reader who still knew her. She was still a student when she made her literary debut. The press rushed to the young woman like water gushing from a spigot. In those days, she suffered from severe menstrual pain, and she held her stomach as she punched at the keyboard. About the time they stopped calling her a new talent and started calling her a rising star, she was struck with an unclassifiable emotional disorder. Her words became disorganized, and memo pads full of incoherent phrases were all that built up. An "emotional imbalance" was all they could call it, and they couldn't determine its name or cause. She couldn't write anymore, managing barely to eke out the book reviews occasionally asked of her. Due to the side effects of her medication, she no longer got the menstrual pain that had given her so much trouble, and she bled less as well. Sometimes in the bathroom she would find her blood trickling down like the water droplets, or the sporadic requests for book reviews. It made her think of a Rorschach test in light black ink of the shape of a uterus.

Her husband took pity on her, and gave up city life to work at his father's bookbindery back in his rural hometown. He thought the relaxed pace of life in the countryside would be best for his wife, now a shadow of her former self, and he hired a maid as well.

To the novelist, though, life in the countryside was not relaxed in the slightest. What was most fulfilling for her was every instant she struck a letter on the keyboard, and just as someone who can memorize music hears each note individually, she remembered each and every letter she struck.

On the contrary, country life flew by. Doctor's orders forced her to go to bed early and not get up until the afternoon the next day, and since she had all her womanly duties stolen away by the maid, she was left with nothing to do but pick herbs from the garden in a medicated daze. The maid used the herbs she picked to make tea. As she ate bits of galette with her husband and sipped on lemongrass tea, the novelist drifted into a trancelike state.

How many years had she been living this idle lifestyle? One summer evening, her husband said, "Look. You can see Antares in the constellation Scorpio." With a yawn, she replied, "Yesterday, we saw Orion, right?" He laughed. "What are you talking about? Orion is a winter constellation. Don't you know the story about the fight between Orion and Scorpio?" But to her now, yesterday was no different from six months ago. Orion had bled when the scorpion stung him, but she was already bloodless. From the seconds counted off by the keyboard, to the monthly deluge of blood, and now even the constellations that separate summer from winter, each and every temporal point of reference within her had dissolved away. It seemed her sanity wouldn't return until the Ottoman Empire came to invade the countryside.

When she visited the factory that day looking like a demoralized prisoner, her husband gave her a warm welcome. "Today my sister and her kids are coming. Did you remember?" she asked. Then he answered, "Of course," and the German-made Pola cutting machine cut within the crop marks on the proofs of some forms currently being printed. Each time her husband answered "of course," the machine would chop off the border of some forms with absolute precision, assuring her of the potential realization of the party she was planning.

"I'm going to make a cake today. Me, not the maid."

"Good idea." Her husband forcefully belted together five orientation booklets for a fitness club. "Are you making dinner too?"

"No," she said. "I'll leave dinner to the maid. Just the cake for me."

"I see," her husband mumbled, and lifted the belted booklets several bundles at a time onto the workbench. There must have been a different number of booklets in each bundle, because they were different heights. "Well then, you'll have to tell the maid there'll be more people coming. You and me, of course," he said lifting two more bundles onto the workbench, "and then your sister, and her kids. The older and the younger." As he spoke, he went on making little bundles and putting them on the workbench.

They looked to her like Russian matryoshka dolls. The way the dolls fit inside each other brought to mind generational gaps, a bloodline, with one matching shape the child, the next the grandchild. Now, though, she looked at the bloodline as mere booklets gradually decreasing in number. Now, she saw the bundle of ten booklets as herself, and the bundle of seven as her younger sister. Living through the era of the ten-booklet bundle, she had experienced going to an expo, but her sister, a bundle of seven booklets, had not. The "space food sticks"—they were solid, biscuit-like things—that she, the older sister of ten booklets, had eaten in the Ferris wheel there were to her seven-booklet sister the product of an absurd future imagined willy-nilly by her predecessors.

However, when it came down to two or four booklets, that is to say her sister's children, it had to be called a new generation. Those solid biscuits once known as space food sticks were now reborn as a low calorie children's snack, which her sister gave to her kids as a healthy alternative, seemingly unaware of their origin. When she first saw them, the older sister was struck with *déjà vu,* but after seeing these Russian dolls of paper, she recognized that the comeback of space food sticks was like from the return of a comet from a decades-long journey.

After saying goodbye to her husband, she went over to the shopping center. It was the kind of large supermarket where they sold cake shortening, unlike the small neighborhood ones in the shopping arcades where the maid usually went.

"Oh, look who it is!" She ran into the neighbor's wife, who held in tow three clone-like white chihuahuas, impossible to tell apart. "Say, who are you voting for for neighborhood rep?"

"I, umm . . ." She pressed a palm to her forehead. She couldn't deal with this woman. There were many reasons.

"You okay? I don't suppose you're one of those headache prone people? As a matter of fact, so am I. I have this great medicine, though. You want to try it? But anyway, the candidates this time, they're all the same, huh? I mean, it's not like we're choosing who to make the son of Caesar, right? If it were, we could just make Octavian the son, and send Antony to Egypt. Just have to make sure Rome gets Egypt in the end. Oh, but poor Cleopatra." She produced a handkerchief and blew her nose. To the novelist, it looked as if she had taken it out to shed tears of sympathy for Cleopatra.

"But, have you heard about the Cleopatra beauty salon? Word is they just recently set up shop around here. They say they use the exact same kind of mud pack that Cleopatra used to use. They make it by mashing up grass from ancient Egyptian times with a mortar and pestle. Wouldn't you just love to try it?"

"Are they doing good business?" As if she had just swallowed something large, the novelist finally managed to speak.

"Why, of course! Everyone's dying to be like Cleopatra. I hear they're all booked up until a month from now."

The novelist recalled an Egyptian mural she had seen in a textbook long ago. In it, a queen was depicted with her face in profile, but her eyes and body facing outward. Following behind her like a parade were human figures, likewise with faces in profile and bodies facing outward. She imagined multitudes of women were awaiting their appointment at the beauty parlor in just the same way. This was far off the mark, since it wasn't as if the women were waiting their turn to ride a Ferris wheel, so there was no need to line up. They could simply make an appointment— enter their name and register it in the computer, or whatnot—and wait for their day to get Cleopatra's mud pack applied, and the rest of the time they could clean the house, go to work, or even go to another beauty salon (though the thought of it overwhelmed her). Still, in her imagination she couldn't help but associate the ranks of Egyptian slaves with the women waiting for their appointments.

The neighbor's wife sneezed again and blew her nose. The novelist was sure getting a mud pack applied would just make the woman's black nostrils stand out in greater contrast.

"Are you shopping today too?"

"Yes," she replied.

"This is definitely the place to go, huh? The one in the arcade near home is no good. They sell fish with cloudy eyes."

At that instant, the novelist simultaneously became aware of the indolence of the maid, who bought cloudy-eyed fish just because the arcade was closer, and the housekeeping prowess of the neighbor's wife, who was going out of her way to make a home-cooked meal. Also, more than the realization that she had been eating cloudy-eyed fish, she was shocked at her own snobby preconceptions toward the neighbor's wife.

"I'm thinking of making a roll cake." She confided her plan to the woman with some affection.

"A roll cake? How nice. I make a *bouche de Noël* every Christmas."

That's right, she remembered. At the neighborhood association's summer camp—which her husband forced her to attend—the neighbor's wife had prepared enough pickles for everybody. She had eaten her vinegar-soaked cucumber without thinking much of it. What untold ages, though, had it taken for that juicy cucumber to undergo the chemical reaction with vinegar and arrive at its final color and texture? She found in the process something similar to calligraphy, or the myriad other arts. People didn't pay the art of pickling any respect, because it didn't seem to require any special training, but in actuality—from the concrete activity of choosing ingredients, to the abstract process of converting experience into a work of art within the conceptual realm—its creation took a long time. In other words, the pickles and works of art she had seen were no more than cross sections of a three-dimensional whole, seen through the tiny keyhole of a given instant, and it was quite impossible in an instant to judge their surface area. Perhaps the neighbor's wife was no different, and the somehow low-class image she gave off was nothing more than a cross section. The frightening thing was that just by looking at a cross section there was no way to determine how wide the surface area was, and it could very well exceed the realistic bounds of temporal order, with the pickle she had eaten something the neighbor's wife had borrowed from the future.

The woman hadn't actually talked about exactly how long the pickling had taken. The pickles were in a glass jar. It seemed quite like the kind of little jar that children like to keep their treasures in. They were things like antique stamps that would fetch a high price someday, or toys made of tin, a reminder of the good old days, and there was something about them that made children want to get together and put them in a bottle. Then, along with papers on which they've written their dreams for the future—why is "astronaut" as unrealistic a dream today as it was back then?—they bury the jar, and they decide they'll unearth it when they're all grown up. Merely by placing inside the junk they call "treasure," the children have the audacity to name the jar a time capsule. (Even if medical researchers were to develop a cryonic life-support system, they wouldn't call it a time capsule.) Discovering the surface areas of pickles and artwork had given the novelist's thoughts some depth, but when she imagined the surface area of a time capsule it seemed altogether too like the present and the future were joined together by a single line, and it made her think of the axis of time as a fragile thread, dangling limply.

"You'll have to excuse me. I have some things to buy for tonight's gratin," said the neighbor's wife. Just how long would that gratin spend in the oven, she wondered, and to where did the space called "oven" adjoin, the past or the future?

Passing through the seafood aisle, the novelist recalled the cloudy-eyed fish and got a faint chill. She made her way to the dairy aisle, by far the freshest aisle in the supermarket, and after a glance at some solid brie, she fixed her gaze on a carton of milk. Knowing that the whipping cream was bound to be nearby and determined not to miss it, she looked eagerly along the row of milk cartons. She found the cartons of whipping cream. In the picture on the front, they had magnificently captured the frothy cream splashing up like a horn.

She gazed at the picture, eyes narrowed. She had experienced this feeling before, of a white liquid becoming solid and visible to the human eye. She lapsed into deep contemplation.

Then she remembered. The source of this *déjà vu* was Vermeer's painting, *The Milkmaid.* The plump maid pouring milk into the pot. She was frozen in that posture, pouring the milk. Everything was stopped. Even the milk going into the pot.

In the painting was a single rivulet of milk on the verge of spilling into the pot. As a student, she had learned that that rivulet shone illuminated by light from the window, and that it held an overwhelming presence within the picture. She had been a model student, and remembered the teacher's words exactly. Now, though, her mind was on something else—something that disturbed her. What sort of neurotic sensibility had allowed the painter to realize that a single rivulet of milk was visible? How was he able to capture the flow of milk as it fell in an instant from jug to pot? Maybe there was a lot of milk in there. Then, like an endlessly flowing waterfall, he would be able to watch the little waterfall of milk flow for a few seconds.

She looked again at the picture of the whipping cream splashing up. She shut her eyes and pressed against them firmly with her thumb and index finger, shaking her head. No, she thought, or perhaps said aloud. That lazy waterfall of milk didn't look like milk at all. It looked like something else, something thicker. The maid's posture was fixed, unmoving. Though she was holding a heavy jug of milk, her stance was stable, not showing the slightest possibility of falling over. It made you wonder if the maid would ever budge again in all eternity. And yet, something that should never stop, a liquid, that is to say the milk, was painted stationary, and it made you think, isn't the fact of the matter that this isn't milk, but something different, thicker, something that could reasonably pause for eternity? Force milk that should be flowing into a stationary space and even its very texture changes. The realization left the novelist dumbfounded.

She put the cream in her basket and hurried away from the dairy aisle like an escapee. Due to a lack of exercise and the side effects of her medicine, her heart started to flutter, and she staggered and came to a stop. She found herself in the children's candy section, with colorful jellybeans in glass cases all around her.

She looked and saw a boy had opened a glass container, and was scooping light blue jellybeans into a plastic bag. She stared vacantly at the boy, or more precisely the jelly beans in the plastic bag. Next he mixed in some yellowish-green ones.

On the side opposite the boy there was a girl a little younger than him, with the novelist in between the two. The boy was boasting to her about how many jellybeans he had in his bag. At that, the girl got serious and scooped some red ones into her own. They seemed very familiar with each other, and to the novelist they looked like brother and sister. The girl was mixing orange jellybeans in with her red ones.

When at last they had both stuffed a satisfactory amount into their bags, they went over to an electric scale in the middle.

There, there was a minor struggle over who would weigh first. They pushed each other with their shoulders, all the while maintaining a firm grasp on their bags of jellybeans, which, as if staking a claim on a plot of land, they each deposited onto the *terra firma* of the platform scale.

Then finally came the moment anyone could have foreseen. Both of their jellybeans were poured out onto the scale. On its surface intermingled the boy's cool colored beans in light blue, yellowish-green, dark blue and purple, and the girl's warm colored beans in red, orange, yellow and peach. The novelist unconsciously tried to read a number from the mix. It looked to her like a testing card for color blindness. On those cards, among the warm colored dots, a number was written in cool colored dots, and the novelist, who was not colorblind, who in other words could differentiate between red and green, could clearly discern the cool colored digit among the warm colored dots. However, these scattered jellybeans were a collection of colors which didn't even represent a digit, the very simplest of symbols, and it made her uncomfortable. The amalgamation of warm and cool colors broke down the two extremes of climate, the temperatures of winter and summer, even the very cycle of the seasons, turning the novelist's past incoherent. She tried to faithfully recall the feeling of stomping the city's pavement with her boots in the winter when she was a little girl. She tried to savor it, to have her fill of it, to stretch it out and remember the series of events that began there. She wanted to write a novel. However, the feeling of the pavement remembered by her foot dissipated before she could remember it for herself, and a memory of how in the summer the elasticity of her rubber sandals absorbed the hardness of the pavement got in the way. The two opposing impressions prevented her from making any observations.

She stood impatiently in front of the register. The machine was reading the barcodes on the cartons of milk and strawberries she had bought. The instant the clerk brought up the price on the display, she got the urge to cry. She wanted to confess that she felt like crying to the clerk, but speedy payment was all he wanted from her. She handed over her bills and took her change, and another clerk put her cake ingredients in a plastic bag, which she carried home in a hurry, mumbling something or other to herself. People passing turned to look at her, questioning her sanity.

When she got home, her sister was there with her children.

"Long time no see, sis!" Her sister was quite healthy, in contrast with the novelist, and blushing she gave her a big hug. "Same old pouty face. You've been thinking about writing again, haven't you?" Her sister understood her better than any other healthy person. "Hey, say hello to auntie,"

her sister said to her oldest, a boy hiding behind her skirt, and made him nod in greeting. Her little girl, still a baby, was asleep on the couch. The novelist put her shopping bag there too.

"I'm over the writing," she said facing away from her sister and lighting a cigarette. "I'm just a little high strung." Her sister turned away from her to peek into her shopping basket. "Oh, you bought stuff for a cake?"

"I was just about to make it."

"Oh, you don't have to go to the trouble. I'll take care of it. Why don't you play with your nephew instead? He loves his auntie, you know." She pushed the boy, shyly holding a picture book, out in front of the novelist, who glared at him and left for the study without a word.

The boy arrived timidly at her study. Despite the fact that she no longer had anything to do, her desk was a mess. She told him to sit on the sofa in front of the desk. She sat down on the chair at the desk and stared at him intently. The boy likes her—the thought of it! Why would her sister lie like that? She thought about it. No, her sister had never lied to her before. Either she'd said it to cheer up her high-strung sibling, or it was just a terribly oblivious and far-flung assumption. Given her sister's personality, both were possible.

"What did you and mommy come here to do today?" she inquired with a sigh. He shook his head. "I don't know. I came cause she said we'd go someplace fun. She said it'd be really fun if I went cause there's a big garden, and a factory, and tons of books . . ."

"And it turns out there's a scary lady like me there. Too bad, eh?" The boy looked down.

"Tell me this," she glared at him. "How did you get here?"

"We came by train," he replied timidly.

"What color train?"

"Green."

"What did you eat during the ride?"

"Marshmallows. Mommy bought them for me."

"What did they taste like?"

"They were yummy."

"It's not a question of whether they were yummy or not." His reply annoyed her almost unreasonably. "What did they taste like? Marshmal-lows . . . right, I suppose they were probably sweet."

"They were strawberry. So when you smell them you think they're gonna be sour, but once you chew them they're sweet."

"Makes sense." This reply had satisfied her. "What was the scenery like outside the train?"

"I don't remember."

"Try harder," she interrogated, narrowing her eyes at him.

"I really . . . I really don't remember," he answered haltingly. "There was chocolate in the marshmallows. It got stuck behind my teeth, so I didn't look out the window." He finished talking and dropped his head.

"Right . . ." she murmured quietly. They claim the marshmallows are strawberry flavored, but it's only the smell that's anything like a strawberry. Once you chew them up, all that remains is artificial flavors and that sweetness unique to marshmallows. In her days, there were only pure marshmallows, but she heard that marshmallows nowadays had jam or chocolate paste inside. She was oblivious to developments in society at large, but keenly aware of trends in the little things. It sticks to the back of your teeth. How about that. The boy was probably telling the truth. He tried to scrape it off, and his eyes went up and down.

"That's it," she muttered, and her eyes popped open, and she threw open the curtain in the window behind the couch where the boy sat. He shot out of the room in a flash. She looked at the view outside. If this room were a railroad car, it would all pass by at a tremendous speed. Chocolate behind your teeth. Try to scrape it off with your tongue, and your eyes roll around, and everything just blends together. The fields, the trees, the houses. It's fast. The speed of it distorts the human senses, makes them dull, ambiguous, and melts together the boundaries between the identities of individual things. It brought to mind hot liquid glass, amoebas, several hard candies sticking together in the can to form a solid mass. The first impression is sour, the taste is sweet, and it sticks in paste form in the end. The marshmallow becomes the scenery, and also an experience. There, the novelist fell into disarray. She lost track entirely of the comparative meaning and importance of things. She couldn't tell which was superior: the view everyone shared out the window of the train, or the individual experience of having chocolate stuck behind your teeth. She wondered to herself why she had chosen the novel as a vehicle.

Wasn't it her job to elucidate the meaning and worth of things, and put their respective values in black ink on white paper? Ah, yes. She had never worried about things like this when she was young.

"Why?" she muttered. She still hadn't noticed the boy's absence.

At last it came time for dinner, and the novelist was called out of her study. As she had instructed, the maid had prepared shellfish *hors d'oeuvres*, a duck *pot-au-feu*, and other large dishes. Whether aware of her plans or not, her younger sister had made the intended roll cake, and not a layer cake. She sipped her sangria, making her plum-like face yet redder, and listened politely as the older sister's husband talked about bookbinding technology. The novelist kept quiet, lost in thought. The boy timidly cast upward glances at this aunt of his.

When her sister went home with the kids, she shut herself up in the study. She felt like being alone. The kind of conversations that make relationships go smoothly, topics everyone understood like the weather or current events, were pure agony to her, and hiding herself away in the study was all she could do to avoid them on nights like tonight when she felt depressed.

There was a blank memo pad on the desk, under the dim light of the lamp. A fountain pen lay beside it, which she hadn't held for some time either. The memo pad, meant to hold material for a new novel, would remain empty for the time being.

Her eyes rolled back as her mind drifted off. The day had exhausted her. Perhaps she wasn't suited to having dinner with people. Should she invite her sister and the kids over anymore? She remembered the way the scarlet sangria had rolled around in her sister's glass, and she gasped and curled up fearfully. She felt restless and couldn't calm down. She was tormented by the apprehension that an indistinct dread was drawing steadily nearer. When she was young, she had written novels to try to escape it. Now, though, even the dread itself was completely disorganized and incoherent. The woman closed her eyes and tried to remember what had happened that day as faithfully as possible. (This exercise didn't have a particular goal, but stemmed from her monomaniacal personality.) Then she tried to remember the series of impressions those events brought to mind. For an instant it made what she had felt into something solid, then like a fragrance it eventually faded away, and the next moment some entirely different impression forced itself upon her. It was similar to trying to follow the cars in an auto race, and it made her think of something like hand-eye coordination. But by the next moment, even trying to recreate the impression seemed ridiculous to her. She felt regret. Why hadn't she tried to take part in the conversation? Maybe the problems of individual perception weren't such a big deal after all. Maybe what was really important was what her sister and husband were talking about: the weather, current affairs and the organization of the bookbindery.

She imagined that she saw a droplet of blood fall onto the blank notebook. It was no more than a dot. It couldn't be spread out, nor could it possibly fill the page with letters. She got a vague feeling of despair. Immediately after, however, an erotic pleasure enveloped her. She had known despair.

But her ecstasy only lasted a few seconds. A knock at the door brought her back to her senses. Her husband came into the study with some coffee. He could never break into the abstract part of her world, so he would break into the physical part like this.

"How's the work coming along?" he asked, putting the coffee cup on the desk. She couldn't determine if her husband, asking her this question when she hadn't had the slightest bit of work to do in over ten years, was just trying to be nice, or was by nature a goodhearted simpleton.

However—she remembered the conversation between her husband and plum-like sister—it didn't matter which was the case. This good man, who daily faced machines and repeated the same tasks, pouring his heart and soul into making beautiful memo pads and receipt forms, surely couldn't even conceive of the sardonic pleasure she had felt a moment ago.

Then he said, "Look," and took a bundle of paper out of a paper bag. There were thirty small holes punched along the edge of the paper, and spaced four or five millimeters away from the holes were perforations. "I made you some loose leaf with leftover paper," he said. "It was a collaborative effort with the hole puncher and perforating machine. You can keep it in a binder, and anything you don't like you can tear out and throw away. I've been trying for a while to think of paper that'd be useful when you're working."

Her husband, for some reason, knew her habit of writing down her ideas in a notepad and throwing away what she didn't like. When she realized that, she felt a tingling embarrassment, like someone had caught her making a silly mistake. To her, "You throw away ideas you don't like, don't you?" sounded the same as "You're crazy about me, aren't you?" She swooned like a young girl, and her normally sickly complexion took on a fruity blush, the same as the sister whose blood she shared. She wanted to cry like a child, without the slightest idea why. She imagined another version of herself, who would confess in detail the series of impressions she had encountered that day, and sob into her husband's lap. She forced down the feelings welling up inside of her. "Thanks for the loose leaf," she said, and sipped her coffee. Then, unbelievably, she said this:

"Starting tomorrow, why don't I help out at the shop? I haven't had any writing work to do in over ten years. You know that, don't you?" She felt like she had lost her mind, talking this way.

But her husband shook his head. "The shop's no place for a novelist," he said.

Keichiiro Hirano

Hirano was born in Gamagori, Aichi Prefecture, but moved to Fukuoka Prefecture at the age of one after his father passed away. He attended Kyoto University where his life revolved around law studies, seminars in politics, playing in a music band, working a part-time job in a bar, and writing a novel. In 1998, while Hirano was at the university, he published the novel *Solar Eclipse* and at the age of twenty-three received the Akutagawa Prize. In 2005, he was nominated as a cultural ambassador and spent a year in France. In 2008, he became the youngest member to be selected for the Mishima Prize.

Tsunami

Translated by Jessiqa Greenblatt

1. "THE BOY FELL ASLEEP IN THE DAPPLED SHADE of the mangrove forest while leafing through J.G. Ballard's *The Impossible Man*/his young, sunglass-sporting parents on either side of him exchanged a lazy conversation"

2. "the morning beach begins to bustle with people on vacation . . . . . ."

3. "young lovers flirtatiously lying about . . . . . . /the elderly donning straw hats . . . . . ."

4. "three topless blondes romp along, tramping over what's left of dead crabs . . . . . ."

5. "the sea, the sun, the clear blue sky . . . . . ."

6. "the boy's dream (I) a far-off, unknown land/a wandering giant in beggar's garb staggers with hunger as he heads toward a village."

7. "the boy's dream (II) the villagers look up in awe/hiding behind his parents in the middle of the crowd, the boy fixes his eyes on the approaching giant"

8. "a buoy with red polka dots bobs up and down atop the waves . . . . . ."

9. "the boy's dream (III) 'Whoa!'/. . . . . . in the midst of stepping over a mountain ridge, the giant tripped . . . . . ./screaming, the villagers fled from the fallen Goliath"

10. "the boy's dream (IV) the earth shook with the impact, fissures cracking open in all directions!/the prostrate giant was wreathed in a cloud of dust—jutting out like a mountain, his protruding shoulders could just barely be seen"

11. " . . . . . . the boy's thumb was wedged in the closed book to hold his place, and on a nearby patch of sand lay a collection of 17 brightly colored shells"

12. "the boy's dream (V) . . . . . . the giant was dying a dog's death . . . . . . /extending for hundreds of meters and streaming out in every direction was a river of blood, but there was no telling whether it was that of the giant or that of the villagers pinned beneath his corpse."

13. " . . . . . . like the blade of a cutting knife, seagulls slice through the sky, one after the other . . . . . ."

14. " . . . . . . the water on the horizon on the water rolls up into a bulge"

15. "one by one, the swimmers on the seashore . . . . . . started to notice the shift in the waters/'What could that be?'"

16. " . . . . . . a middle-aged couple who came to stroll along the coast talk about the ocean's odd behavior, their video cameras rolling/. . . . . . the mangrove forest gives a quiet shake . . . . . ."

17. "a white spray whirls up high in the sky, reaching ever higher, bit by bit . . . . . ."

18. "Hearing countless screams and cries, the mother looks back towards the sea for the first time/'Hey, look at that . . . . . . What is it?'"

19. " . . . . . . like a fierce herd of massive beasts blindly charging forward, the white capped wave breaks violently, roaring louder and louder with its approach"

20. "'Run for it! Let's get outta here, go!'"

21. "the father gradually gets up, takes off his sunglasses and squints his eyes"

22. "one after another, young men on body boards disappear into the wave like leaves of a tree"

23. "behind the shrieking, panicking people, the wave stands like a fortress on the verge of its collapse . . . . . ."

24. "'Get up! Just go! C'mon, hurry up!'"

25. "the boy opened his eyes, his thumb still holding his place in the Ballard book/the instant his mother took him in her embrace, salt-water came raining down as if the sky above had shattered . . . . . ."

26. " . . . . . . the wave . . . . . . swallowed up the entire shore . . . . . . (I)"

27. " . . . . . . the wave . . . . . . swallowed up the entire shore . . . . . . (II)"

28. "after being struck by the second wave, the town goes on to meet its destruction in the path of a muddy stream, swollen with immense strength and speed/a man stranded on the roof of a submerged bus stretches out his hand . . . . . ."

29. " . . . . . . the women . . . . . . weep and howl on hotel balconies . . . . . ./ . . . . . . one by one, the townspeople are engulfed by the water . . . . . ."

30. "several days later . . . . . . countless rotting corpses are left buried

beneath the mud . . . . . . /the sun beats down . . . . . . /they are excavated
. . . . . . and form a line of cadavers on the ground . . . . . . / . . . . . . still
and silent . . . . . ."

31. " . . . . . . people break down in tears . . . . . . / . . . . . . a sweeping torrent
of video cameras reflects glints of sunlight . . . . . . "

32. "cars on the beach, tires reaching for the sky . . . . . . / . . . . . . shells . . . . . . /
. . . . . . the now gentle waves lap onto the shore . . . . . ."

Yoko Ogawa

Yoko Ogawa was born in Okayama Prefecture and graduated from Waseda University. She lives in Ashiya with her husband and son. Since 1988, she has published more than twenty works of fiction and nonfiction and has won every major Japanese literary award including the 1988 Kaien Prize for her debut novel *Disintegration of the Butterfly*, the 1990 Akutagawa Prize for *Pregnancy Calendar*, the 2004 Yomiuri Prize and the 2006 Tanizaki Prize.

Her novel *The Professor and the Housekeeper* was published to great acclaim in the United States. Yoko Ogawa's fiction has appeared in *The New Yorker, A Public Space,* and *Zoetrope.*

The Sea

Translated by Stephen Snyder

IZUMI'S FAMILY HOME WAS FARTHER FROM THE airport than I had imagined. We rattled along for more than an hour in a van and then transferred to a local bus for the last few miles along a riverbank, past paddy fields and a Self Defense Forces base.

It was our first trip together, the first time we would be staying overnight on the road, but unfortunately it was hardly shaping up as a romantic getaway. The bus ride made her carsick, and I rubbed her back trying to comfort her until my arm was numb. Finally, she couldn't stand it anymore and we got off three stops short of our destination and walked the rest of the way, pausing along the highway from time to time to rest.

Her face was pale and she said almost nothing. Her back seemed so frail I worried that I'd rubbed it too hard. A reed-choked river snaked along to our left, and on our right, a string of hills was covered with what appeared to be groves of fruit trees. After the bus drove away, we saw only a few trucks bringing farmers back from the fields, but no one else walking on the road at all. The sun would be setting soon.

Izumi's family was waiting for us outside the gate. We were later than we'd planned and they must have been worried. They stood watching as we approached: her parents, her ninety-year-old grandmother, and her "baby brother." (He was ten years younger and she always referred to him that way.) Even from a distance it was clear that they had been anxious. The first to spot us was the grandmother—whose eyes should have been the poorest. Ignoring her drooping sleeves, she stretched her arms toward us, bending forward and greeting us by rubbing her palms together.

I didn't know much about Izumi's family. Just that they had once grown grapes, but her grandfather's losses in the stock market had cost them their land. Her father had been forced to become a bureaucrat, and her younger brother, who was twenty-one, was a musician of some sort. That was the extent of my knowledge. I had noticed a slight tremor in her voice whenever her family came up, so I had resolved to avoid mentioning them.

When we did have to talk about them, we treated the subject like a peanut that drops from a bowl. We merely had to gather it up, shell it, and pop it in our mouth to be done with it. That was the simplest way to avoid unpleasantness. But now that we were taking time off with the express purpose of visiting her family, that attitude was hardly appropriate—even less so given that I was going to ask their permission to marry her.

The house was old and quite ordinary, but solidly built. A zelkova tree spread over the modest garden, its leaves trembling in the pleasant breeze blowing from the orchards on the slopes above. The preparations for our arrival had been meticulous. The house was spotless, flowers had been set here and there, and the slippers lined up inside the door were brand new. Everything was perfect—so perfect, in fact, that I had the feeling this wasn't a house that was used to receiving visitors.

"Such a long trip, you must be exhausted." "Please come in, make yourself at home." "Can I get you something to drink?" Her mother and father immediately began a welcoming litany, as though competing to see who could be more hospitable, and giving me no opportunity to apologize for our late arrival. What's more, they were so solicitous of me, they completely failed to notice that their daughter was feeling ill. The grandmother continued to rub her hands together, while baby brother stood to the side and said nothing. Though he was hardly a baby. He was a full head taller than me and, from the look of him, half again my weight.

Dinner was served almost immediately. A vast feast was set out on a table covered with a starched white cloth. Nor was it simply vast; a great deal of care had clearly been paid to every detail, down to the color combinations of the food and the arrangement of the dishes. Her mother hurried back and forth between the kitchen and the dining room, while her father sat and encouraged me to keep eating. Izumi's color had finally returned and she seemed to be feeling better, but she ate little.

She had told me that her father was a public health inspector. "That's why he's always on the road. He stays at hotels and inns and checks to see whether they're complying with the health codes. Then he gives them a rating, A or B or C."

"Sounds like fun," I said, not really meaning anything by it. But she shook her head and grimaced.

"Fun? Running a Q-Tip around a toilet seat or rooting around in garbage or collecting pubic hairs in locker rooms sounds like fun?"

For a man in his fifties, her father's face was heavily wrinkled, with a retreating hairline and dry, powdery skin. He had none of the worldly composure usually seen in people who travel for a living, but seemed rather withdrawn, reserved and almost awkward.

He popped a fava bean from its pod. "So, how are things in the middle schools these days?" he asked.

"Not bad, I suppose," I said, taking a sip of beer to cover my embarrassment at having nothing more interesting to say.

"And what exactly does a 'technical arts' teacher teach?" he said as his wife refilled my glass.

"Computer basics, for the most part. And woodshop—I show them how to make a chair. And some electrical circuitry; we make simple robots. That kind of thing."

"Sounds like a wonderful job . . ."

The conversation was faltering, but as if in an effort to cover the silences, Izumi's mother kept running off to the kitchen and returning with still more plates to squeeze onto the table. Her father looked as though he was wracking his brains for another question to ask, but ended up merely repeating that I should "keep eating."

I tried imagining the man sitting in front of me with a Q-Tip and some pubic hair in his hands—and oddly enough this made him seem more impressive.

I glanced at Izumi who was seated next to me, a bit irritated that she hadn't intervened to smooth things a bit, but she was clearly still under the weather. Her lips were pressed together. I stared at them. They were full and moist, with an arch that made you want to trace them with your fingertip—strangely pneumatic, as though they concealed every sort of unimaginable word. Shortly after we'd started dating, she had asked me what I liked best about her and I'd said it was her lips. "Your lips when you whistle for the children to get in line." Izumi teaches phys-ed, and the whistle she wears around her neck is almost always moist from her lips.

Her grandmother and her brother seemed to be having a separate dinner all their own. Their appearance could hardly have been more different—the grandmother with her head barely protruding above the table even though she was kneeling on her chair, and her grandson who could have lifted her bodily in his hands—but their table manners were identical. Making no more noise than absolutely necessary, in rhythm with their breathing, they inhaled bite after bite. Vegetables, tofu, sashimi, seaweed, everything disappeared quickly and discreetly into the dark recesses of their mouths, in quantities that made me worry they would make themselves sick, if not the brother then surely the tiny grand-mother. But no one seemed to be paying any attention, not even Izumi. They would pull a plate closer, flutter their chopsticks, clutch the bottle of soy sauce, and then reach for the next plate. Their hands pushed and pulled across the table, tracing wonderfully choreographed tracks in the tablecloth.

The grandmother suddenly spoke up. "When do you suppose our guest will be coming?" Her question added an odd accent to a conversation that moved in fits and starts at best.

"He's been here for some time now," said the mother, rearranging the old woman's napkin. It had been tucked into her collar and was dotted with grains of rice, bits of beef, tiny fish bones.

"Is that so?" said the grandmother.

"Look," said the mother, "he's sitting right here next to Izumi."

"Is that so?" repeated the grandmother. "You might have told me sooner." The lids of her eyes, buried deep in wrinkles, opened wide, and her pupils, like tiny, dry pebbles, peered over at me. Then she leaned close to my ear, as I swallowed a bite of mushroom tempura. "Be careful," she whispered. "It might be poisonous."

At bedtime, it was apparent that Izumi would be sleeping in the room she had occupied until she had left for college, while I would be with "baby brother." To be honest, I didn't think much of this arrangement. I would almost have preferred to sleep with the grandmother. Baby brother had not said a word since our arrival, and, having no brothers of my own, I had no idea what we would talk about. I had decided I would plead exhaustion and go right to sleep.

Two futons had been laid out in the room, which was otherwise empty, except for an immaculate desk and an out-of-date video player. Baby brother had changed into pajamas and sat on a futon with his legs stretched out in front of him.

"So . . . ," I said, not sure what would come next. He looked down at his lap, fiddling with the bottom button on his pajamas.

It was bothering me now that Izumi had insisted on calling this large man her "baby brother." Every time she had used this pet name, she had said it as though picturing a small, frail figure that might be blown away if she breathed too hard.

"Feel the poison?" he murmured, still looking down at the button. "Granny said you might."

"She did at that. But so far so good." I flexed my fingers and rolled my head on my neck to show him I was all right.

"That's good," he said, looking up at last.

"I appreciate your concern. But you must have good ears; she was whispering pretty quietly."

"Not really. But I'm a musician . . . You want some soda?" he said suddenly.

Before I could answer, he opened the desk drawer and pulled out a bottle, an opener, and a glass.

"Nice hiding place."

"Mother won't let me drink them. She says cold drinks give you diarrhea. Sorry, I've only got one glass." With a practiced motion, he gripped the bottle between his knees and popped the cap. Then he filled the glass, handed it to me, and took a drink from the bottle. The warm liquid tasted like rainwater. The glass had apparently not been washed in some time and was slightly sticky.

The house was quiet. Our throats gurgled one after the other in a kind of rhythm. Outside the window, the night was black, and the wind continued to blow.

"Let me know if you want more. I've got another bottle in the drawer."

His voice was, in fact, that of a baby brother, so soft it seemed to disappear down the mouth of the bottle, dissolving quietly in the bubbles. He had pale skin, short hair, distinctively shaped ears. As if fearful that his overly large body would bother his guest, he sat with his neck bent, his back hunched over. His pajamas were decorated with giraffes. He swirled the last sip of liquid in the bottle, apparently wanting to save it as long as possible. Having missed the moment when I could have suggested that we go to sleep, I looked around the room again.

There was nothing even vaguely connected to music. No audio equipment, CDs or instruments, let alone a metronome, a music stand or concert programs. But then again there was nothing much at all. Nothing that would provide a glimpse into his life, no hints as to the kind of person he was. No half-read magazines, souvenirs from trips, photographs of favorite stars; no broken-in baseball glove, dusty plastic models . . . I looked around for the tiniest clue, but it was useless. The large form in giraffe pajamas swirling the last of the soda was the only proof that this was baby brother's room.

Izumi was probably already asleep. I listened for any sound from the next room. As we had come up stairs, she stopped me. "I'm sorry," she said.

"Don't apologize," I told her. "Just say good night."

"Do you want some more?" baby brother asked again.

"No, I've had plenty, thanks."

"Guests are always hesitant to ask, so you have to keep checking," he said.

"Who told you that? Your mother?"

"No. I think it was granny."

"Well, I wouldn't hesitate, so you can relax," I told him.

He gave a little yawn and then burped. There was a rustling in the next room, as though someone had turned over in her sleep. A dog barked in the distance but then fell silent, and it seemed even quieter than before.

"Would you mind if I watched a video?" he asked, sounding hesitant now himself.

"Not at all," I said, happy for anything that might break the silence. "It's your room. Just do what you'd normally do."

He took a tape from the drawer and slipped it into the player. After a few moments of static, the strains of a theme song filled the room and images of a savannah, a jungle, and the ocean floor played across the screen. The picture was a bit jumpy and the soundtrack skipped occasionally, perhaps because the tape had been played so many times.

Animals are our key to unlocking the mysteries of nature. They teach us about the beauty of our physical world. This evening again, Animal Wonders *will be your guide to our miraculous planet. Tonight's episode is entitled* Playing Dead.

"I watch an animal show every night before bed. Dad tapes them for me." Baby brother put the soda bottle next to his pillow and turned to face the TV. I stretched and folded my legs under me.

Animals have developed all sorts of techniques for protecting themselves from their enemies. Some wrap themselves in protective armor while others use camouflage to hide. Some send out warning signals, or shoot streams of poison. Still others are content to simply flee. But among all these techniques, one of the most strange and astounding is the practice of playing dead.

The middle-aged woman narrating the program had a deep, gravelly voice.

"You do this every night?" I asked. "Drink soda and watch a video."

"Every night," he said.

"Why do you like watching animals so much?"

"It's not that I like it," he said, shaking his head. "But watching them helps me get to sleep."

"Why's that?"

"I'm not sure. I guess I feel happy knowing animals that live so far away, someplace I've never been, still look a little like me, and they still eat like me, and have families, and sleep and die, just like me. Is that funny?"

"Not at all," I said. His face, illuminated in profile by the fluorescent lamp, was close enough for me to reach out and touch. He studied the screen, barely breathing.

The champion at playing dead is the American opossum. When attacked, the opossum fights back fiercely. It lets out a menacing cry and snaps its sharp teeth. But if the attacker fails to back down, it quickly resorts to playing dead; and when the opossum adopts this strategy, the onset is sudden and dramatic.

I was seeing an American opossum for the first time in my life—an unimpressive creature with sparse gray fur, like a cross between a rat and a badger. But as the announcer had suggested, it was truly gifted at playing dead. Flat on its back, legs stuck out a random angles, claws grasping in vain at the sky, and a certain air of hopelessness in the half-closed eyes and protruding tongue, as though it was wondering how things had come to such a pass.

Baby brother stared at the opossum, lips and hands clenched, afraid perhaps that the animal might actually die from such a perfect imitation of death. He turned to me for a moment and started to say something, but the words died in his throat and he turned back to the screen.

You may think the opossum is foolish to expose itself like this, completely defenseless in front of its adversary, apparently simply saving it the trouble of a fight. But you could hardly be more wrong. We know that the brain waves emitted by the opossum when playing dead are identical to those the animal produces in an alert state. The animals are not falling recklessly unconscious, nor are they surrendering. They are fully conscious and cognizant, and perhaps they even realize that the majority of predators only respond to moving prey. Predators are searching for fresh, healthy meat; so by playing dead, the opossum suggests that its body has already begun the process of decay . . .

At that moment, the opossum on the screen suddenly came back to life. Baby brother let out a little cry, and the opossum ran off into the brush.

The strategy is a success. The enemy withdraws, providing the split second our opossum needs to make good his escape.

"Where did he go?" Baby brother asked.

"Back home where he can be safe and go to sleep."

"Really?"

"Really. He'll be fine now."

He breathed a long sigh of relief.

After we had climbed in the futons and turned off the light, I asked him what instrument he played.

"The *meirinkin*," he said.

"Mei . . . rin . . . kin?"

"Yes, you write the characters like this." He held out his hand to trace the word in the air, but in the dark I couldn't make it out.

"It must be quite rare," I said.

"I suppose so."

"Where does it come from?"

"From Japan. Right here."

"Is it an old instrument?"

"No, not very old." In the dark, his voice seemed even fainter. His quilt was pulled up around his neck, and I could just make out his face turned toward me.

"What does it look like?"

"It's a little bigger than a rugby ball, you can just hold it in two hands. They make it the air bladder of a humpback whale. The surface gets covered with fish scales, and they stretch it inside with the fins of a flying fish. When you play it, the fins vibrate out to the scales."

"Do they always use the same kind of scales?"

"The sound is richer when they use lots of different kinds."

I realized then that *mei-rin-kin* must be written with the characters 嗚 meaning cry, 鱗 meaning scale, and 琴 meaning harp. "You're the first *meirinkin* player I've ever met," I told him.

"Of course," he said. "I'm the only one in the whole world who can play it. In fact, I invented it. I'm the inventor and only player."

As my eyes adjusted to the dim light, his face seemed even closer. A narrow band of moonlight from the crack in the curtains fell on the quilt between us. There was no sound now from Izumi in the next room.

"When do you play it?"

"Whenever you want, but it has to be by the sea. You have to have a sea breeze to make the sound. After all, it's made out of sea creatures."

"Do you have one here?"

"Of course, in there, in a box." He pointed to the desk drawer from which he had produced the soda.

"I'd love to hear you play," I said.

He looked at me for a moment, then rested his right hand on his chest before answering. "I'm sorry. I can't right now. Not without a sea breeze." He sighed again. "There's a long, narrow crack down the side of the bladder, and when the air passes through it, the flying fish fins vibrate. As the force of the air changes, the pitch rises and falls. The player—that's me—blows into the mouth of the bladder, but you have to be careful not to interfere with the air from the sea. You join with the movement of the bladder and send the sound to the scales. So even though I say I'm playing it, I don't make the melody. The wind really plays it—the wind from the sea."

"I'd love to hear how it sounds."

He folded his arms to form a cavity in front of his chest, puffed out his cheeks, and puckered his lips. Then he blew softly into the darkness of the cavity.

He was neither whistling nor singing, but the sound that emerged was soft and steady. It made me think of the comfort you feel when reaching the end of a long voyage—from the depths of the sea—but also the boundless sense that the voyage goes on forever.

I tried to imagine him standing on the beach, his feet planted firmly in the sand, his hands wrapped gently around the instrument. The breeze was drawn to him as though aiming at a target, as though all the wind from the sea were seeking the warmth of his palms.

His lips continued to send vibrations through the shadows. They were exactly the same shape as Izumi's, the lips I loved so dearly.

It was still some time yet until dawn but probably well past midnight. "How do giraffes sleep?" I asked, to find out if he was still awake. There was no answer, just the regular sound of his breath.

I slipped out of my futon and moved over to the drawer, making as little noise as possible. As I opened it, bottles rolled around inside. At the bottom of the drawer was a wooden box about the size he had described. It was simply varnished with no label or design. The finish was chipped in places, the latch rusted.

I turned to look at baby brother, who had gone off to the land of sleep, led away by the opossum's imitation of death. I reached out for the box and pulled it close to my chest, standing frozen for a moment. Traces of sound from the *meirinkin* echoed in my ears.

Then I returned the box to the drawer without touching the latch, and the only thing I could feel in my hands was the weight of the breeze from the sea.

Tomoyuki Hoshino

Tomoyuki Hoshino was born in Los Angeles, and his family returned to Japan in 1968. He graduated from Waseda University's Department of Literature in 1988. After working for the *Sankei* newspaper as a journalist for two years, he left Japan to study abroad in Mexico from 1991–92. Hoshino's debut novel *The Last Gasp* was published in 1997 and awarded the Bungei Prize. His second novel *The Mermaid Sings Wake Up* was published in 2000 and awarded the Mishima Prize. In 2003, he was awarded the Noma Literary Prize for *Fantasista*, a collection of three novellas. Hoshino was nominated for the Akutagawa Prize for new writers twice, once for the novella *Sand Planet* in 2002 and again for *The Examination Room for Plants* in 2007. From 2004–2007, he taught creative writing at Waseda University.

The No Fathers Club

Translated by Brian Bergstrom

THE NO FATHERS CLUB GOT ITS START NOT ONLY because my days were filled with free time, but because my friend Yôsuke took me to see a game of No Ball Soccer.

No Ball Soccer was just like normal soccer, only there was no ball. The five members of the team would pass and shoot as if one was really there. The opposing side's goalie would jump and make a save as if intercepting a ball actually flying toward the net. The shooter would be crushed. And the crowd would go wild, raising their voices to the heavens as if they truly had just witnessed an unbelievable save.

I was the only one who couldn't see the ball. The players and fans and referees all watched the non-existent ball. They'd steal this absent ball from each other, dribble it between their feet, feint one way then move the other, leaving their opponents to overcompensate and fall. Careful not to overlook a gap in the defense, the offensive player would find one and shoot the absent ball through it like a bullet. It would hit the bar. The offense would raise their hands to their heads and shouts of "GOOOAAALLL" would fill the air. A ring of celebrating players would form. The invisible ball rolling around near the net would get a kick from the sulky, defeated goalie.

At first I felt uneasy watching, thinking I was being tricked, that everyone was in on a joke that excluded me. Or like I'd been invited unsuspectingly into a cult, listening blankly to a charismatic zealot's overheated sermon. But as I kept watching, at some point I started to catch the fever too, to stand up and cheer with everyone else for a particularly spectacular play or boo and give a "thumbs-down" to a bad call. I still couldn't see the ball, but it was really there. I even began to hear the faint thump as it connected with a player's foot.

I hadn't been this excited since I was in sixth grade, playing chicken in the dirt-filled expanse of an unfinished housing development during the summer and winning. The game was to race along as fast as our bikes could carry us, aiming for the furrows and jagged protrusions that scarred the area and launched our bikes into flight, and the one who could go the longest without braking was the winner. I wore my red windbreaker and practiced my falls for when I wiped out, and in the end I held victory in my hand, the rest of my body bloody from being scraped across the ground.

I'd just been killing time, perhaps, since the day I was born. I was raised in aimless plenty, average in my academics and athletics, in my looks and my conversation, in the economic status of my two working parents. Maybe that was why my passion had thinned. Despite my youth I already felt like I was just living out the rest of my days. When my father died in an airplane crash when I was eight, I felt as sad as anyone, but he'd hardly ever been home and I barely had any memories of him playing with me, so I became accustomed to his now eternal absence soon enough. He left a small inheritance and some life insurance money behind for us, and between that and the settlement from the airline, there was no danger of falling on hard times, so, though both my younger sister and I felt a bit uneasy about it, our days continued to overflow with leisure just as before.

Though I should have had my time occupied when I enrolled in a mid-level high school, my free time only increased exponentially, and it started to weigh heavily on my body. It got hard to breathe. I joined the soccer team, but the interactions I had there were just like in any other school activity, and as if flipping switches within myself I first played the role of newbie, then that of the experienced senior two years later. I'd wanted to play flat out, wild and willful like Brazilian players did, but it was impossible for someone as lacking in passion as I to even figure out how to act willful or wild in the first place.

I started hanging out with Yôsuke when I found out that his father had gotten sick and died when he was in fourth grade. Don't get me wrong, though, it wasn't like we found each other and started sharing our tales of woe about our single parent households or anything.

One evening in early spring, near the end of our freshman year in high school, a particularly tiresome older teammate was threatening to keep us late after practice and Yôsuke tried to excuse himself, saying, "My father's coming home tonight after being away for a long time, so I have to be home in time for dinner." The older boy responded angrily, "What are you talking about, idiot? You don't have a father!" Yôsuke dipped his head and gave his accuser a dark look. Everything grew quiet around them. Feeling bad, the older boy muttered, "Sorry," to which Yôsuke drew himself up and replied fiercely, "He's expecting me," then gave a curt nod and left.

The next day, I greeted Yôsuke in a loud voice when he came through the door. "So was your father glad to see you?"

After a beat, he twisted his lips into a grin and said, "He gave me a whuppin', 'cause I was late."

"He hit you? Even though he comes home so rarely?" I pressed him, and he replied, "Well, it didn't hurt much, since he's dead and all."

"Yeah, I know what you mean," I said, going along, "I massage my dad's back sometimes, but it never gets any better, 'cause he's a corpse."

"You too? Don't worry, it's just your mind playing tricks on you. His back's not stiff, he's just dead."

"But I press down and it doesn't give! So you're saying he's not stiff, he's frozen?"

We couldn't help but go on and on like this.

It was thrilling. No one else could join in. First the older boys, then everyone stopped talking to us. The atmosphere of the place grew frosty, the air palling balefully around us. Even though it seemed like we were making everyone angry, we couldn't stop.

After that, Yôsuke and I would talk about our fathers from time to time. Regardless of whether anyone was around to overhear, I couldn't suppress the breathless excitement I felt when we started to get carried away with our father talk. When we became sophomores, we performed a two-man stand-up routine at the welcome banquet for new members called "Let's Talk About Papa." Naturally, no one laughed, and we even heard people muttering darkly to each other, "It must be nice with their parents dead, no one to bother them. They should think about how we feel." The two of us felt our teammates' anger swell almost to bursting as we chattered away.

It was around then that I watched my first game of No Ball Soccer. It occurred to me as I did that we could use this approach for our problem. If a ball could materialize out of thin air that had more substance than any real ball just by having everyone agree to act as if it was there, wouldn't a father more real than any real father materialize if we just acted as if we believed he was there with every fiber of our beings?

So we quit our increasingly hostile soccer team and started the No Fathers Club. We admitted only those whose fathers truly didn't exist in this world, so children of divorce were out, though illegitimate children who didn't know their fathers were in. The idea was to pretend we really had fathers every second of every day, leaving no room for sharing feelings or talking about our pitiful situations, so to those seeking therapy: sorry. We announced our conditions and even required the production of official family registers as proof, so we were shocked when we ended up admitting nineteen members, including some from other schools.

At our inaugural meeting, everyone introduced themselves and then we opened the floor to a discussion called "My Father's Like . . . . . ." We shared the problems and conflicts we had with our faux fathers and discussed together strategies for dealing with them. I told everyone how my father was perhaps too understanding, and that while it was nice that he let me do as I liked, I sometimes wondered if he really just didn't care.

"So when I came home all bloody from playing chicken with my bike, my mom chewed me out, but my dad just said, 'If he dies, he dies, what can we do?' I thought, is that what he'd say to the papers if I committed suicide? And then later, when I drove the car around even though I was only fourteen, all he said was, 'In Mexico they let kids your age learn to drive on their own and just get licenses for them later.' It makes you wonder, right? Aren't parents supposed to judge their children's behavior just a little, teach them right from wrong?"

And the girl who then said, "Actually, I'm envious of you, Joe. Your father sounds like he really understands children," was the girl I ended up dating, Kurumi Kunugibayashi.

"If you told a kid who had a real interest in cars that driving around when you're fourteen was no big deal, he'd keep driving, right? But if that kid was just trying to act big by doing it, he'd lose interest. With just a few words from your dad, you lost interest and stopped trying to sneak the car out, right Joe?"

I was dumbstruck. You got me, I thought.

"Well, actually, yeah. That's what happened, I heard him say that and I stopped trying to drive."

And I even muttered to myself under my breath, yeah, that's right, my dad was right all along. Muttering to myself like that really did the trick. At that moment, my father truly felt real to me.

"Yes, he was right all along," agreed Kurumi, overhearing me. She went on.

"So that's why I was thinking, maybe all the issues with our dads that we've been talking about only seem like problems 'cause we're still just kids. We just don't understand what they're trying to do yet. In my case, it took five years after the issue came up before I could look back and see what he was trying to do, to come to terms with it."

When Kurumi first got her period at eleven, her father gave her a rather explicit sexual education. Showing her all sorts of things, from Hollywood sex scenes to pornographic woodcuts, he explained that it was just a natural part of life, like eating or drinking or breathing or menstruation, so there's no need to make a big deal of it. It was just that if you're too careless eating or drinking you'll end up poisoned or dying young from alcoholism, so by the same token, if you're careless about sex, you'll end up pregnant before too long, so to avoid getting into trouble you should be slow and careful as you progress along past your first time. It's just like how you only start eating real food after getting slowly weaned from your mother's breast, he explained.

"It was like torture. While he was showing me the woodcuts I kept thinking of all sorts of things, like when we'd go into the bath together when I was little, stuff like that. He started seeming dirty to me, and I was embarrassed and so angry I thought I'd explode, but he wouldn't let me run away. I didn't speak a word to him for a while after that."

Kurumi paused, and surveyed the room.

"But what I understand now is that my father was also fighting down the same explosive embarrassment I was. It wasn't that he wanted to talk about those things with me, it was just that my mom had dropped the ball and wouldn't do it. So my dad had to take the dirty job and give me the information I needed. Though if it was appropriate to do it so explicitly to an eleven-year-old girl, I don't know. But I do know that thanks to him, I'm well prepared for how perverted boys can be."

At that point, the boys in the group chuckled a bit, though I was moved by her words once more. "Your father was trying to become your mother too," I said, almost at a whisper. Kurumi's eyes opened wide in surprise as she looked at me, and she nodded her agreement.

The only thing that intruded on the intimate space forming between us was the guy who then asked, "But that never happened, right? Were you talking about your made-up father? Or were you remembering when your real father was still alive?" In response, I warned him, "You're about to lose your membership here, saying things like that. The rule is that we act like we truly have fathers, every moment of every day, in our thoughts and words and actions." Guys like that, with weak powers of imagination who couldn't keep up their concentration, ended up dropping out of the club before long.

Though, even I had trouble at that time thinking very deeply about what kind of person my father really was. The father I created now didn't have to be a continuation of the father who died nine years ago. The way he parted his hair, how far his belly stuck out, what health problems he might have, how he romanced my mother when they were young, what he was like when he was in school, how old he was when he lost his virginity, all these things, even things a son would never know about a real father, if I didn't create them for him he'd remain insubstantial. Imagining myself having to create absolutely everything, down to how he acted as a child and what kind of people his parents were, I felt faint at the prospect of the potentially endless labor ahead of me.

Even so, as we kept meeting and sharing tales of our fathers, the words began to come more easily, like flowers blooming, and my father began to take on an independent existence, to "take his first steps," so to speak. The most important thing at this point was the responses I would get from the other members. Especially Kurumi, when she gave her interpretations of my father's actions I felt I got a whole new perspective on him I'd never had before.

We started going out after two months passed, when summer started, and 70% of what we talked about was our fathers. Nervous, I made up all kinds of things, last weekend I drank beer with my dad, he told me about trying to start a small textile business, he's Hong Kong-crazy and knows everything about Hong Kong movies, I rattled on and on. Kurumi responded in kind, happily jabbering about skipping school and helping out at the supermarket her father manages, about the things the other workers would tell her about him, about how he's pretty popular with the ladies there but he's too pure-hearted to notice, things like that. Our conversations were so taken up by talk of our fathers, we hardly knew anything regular couples knew about each other, not our interests or backgrounds, nothing. We went on a trip, just the two of us, to Hokkaido during summer vacation, and even then we'd do things like imagine how we'd be acting if our fathers had come along, buying picture postcards and souvenirs for them, and we ended up seeing the sights as we traveled half through our fathers' eyes.

Thinking back on it now, that might have been the peak of our relationship. The membership of the No Fathers Club took a sharp dive at the beginning of the second school term. All sorts of excuses were given, "I'm busy with my job," "My schedule's full with school activities," "My father's sick," but what was really happening was members getting tired of the faux-father game. When even second-in-command Yôsuke stopped coming, I confronted him, asking, "What about your responsibilities as a leader?" Yôsuke replied with a serious expression. "My father died." Appalled that he'd say such a thing, I shouted at him harshly, "If he's dead you can just bring him back, can't you? That's what we do!"

"It was a suicide. He drank a bunch of poison. He left a note saying, 'Let me rest in peace.'"

"That's impossible. A made-up father has no right to die. We've put so much into creating and supporting him, he can't just disappear like that. If he did, it's 'cause your commitment is weak, Yôsuke. Just try again, do it like we started all this, like playing No Ball Soccer!"

"I started that, you know. 'Cause I wanted to play soccer. I don't want to live with a fake father forever. So, I quit. Say hi to your dad for me."

And with that, the No Fathers Club shrank to just Kurumi and me. I told myself that the others were just jealous of our deep connection. Just overwhelmed by the extreme realness of our fathers.

It was a mild, sunny day in early autumn, and we were discussing once again how we'd take care of our fathers in their old age. As we were imagining ourselves nursing our elderly charges in the future, the words "But we'll still be together then, right?" escaped my lips before I quite knew what I was saying. Kurumi looked me slowly up and down, then tilted her head slightly and said, "Well, I'd always thought so. You know what, I kind of want to meet your father, Joe."

Meet my father? Not knowing how to respond, I sat there for a bit in stunned silence. Kurumi added, "I think our fathers would get along, don't you?"

"So we'd all get together, the four of us?"

"Yeah. Why don't you come by my house next time? I'll play host."

"Well . . . Dad's kind of busy . . ."

"So's mine. That's why if we don't do something about it, they'd never get a chance to meet. You haven't said anything to your father about me, have you? I've told mine all about you. He seems to want to meet you too, and your father."

I flinched. I didn't know if I had it in me to start talking to my father alone at home. I could think up all sorts of details about my father to talk about with Kurumi, but it seemed impossible to start a conversation with him when I was by myself. Kurumi's father suddenly seemed more grounded, more real than the one I'd created, and I felt passed up by her. Or, to be more precise, by the unwavering firmness of her commitment to her father.

"In any case, I'll talk about it with my dad," I said, then fled.

As I climbed into bed that night, I tried as hard as I could to imagine Kurumi in her house having a conversation with her father. If I couldn't even imagine that, I'd surely misspeak when the four of us all met, and Kurumi would coldly criticize me, say things like, "Who do you think you're talking to? My father'd never say something like that," and that would be the end of it. Just like when you play No Ball Soccer, if Kurumi and I weren't completely synced up, we wouldn't hear the words of the silent conversation the same way.

Telling myself I couldn't fail, I peered into the darkness and hesitantly started to speak to my father made of air. There was no answer, but still I launched myself into conversation. At first I was afraid of the silence and devoted myself to filling the air with words, most of them about Kurumi.

After a while, I started to get into the rhythm of the conversation, and suddenly my father began to talk back. The things he said caught me by surprise.

So this Mr. Kunugibayashi, I think I know him. He manages the Maruhan supermarket in Yoshino-ga-oka, right?

—Uh-huh . . . I muttered, and left it at that, his words leaving me otherwise speechless.

I've never dealt directly with him, so we've never talked, but I've seen him around. I might have seen his daughter, too.

Now that I thought of it, they were in industries that would bring them into contact. Of course, that was before they both di—I put a lid firmly on the doubts that started to boil to the surface, and told myself that I could do this.

—*So, do you want to come with me to visit the Kunugibayashis?* I squeezed the words out.

I do.

—*'Cause you want to meet my girlfriend?*

*It's you, Jôji, who's being childish. I know what's going on here. Kurumi
looks at her father and sees that men our age don't have very many true friends.
A man preoccupied with his work mistakes the other men he works with for
friends, but in truth he has no one he can really rely on. It's actually easier to
work that way. But no one wants to face such a lonely truth, so everyone acts
like they're buddies. It's sad, but what can you do?*

—*So Kurumi's trying to give you and her dad a chance to make a real
friend?*

Isn't she?

—*And you don't have that many friends either?*

What do you think, Jôji?

—*Well. I don't know.*

I wouldn't think you would.

—*Am I too much of a child?*

Do you have many friends, Jôji?

—*You've gotten rather talkative all of a sudden, haven't you Dad?*

*It's just because I'm looking forward to meeting Kunugibayashi and his
daughter. Set it up, would you? I'm asking you seriously.*

—*I don't know how dependable I am, but I'll try.*

Good. Well, good night, then.

—*Good night.*

As I fell asleep, I was absently aware of my father's presence receding
before it finally faded from the room completely.

I didn't have a chance to talk with my father again before the big get-
together, but my excitement continued to build, a ceaseless fluttering in
my chest like blades of grass shivering in the breeze. Confidence suffused
my body from head to toe.

When the big day arrived, I bought a cake large enough for four
people to share and went to the Kunugibayashis' house accompanied by
my father. Kurumi's dad was quite a bit taller than mine, and he welcomed
us into the house with a booming voice and a hearty shake of his firm,
thick-skinned hand.

Just as Kurumi had predicted, our fathers got along swimmingly. They
began by talking about work, but, sensing that they were squandering
their opportunity to get to know each other, they began talking about

us instead, and then my father asked, Is it true you like soccer? Soon we were all swept up in hotly debating which J-League team was better, JEF Chiba or the Urawa Reds, and then the discussion jumped to Hong Kong movies after someone brought up Shaolin Soccer, and before we knew it we were planning a four-person trip to Hong Kong for the beginning of the new year. Soon there was less and less room for Kurumi and I in the conversation, and our presence became unnecessary to keep it going. Kurumi, smiling ear-to-ear, refilled our teacups again and again. My father started visiting the bathroom frequently, probably from drinking too much tea. When he did, Kurumi's father would turn to me and say things like, *Your father's a nice guy*, or, *What a jolly sort*. I'd reply, *No, no, you're the one who's a cheerful soul*, things like that. And I'd mean them.

Kurumi's mother was about to get home, so that day we left the Kunugibayashi household before dinnertime.

My relationship with my father grew ever more profound. It was probably for just that reason that we had our first big fight.

It was over something little. I was talking to him about how I wanted to live my life on my own terms, and then it suddenly came to me that a student's life was not for me, so I made up my mind not to continue on in school. I said as much to my father: *I think my boredom with life comes from always being at school, and I think I'd be more fulfilled if I worked in the real world. So I'm not going to apply for college, I'm going to look for a job instead*, I said. My father erupted like a volcano.

Don't be naïve! You don't know what you're saying, you just like the way the words sound! That's the worst. You're just being gutless, using "getting a job" as some kind of out. Whether you go to school or go on the job market, I don't really care, but you have to take your decision seriously. You think your parents will just give you money if you decide to go to school, right? How can you hope to succeed in the real world with an attitude like that?

With these last words came a slap across my face. The span of Dad's palm was the width of a fan, and I flew back and hit the wall behind me. I cracked the back of my head hard and things went black for a second, and after I came to, my father was nowhere to be found.

I was shaken. I ran my fingers again and again across my cheek where it was hot and tingling painfully, and I cried as I drank the blood from my split lip that filled my mouth with the taste of iron. So this was how substantial my father's presence had gotten? He was able not only to converse with me face to face, but could even slap me around?

I wanted to share my excitement at this development with Kurumi, but for some reason I hesitated. I had the feeling Kurumi would do something to dampen my mood. So I never mentioned it. But it seemed impossible to have a secret just between my father and me. Kurumi and I could have secrets, but how could I with him? And yet, now I had one, and I felt guilty about keeping it.

In return for the previous invitation to their house, this time we had the Kunugibayashis over at our house in the middle of the winter, right when JEF Chiba became first-time J-League champions. We gathered around the clay *nabe* stewpot and started drinking at noon. Though Kurumi and I were only allowed one glass of beer each.

After a while, Kurumi's father, still in high spirits from JEF Chiba's win, started telling the story of his bungled, premature attempts at sex education with his daughter, making us all laugh.

Sure it's a funny story now, but at the time I thought I'd never be close to you again, Dad. It was really hard.

—These days, I'd probably be accused of sexual harassment, or child abuse. It sounds weird to say it, but when I met Joe here, I was relieved from the bottom of my heart. I could die without regrets, I thought.

I laughed, a bit unnerved.

We're only sophomores, Dad.

—Age is hardly a factor in these matters.

Kurumi's dad really was a pure soul. Compared to him, my father seemed positively lewd.

You two seem as close as if you've been together for decades. Doesn't it seem like we've been friends that long, too?

—It does, it does. We're blessed as fathers, aren't we?

We sure are. Want another, Nobuo?

—Sure, sure, Hisashi. Here.

. . . .

— . . . . aaaah.

You know, it took a lot of courage to do that as a father, Nobuo. A lot of confidence. That's what I thought when you told that story, anyway.

—Ha ha. Well, thanks, but let's not talk about that anymore. How to be a good father, things like that. You just try to be the best parent you can, you know?

When I opened my eyes, the room was pitch dark. I felt like I'd been sleeping for a long time, tucked under the *kotatsu*'s heated blankets, but when I looked at the clock it was only five in the afternoon. I turned on the light, woke Kurumi, and turned on the gas heater.

"Where are our fathers?"

"They went out for a walk to clear their heads."

They were nowhere to be found. The food in the cold *nabe* looked almost completely untouched. The beer was about half empty. Kurumi and I exchanged a sheepish, somewhat awkward look.

"Well, we should . . ."

"Yeah."

It was almost time for my mom and younger sister to come home, so Kurumi jumped to her feet even before I finished my sentence and pulled on her coat.

"Sorry for leaving you to clean up."

Kurumi said this at the doorway, looking at me with a lost expression on her face. *Say hi to your dad for me,* I almost said, but stopped myself. I just stood in the doorway for a while instead. I heard a sound like a walnut cracking somewhere in my chest.

The four of us never got together again after that. Kurumi and I decided that our fathers were getting along so well that there was hardly room for us in the equation, and they spent all their time out drinking or going on little trips together. Our fathers wouldn't talk about things like that with their son or daughter.

"So that's true friendship, I guess. I think it's great. That's what I wanted to have happen." Kurumi's face was expressionless as she said this to me.

"Yeah. I don't talk much to him about what I talk about with you, or what we do together anymore."

"I do, a little. Just enough to be polite."

I wondered if Kurumi was talking less and less to her father as well. Or, not just talking less, but finding it impossible to talk to him even when she wanted to. Because he wasn't there anymore. The sight of the cold, untouched *nabe* appeared behind my eyelids once more. It seemed that day we'd gone as far as we could go with this.

"The Hong Kong trip looks like it'll be put off, too. Well, they're both busy men, so what can you do? Besides, we have our entrance exams starting then. Maybe we can go during spring break, though."

Irritated at Kurumi's refusal to accept the end of things gracefully, I told her about the incident I'd told myself I'd keep secret.

"Dad's grown pretty independent of us, so I guess it doesn't matter if I tell you this. He hit me once, you know. Split my lip on the inside, the blood really gushed out. Here, look."

I folded back my lip so she could see the inside of my right cheek.

"I kind of get what you mean, but I also kind of don't . . ."

"It was swollen up all that night, like I had the mumps. I said I didn't want to go to college, that I wanted to get a job instead, and he was like, 'Don't be naïve! How's a kid as immature as you going to hack it in the real world?!' And then, WHAM! It really opened my eyes. Dad's trying to show me what it means to stand on my own two feet, so he's ignoring me on purpose and paying more attention to your father."

"I think your father was right," said Kurumi with a sigh, looking at me with a mix of sadness and irritation. "So did you decide to take the entrance exams?"

"Well, you know . . ."

"Let's both promise to take them, for the sake of each other's independence."

I groaned. "Isn't it kind of early for that?" I protested weakly.

"I've already signed up for the spring training course."

The No Fathers Club, already down to just Kurumi and me, fell apart completely. But I was satisfied it had served its purpose well: our fathers had come back and attained an independent existence, and we'd filled our free time with rich, rewarding days together.

It was after school on the first day we'd come back from spring break to start our junior year. I decided to accompany Kurumi on her way home. We made small talk about little things like the entrance exams and such, and then I asked her a question.

"Do you still talk to you father?"

Kurumi shook her head.

"Don't you think that's a good thing?"

Kurumi drew a deep breath, and then let it out.

"Our connection was always through our fathers, wasn't it? If they disappear, we don't have anything in common anymore, do we? I don't understand what you're trying to say, Joe."

"But if our fathers disappear, doesn't that just give us room to get that much closer to each other? We can't always relate to each other through our fathers, can we?"

"The idea was always to be a foursome, though. Remember? We were going to stay together to take care of our fathers when they got too old to take care of themselves."

"Take care of who? I'm going to have to care for my mom, but other than that . . ."

"All you ever really wanted was to say goodbye to your father. He disappeared before you could do that, so you forced him to come back and let you perform some sort of farewell ceremony with him. Now that's done, so you don't have any use for him anymore and you feel like you're your 'own man.'"

"It didn't matter to either of us if we had fathers or not! We were just trying to pass the time, so we wouldn't go crazy with boredom! But what's gone is gone, there's no denying that."

"So you were spending all that time with someone who didn't matter enough to you to even care whether or not he really existed? You really are a shallow one, Joe. Is that what you think building a deep relationship with someone is? I promised a bunch of things to my dad. Like if I met someone more wonderful than him, that's who I'd spend the rest of my life with."

"Then you'll spend the rest of your life alone, Kurumi! Your father's just some ideal man you've made up in your head!"

"Maybe. But I'd rather have it that way. It beats putting up with someone with passion as thin as yours for the rest of my life, that's for sure."

"If your father really was still alive, maybe we could have met as two self-sufficient individuals."

Kurumi looked at me with a scornful look on her face. "And what, exactly, is a self-sufficient individual?" she snorted.

"If our fathers were alive, there wouldn't have been anything to bring us together. It's ridiculous to think we'd have gotten together without them."

I sighed. "Maybe you're right," I agreed. And as a parting shot, I said the line I'd forbidden myself from uttering: "Say hi to your dad for me." Kurumi's final words to me were, "I'll pray for your father's health and happiness." It was like attending my own funeral.

Hitomi Kanehara

Hitomi Kanehara was, at the age of 20, one of the youngest writers to win the Akutagawa Prize in 2004. Her reputation as a social deviant and truant began when she was in the fourth grade, and by the age of 15 she was a high school dropout. Kanehara began writing stories when she studied abroad in San Francisco. She was awarded the Subaru Prize for her debut novel in 2003, *Snakes and Earrings*. Her many novels are written in the first person using contemporary urban slang and a gritty style. Kanehara's stories are mostly about women in their 20s and are often highly erotic. She often writes about mutilation and women's obsessions with their bodies as vehicles for self-expression.

Delilah

Translated by L. Hale Sterling

THERE WERE EIGHT COUNTER SEATS AND THREE tables. I smiled contentedly because I felt like I had some special talent for guessing this the instant I opened the door. There was no sign of anyone inside the bar, but from beyond the black curtain separating the kitchen from the counter, I heard a loud noise.

"Excuse me." The tiny reverberation of my voice was drowned out as the noise became even bigger. It was a rustling noise that sounded like someone was putting hot towels in the warmer. The thought vanished instantly, replaced in my imagination by a plastic bag wrapped around the dead body of a fully naked man in his thirties. He had taut muscles and tanned skin. He must have been strangled. He wasn't bleeding. His erect penis pushed up the plastic bag. For instance, what if there were dried sperm stuck to it? I would probably put my fingernail to the head and scrape it away. As I let my imagination go, the tip of his penis became my clitoris. Ouch. I felt a leaping pain wrap around my lower body . . .

but then I remembered I had to call out to the person in the kitchen. If I just stood here and let my imagination expand and start playing its devious little game, I'd forget to call out to the person in the back who was putting the towels in the warmer, or wrapping the dead body in plastic and stuffing it in the freezer. Whichever, if someone came out from behind the black curtain and found me just standing here at the entrance in total silence, they might think I was insane.

"Hello . . ."

As I said this and walked further into the bar, the loud noise stopped. A middle-aged man in a T-shirt and jeans came out holding three hot towels in his hand. I realized that my original assumption was correct. As he came out and just stood looking at me suspiciously without saying a word, I thought I should tell him why I was here.

"Umm . . ."

"We don't open until seven."

"Oh, I'm not a customer. I saw the flier outside."

The minute I said I wasn't a customer the man's expression turned slightly sad. The minute I got the I-saw-the-flier-outside part out of my mouth, his expression turned even more complicated.

"I'm not the owner, just the day manager, so I wouldn't know much about that."

"I see."

"I'll go ask him. Just wait a minute."

The gruff manner in which the man referred to himself as "I" made me feel strange, like he was speaking down to me. I wondered how this man, who looked to be in his mid-forties, could refer to himself in a way that would make me feel comfortable. I craned my neck around while I thought. If he said it too boyishly it would seem odd, but he wasn't dignified enough to refer to himself in a very fancy manner either. I guess that his rough "I" was appropriate. I took a seat at the counter where he directed me to wait, pointing with his hand that still held the hot towel, and soon heard the sound of talking from the other side of the black curtain.

"Yeah, yeah. Looks like she's looking for part-time work. Yes, yes. Oh, I see. Yes, yes. What? Oh, yeah, yeah."

There didn't seem to be any emotion in the man's voice as he repeated "yes, yes," over and over again. Finally, I heard the sound of him hanging up the receiver, and after ten or twenty seconds of silence, the man showed up from behind the curtain. He wasn't holding the towels any more.

"He says you're hired."

"Really?"

"He said that as long as you're a girl, we could take you."

"Thank you very much."

"Well, give me your name, address and telephone number."

As I took the pen and paper the man held out for me, I noticed that the paper was a sales slip. I thought about writing my information purposely in chicken scratch, but about halfway through writing my self-consciousness took over, saying to me "that's such a stupid idea." I managed to get my information down to a legible degree.

"Have you ever tended bar or waited tables?"

"I've waited tables before."

"All right. I'll teach you how to bartend."

" . . . Okay."

"Just pay attention and remember what I teach you."

Answering yes, I observed the man. His mustache was streaked with bits of grey, as was his entire head, about ten percent I would say. Both were tastefully styled. His eyebrows were thin and unkempt. The hair on his fingers was a shade darker than the rest.

"Oh, what's your name?" In response to my sudden question, the man looked up from the paper I had written my information on and in the same cool, emotionless voice as before said, "I'm Kaizu."

"Your writing is pretty crazy," Kaizu said, as he looked at the characters I had written. He laughed happily at my response of "I get that a lot."

I looked closely at Kaizu's mustache and there was white foam on it. This meant he was already having a beer before opening time. Or, perhaps it was the remainder of his facial cleanser; or maybe he'd been frothing at the mouth and doubled over until I arrived . . . who knows.

"Do you have a driver's license or some kind of ID card?"

"I have my health insurance card."

Without a word, Kaizu just held out his hand in a gesture that said give it here. I took my insurance card out of my wallet and handed it over to him.

When I touched Kaizu's hand, it gave off a very unusual heat. I held back my violent, dizzy pulse like I was reacting to a lit cigarette ash touching my skin, stopped my body from jumping back in immediate surprise, and nonchalantly let go of his hand.

"Yu Kanda," Kaizu nodded as he stared at my health insurance card. He seemed content that the Chinese character for my first name "Yu" was the same as the first character in the word for "depression."

"When can you start? Today is fine, tomorrow . . . you want to start training now?"

"Yes."

With this simple conversation, the course of what I would do with my life over the next few hours was decided.

"All right, let me make a copy of this," Kaizu said, as he flattened out my health insurance card. When he disappeared once again beyond the black curtain, I took a deep breath and looked around the bar. The moment I set my elbow on the counter, the progress of all the day's events flashed before my eyes. As I kept feigning unawareness, working to keep my calm, I realized just what a strange condition I was currently in.

The moment I woke this morning I was resolved. I was full of volition that today for sure I would go to the mental health clinic. For almost a month since the beginning of June I had been struggling with depression again for the first time in a few years, and until yesterday I was full of despair that there was nothing left to do but die. When I woke up today, I felt slightly better and thought that if I let this opportunity pass I would certainly die. I will certainly die. I will certainly be dead by tomorrow. With that compulsion I drove myself slowly, without breaking the sedation of my depression, as if taking hours to walk all the way across a single balance beam, to meticulously, painstakingly get ready. By five o'clock in the evening and after a great struggle, I was finally able to go outside. However, as I was heading from my apartment to the hospital across from the train station, in other words a brief few minutes ago, I saw this bar's sign saying "Now Hiring." As if drawn in by some strange force,

I pushed open the wooden door. What exactly had I seen in that sign? Why had I been hired? My stomach fluttered with the foreboding that my depression was about to relapse.

My depression came with every change of season. The fact that it was hiding deep inside me for so long led me to believe mistakenly that my mind was strong. I was going to the mental health clinic because of a sleep disorder, but for over three years now I had just been living on sleeping pills. But since June I couldn't even leave the house to get my prescription refilled. Three and a half years ago, this sudden spasm of depression that began plaguing me at the very end was more extreme than what I experienced previously, and certainly for that reason, when I overcame it, I was surrounded by a warm feeling of omnipotence. I had been soaring through life the past three years on the wings of this all-powerful feeling. However, my certain reality was, as always, depression.

I noticed a few books of matches laying on the edge of the counter and casually picked one up. On the back was written the single word "Delilah." At that point I realized I was hired without even knowing the name of the bar. Delilah . . . it was certainly a woman's name.

Lonely Delilah had two dogs, and her hair in an Afro perm. Her one and only enjoyment in life was slaughtering everyone that called her a gorilla. One day Delilah cut open their corpses and used their bowels as bags in which to put her beloved canines' shit. Looking somewhat proud, Delilah carried the hose-like shit bags with her while taking the dogs out on walks. The scene of Delilah playfully twirling the bags as she walked was the talk of the town. Bags made of human innards and used for dog shit. There wasn't a big difference. This is what Delilah thought. Destiny comes to everyone . . . until that day.

For a brief moment the dimly lit bar brightened, and I raised my head mechanically in response. The kitchen light penetrated the darkness when Kaizu returned through the slit in the black curtain. Saying thanks he returned my health insurance card. In his right hand was the mug of beer that he'd probably been working on since before I arrived. He didn't seem to be particularly worried about being seen carrying it. I nodded my head in response to his "One for you?" and he immediately handed me a fresh golden mug of beer from the tap.

"Well, then."

At this signal from Kaizu, I touched my mug to his in a toast, and then drank.

"Congratulations."

Not having any idea what this meant, after my momentary astonishment faded, I remembered that even if it was only part-time, I finally found something to do. However, in reality what I desired wasn't work. If it came to money, I still had some in the bank, and a few guys I could leach off came to mind. I guess I just wanted a place to go every day. A place to go, no, a place I had to go, or no, a place I should go . . . . no, a place it was acceptable that I went to every day. I wanted a place that would make me come to it every day. I wanted a place that even if I went to it, nobody would complain.

Still seated, I looked up at Kaizu standing behind the counter. As I finished saying thank you, I felt uncomfortable wondering after I said those words, whether or not my smile seemed genuine. When our eyes met, I noticed there was no gleam in Kaizu's. Even a human being with eyes so devoid of hopes and dreams like his managed to sweat and labor to survive. With this thought in mind, I searched within myself for a way to live my life. On the other hand, I realized that the usual result of ongoing attempts like this was failure. I saw my depression rear its head and cast a flattering, upward glance at me as it curried my favor.

"Sorry, where is the bathroom . . . ?" I asked, after taking half my mug of beer down in one gulp.

"Over there, that way," Kaizu said to me, his words mixed with hand gestures.

I picked up my bag, went to the bathroom and stared intently at my face in the mirror above the sink. The light from the incandescent lamp hanging on a clip lit my face at an odd angle. I adjusted it slightly and stared into the mirror again. As I stared straight at my wide-open eyes, I felt like vomiting. I pulled some sleeping pills out of my pill case and after checking to see that none of them fell anywhere, I put them on the sink tile and crushed them up with the back of my cigarette lighter. I have to hurry or they'll wonder what I'm doing, I thought, as I tucked my bangs behind both ears, brought my nose down close and fiercely sucked the powder in through both nostrils. I could tell that the unevenly crushed pieces stuck to the mucous membrane inside my nose, so I rubbed my nostrils to loosen them up and help my breathing. Tears formed from the pain and mucous started building up from deep within my nose. I swept up the remaining particles from the tile, and with the sudden buzz of a mosquito near my ear, my body shook briefly in self-repulsion.

"That's pretty intense."

"What do you mean, 'that?'" I said suspiciously to Kaizu, his finger pointing at something.

Was he talking about me? Kaizu, who had moved to a seat at the bar counter, nodded "No, no," and pointed at my back. I felt relieved when I immediately realized he was pointing at the spider web-patterned camisole I was wearing.

"The only thing that looks S and M about me is my back, right?" I said, as I sat down next to Kaizu and showed him my back. I sensed my elevated body temperature behind the stitch holes, and felt like leaping in ecstasy again.

"I like it. It's pretty sexy."

His finger only touched my back for a moment, but where Kaizu had touched was so hot it felt like a burn.

I suddenly remembered the days when I worked at the cabaret club. I had heard there were women furious at being sexually harassed at the office. But for just being touched or slapped a little, if you get treated well, didn't you get what you wanted in the first place? Well, women who work at companies are intelligent, which is why they get upset, but I'm not intelligent and don't have any real talent, which is probably why I have to live on physical strength alone, just like a man who does physical labor because he isn't cut out for desk work.

Kaizu kept staring at my back, so I put my left elbow on the counter and twisted my body around so he could look while I continued drinking my beer. As our eyes met again he muttered "Pretty sexy" once more and faced forward. I followed suit, but my back still prickled with a hot, burning sensation where his finger had been. I fell into the momentary illusion there was some kind of special device attached to Kaizu's finger that made me so hot. I studied his hand, but it was neither fat nor thin, his fingers neither long nor short; of course they were just ordinary fingers.

"I'll show you around the break room," Kaizu said. I followed him from the counter behind the black curtain into the bright light of the kitchen. The tile floor was white, and left the impression of being sanitary to some extent. Going farther into the back of the kitchen there was the employee bathroom and break room. Before entering the break room, Kaizu pointed to a door at the end of the hall, and with a nod that seemed to say "alas," opened it to show me what was behind. A cacophony of sounds filled my ears, and I was overwhelmed by the void of the "outside." With the total fear of a bird thrown out of its cage into the unlimited, what you could call colossal territory that suddenly reveals itself in the outside, I silently pleaded, "Hurry and shut the door! Hurry and shut me in!"

"This is the back door. I'll give you the code for the lock later," Kaizu said, as he shut the door. My head was spinning as I followed him back to the break room. The strength had gone out of my neck, and I felt like I couldn't hold my head upright in one place any longer.

"You all right?"

I nodded, as I held my head in place with my right hand so Kaizu wouldn't think anything was wrong.

"Sorry. My inner ear is a little bad . . ."

Kaizu just grinned at my excuse. He handed me my uniform in the break room. I took it into the changing room, which was about the size of a toilet booth and set up like the dressing room of a clothing store. After going back and forth as to whether I should wear my uniform blouse by itself or wear it with my camisole underneath, I decided to wear just the blouse. The tight skirt was long and I noticed that the balance with the blouse was off, so I folded it over at my waist. When the black skirt was set above my knees and the white blouse finally fit how I wanted it to, I left the changing room.

Seeming to have changed while I was in the other room, Kaizu was also dressed in a white shirt and black pants. After having seen Kaizu in his disheveled T-shirt look, I was quite surprised that with just his clothes alone, he was able to change my impression of him so much. Concealing my surprise, I asked how I looked.

"Yeah, looks right."

"The way I'm wearing it?"

"Yeah."

While Kaizu was in the bathroom, I put my things in a locker and returned to find a young man sitting at one of the table seats of the bar.

"Ummm . . ."

"Hey, who are you?"

"Oh, I'm Yu Kanda. I just started working here today."

"Oh, okay. I work the kitchen and tend bar. Name's Utsui."

I studied him as we made our introductions. He must have been about the same age as me. I admired his stature when he stood. He had a good, model-like style at about five feet nine inches tall. In his right hand was a mug of beer just like Kaizu and I had been holding before. As soon as Kaizu came back, he glanced over at Utsui and the mug of beer in his hand and immediately looked away. My gut feeling told me that Kaizu didn't like Utsui.

"Hey, let's make a toast."

Kaizu sat down at the counter and got another mug ready, almost as if encouraged by the elated Utsui. At all the cabaret clubs and restaurants I had worked at before, I always got pissed at the hard-headed owners, but with guys like these two, their businesses would have been swallowed up for certain. I don't really know why my mind was drawn to management issues at a time like this.

"Cheers!"

We all put our mugs together at Utsui's toast. Just as I had drained half my mug and was about to take a breath, I heard Utsui comment on how well I had taken the first half of my beer down, and decided to pound the whole mug down in one shot. Without a word, Kaizu poured me another.

"Uh, right. Yu, are you in college?"

"No, I'm just job hopping right now."

At Utsui's response, which seemed to have meaning, I asked, "Are you a college student?" and a pleased expression crossed his face.

"I want to conquer the world."

I sensed my words weren't being understood, and I felt dizzy from the unbearable distance to the outside world. I felt something hot just above my hips.

Looking out the corner of my eye, I saw Kaizu rubbing my waist. On the other side of the counter, Utsui seemed oblivious to the sexual harassment afoot, and was speaking passionately about his world conquest. However, everything he said went in one ear and out the other before I tried to chew it up in my mind and spit it back out.

"Miss Kanda, if you were going to attain world domination, what would you do it with?

" . . . . . . probably nuclear weapons, bombs, stuff like that I guess."

"Ah, I see; the destructive type. I'm more of the mind control type myself. What about you Kaizu? You were the virus type, weren't you?"

"Yeah, that sounds good. If the three of us get together tag-team style with me as God, I'd be able to handle all the issues in the world, right? The fact that all this power has come together in this store is nothing short of a miracle. It's great isn't it?"

Why didn't I get to be God? Why didn't Utsui even raise the possibility of me being God? I sensed a very serious lack in Utsui's imaginative faculties.

"Gotta open up soon," Kaizu said expressionlessly.

"I'll go change," Utsui responded. Kaizu took his hands from my waist. It felt like Utsui, with his hand on the black curtain behind the counter looked back for a moment, and when I looked in his direction he just kept staring at my hips. It seemed he was having second thoughts as he disappeared into the kitchen, but I couldn't help but think his gaze had meaning. Even if it didn't, I wasn't the least bit suspicious as I hurriedly finished off my beer.

"What a freak."

I thought it sounded sarcastic that up until that very moment I was commenting to the freak who had been sexually harassing me about the strangeness of another freak, but I couldn't help but say it.

"Ms. Kanda, you're a freak too, you know."

"Really?"

"Do you wear your skirt short like that to attract guys?"

"You can think whatever you want," I tried to reply as if to say, "You're the sexually harassing manager!"

Not to be outdone, Kaizu fixed his eyes on mine with a bullish stare. "It's working for me."

A disquieting air like the one that appears the moment before the morning dew swirled around in my brain. I had to talk about something else. For some reason I was in a cold sweat. I searched my mind for topics, thinking that I needed to break this conversation up into different branches and stretch each one to a far separate place from its trunk. There they would eventually bear fruit. In the end I had to knock that fruit to the ground to make a new and independent tree.

"Kaizu, you go back and forth with the way you talk about yourself; sometimes it's so gentle and sometimes so tough."

"Most men are like that."

I felt uneasy as he seemed to be just slightly missing the meaning of what I was talking about, but didn't say anything because if I tried to clear up what I meant, I was sure our conversation would just end up getting even more off track. My mind was completely mixed up. It had been quite a while. Yes, this evening I left my house for the first time in almost a month, found the Help Wanted sign on the door, got hired, and from that point on for less than an hour I was surrounded by these two freaks. I was so confused. No. Maybe it was just like Kaizu said. I'm just a freak and the other two are just ordinary. Perhaps my judgment was dulled because the two of them were so strange and walked such a fine line, or maybe my senses were just screwed up. I was at a total loss. Yes, if you only looked at what was currently happening at this bar, it didn't seem all that strange. I could easily say that Kaizu was just a dirty old guy who liked to sexually harass, and all the same Utsui was just an air-headed young punk. Yes. The womanizing dirty old man and the young kid who grew up holding on to his sense of omnipotence in regard to the outside world were nothing special. So, then it was no mistake that it was me in all my overreaction that was the source of this madness. If that were the case, then I felt like I should apologize to Kaizu for my negative attitude, and at least do something about my bad mood.

"I'm tired of beer," Kaizu said, and took out a glass from below the counter.

"I can make simple stuff when it comes to cocktails."

I said this, desperate for any sort of reprieve because I was feeling lousy just sitting here empty-handed. A mild look of pleasure crossed Kaizu's face.

"All right, how about a gin and tonic?"

"I think I can make one."

I pulled two glasses from the bar, filled them with ice, squeezed in the lime I had seen in the glass-door refrigerator, and filled each one a fourth full from the bottom with Bombay Sapphire. As I did this, Kaizu wrapped his hot hand around mine that held the bottle, and poured more gin into the glasses.

"Make the gin shot a third."

After we poured the gin into the glass to Kaizu's satisfaction, his hand on top of mine, he finally let go. The tonic water here was squirted out of a server hose, not poured from a bottle. I didn't know how to work it, so I looked up at Kaizu with an embarrassed look and said, "Teach me." The fact that he understood my eye contact didn't make me feel good, but Kaizu covered my hand that held the server hose with his, and again I was perplexed by that intense heat. Our right hands one on top of the other, the tonic water hissed as it spurted out. Kaizu's left hand felt its way around my waist. In an instant I noticed Kaizu's face only an inch from mine, and immediately there was the faint sound of my hair brushing close to my ears.

"You were snorting something in the bathroom just a minute ago, weren't you?"

My face tightened suddenly and then the muscles relaxed, floating into a thin smile. Kaizu's right hand pulled away from mine, and I instinctively pulled mine back as well. The server handle fell into the sink with a thud. I thought for a moment I was being gagged as Kaizu's right hand covered my mouth, but it soon moved, as if searching to touch my nose, which he rubbed almost as though pinching it in stimulation. The remaining bits of the sleeping pills melted sharply into my nose, and tears welled up from the pain, blurring my vision. I sensed a bitter taste in my throat and quietly let my breath out.

"Is there some reason you need to act like such a fucking victim?" Kaizu said, as if fed up with my antics. I felt relieved by his words. I was relieved I found someone more messed up than me. The hair on Kaizu's face brushed against my right shoulder, and I felt like I was being pressed against a heater. His left hand, which had been around my waist, made its way past my skirt and inched closer to my crotch. Following the route Kaizu's hand had taken, the remaining heat oozed up wet like the path a slug leaves when inching across your skin.

"The gin and tonic's done."

He ignored my words, as his fingers that were groping my crotch lifted my skirt. The moment his fingers touched me from under my panties, I was shocked to realize that their heat was the same temperature as my body down there. I felt the heat move away from my shoulders, and when I turned around his head was gone and Kaizu was kneeling down in front of me. I lifted the gin and tonic to my lips and took a drink. I pulled the glass away and saw some lime pulp stuck to it where my mouth had been. I licked it off with my tongue. I crushed the pulp between my upper and lower canines, and the acidity tickled my tongue. I stood stiff as a rail and stared straight forward. Kaizu's tongue found its way all over the outside of my panties. My dry pubic hair was pushed around smoothly and then dampened with his saliva. I was surprised. I thought the soft feeling of my pubic hair would last for a while, but all of a sudden it was completely dampened, and I was taken aback by the amount of saliva he produced. From my thin nylon panties I heard the sound of my pubic hair being moved softly around, soon replaced by the sound of Kaizu's spit. The icemaker let out a dull mechanical howl. My body quivered as Kaizu's tongue found its way to my clitoris. Embroiled in the total confusion of the moment, I kept drinking the gin and tonic, breathing in and out heavily, and from time to time checked the abnormality of the situation by touching Kaizu's head buried between my legs. He pulled my panties to the side and his tongue crept further. Each time his tongue touched my inner thighs, I couldn't tell if it was my pubic hair or Kaizu's mustache brushing against me.

How had everything ended up like this? Around the top one third of my field of vision a single line came into view. From that point to the bottom, everything I saw slid several centimeters to the side. After a few moments a line came into the area of the bottom third of my vision and that slid to the side as well. I blinked in an attempt to return my fragmented vision back to its original state. With each short smarting little blink my vision returned to normal. Blinking faster than I ever had in my life, the reality before my eyes unfolded like a scene from a stop-motion comic strip. I felt the light suddenly pierce the darkened bar room again and searched for it out of the corner of my eye. The black curtain was undulating. I knew it had to be Utsui, but he didn't come out from behind the curtain. He must have been on his way back when he saw what was going on and now couldn't leave the kitchen. How could Kaizu be doing this when he knew that Utsui would be coming back? I let out a loud moan as I felt my orgasm approaching. I felt I had to tell Kaizu, so I put my hands on his head. As I was about to speak the light shined in again from the kitchen, and I sensed my ecstasy becoming more remote. I noticed the sliver of light from the kitchen continuing to shine into the room and when I looked again in the direction of the black curtain, I saw Utsui staring from a thin slit in the curtain. His body was moving frantically, and when I looked down I saw his hand rubbing up and down his penis. Perhaps this was what Utsui had been imagining when he talked of being God.

However, somewhere in my mind I knew only that this was the natural course of events. Or was I Utsui? I felt something watery suddenly run out of my nose and held it back with my hand. I put my index finger to my nose and the transparent liquid stuck to it. There was the dull sound of wood and at the same time the stagnant air in the room completely changed for a moment. The air came in, and I saw the outside framed squarely in the open door. Then from within the jumbled noise from the outside, I heard the sound of people's voices.

"Come in." As I planted my weak, wiggly legs and shouted this phrase out towards the door, I was alarmed that my voice might have sounded hollow. Kaizu's tongue seemed to only get hotter. Both customers wore suits. They asked, "Is here okay?" and sat down in front of me at the counter. With great sensitivity I shifted my gaze away from them, and as I looked back toward the kitchen again, Utsui's semen came flying in my direction. Marking the wet spot on the floor, I imagined myself slipping and falling on it.

"I'll have a gin tonic ... and ..."

"I'll take a Budweiser."

I was out of control with ecstasy as I took their orders. As my vagina quivered, I said, "Gin tonic and Budweiser, right?" Lost in the intense quivering sensation in the center of my body, I mindlessly took two glasses from the bar.

I squeezed the lime between my fingers, and as I watched it spray out and drip into the glass I thought: depression is bliss. Then I thought: I'm so funny. I had to say there are days that end this way too. I made the next gin and tonic without any trouble at all.

Noboru Tsujihara

Tsujihara grew up in the town of Inamicho in Hyogo Prefecture, graduated from Osaka High School, and then moved to Tokyo to study literature. His many awards include the Akutagawa Prize in 1990 for the novel *Name of the Village*, and the 1999 Yomiuri Prize for *Fly, Kirin!* In 2000 he won the Tanizaki Prize, in 2005 the Yasunari Kawabata Prize, and the Osaragi Jiro Literary Prize in 2006 for his novel *The Best Flower is a Cherry Blossom*. In 2010, he won the Mainichi Literary Prize for his novel *The Unforgiven* which depicted people's lives before and after the Russo-Japanese War. His most recent work is *Deep Inside the Darkness*. He is currently a professor at Tokai University.

My Slightly Crooked Brooch

Translated by Tyran Grillo

WHEN THEY RESUMED WALKING, SHE WAS A FEW STEPS ahead of him, basking in his gaze. She cast her eyes to the ground, an anxious smile upon her lips. Overhead, the whoosh of a passing monorail. The regular interval between trains told her that twenty minutes had gone by since they'd gotten off at the station. It usually took about fifteen to walk the hill to its summit.

Mizue suddenly raced to the top, taking in the enchanting view spread out before her. She picked out the lights of the little town of Koshigoe, wedged between Mts. Katase and Kamakura, and the calm sea beyond. A gibbous moon hung in the sky, shining its light across the ocean's surface and pouring down through the hill's dense cover.

"Looks like moon's almost full," said Ryō, standing to her right.

"So it is."

"You're not chilly?"

Mizue said she was fine, but tightened her scarf as if only now noticing the cold.

"You're fine with this, right?"

"With what . . . ?"

"The fact that I'll be with her tomorrow."

Mizue kicked softly at the ground with her left high heel.

"I suppose so."

The moment she said it, her smile faded.

The path made a wide curve to the left and wound its gradual way back down the hill. Their house was on the left at the lowest point before the path resumed its ascent. As the two of them made their way home, Mizue hooked her left arm into her husband's right. The monorail came from the opposite direction on its return loop, passing over their heads with another rush of air.

It was a rare Friday night off for Ryō, who worked a corporate job in Ōtemachi. He and Mizue had met up at Yokohama Station, grabbed some Cantonese in Chinatown, and returned to Ōfuna from Ishikawa on the Negishi line. While walking the concourse, they'd made it as far as the monorail station before Ryō told her he was in love with another woman. Mizue only walked on in silence, buying her ticket at the machine and making her way hastily past the ticket inspector. The monorail lurched back to life and was off. There were no seats in any of the three cars, crowded as they were with homebound businessmen, leaving them no alternative but to worm their way over to the car connector and make an awkward grab for a hand strap.

The monorail was a SAFEGE, or suspension train. Unlike its land-bound cousins, the monorail's vibrations came from above . . . Ryō said it would be a nice change of pace: riding the Yokosuka line from Tokyo—which for some reason was never as smooth as the Tōkaidō running parallel to it—for 45 minutes before switching to the monorail for another 15-minute leg to Kataseyama. "I'll be the only one of the 3000 employees at my company," he said, "who commutes to work this way."

As they swayed back and forth in the monorail car, he told his wife of ten quiet years that he'd been having an affair for the past year. During dinner he'd been his usual self, remarking only about the lack of cilantro flavor in their meal. He gave no indications that anything was wrong.

She was a college student, he told her, just getting ready to graduate. Once she was finished with school, her parents had arranged for her return to Matsuyama on the island of Shikoku, where she was to get married. They'd already screened the groom and gone through with the engagement ceremony last fall. She and Ryō had decided a clean break would be best. But until then she wanted to live together during her final month of freedom, so he had agreed. It's what they both wanted, he said.

At this, Mizue laughed a little. They arrived at Kataseyama, going down the long stairs amid a throng of passengers. And just like that, her laughter had hardened into that same anxious smile.

They descended the sloping path and were home. Mizue went in first and turned on all the lights. Ryō watched in silence. They got changed and sat together on the living room sofa before getting down to the matter at hand.

"Starting when?"

"Tomorrow."

He would be gone for a month. Not a day, hour, even a minute more. That was his promise. They checked the calendar.

"That's the twenty-fifth of next month. Saturday night, six o'clock."

Mizue smiled and gave a small nod.

"Make sure to call me every night at nine."

"Of course."

He told her to have any work-related correspondence forwarded to the company, and all his personal mail kept at home.

"And feel free to open any of it. I've got nothing to hide."

"Oh, you're one to talk. This coming from someone who's been hiding the worst secret of them all."

In case of emergency, she was to call the company.

Stroke by stroke, Ryō painted a picture of how they'd met.

Last April, at the Tokyo Station Gallery, there had been an exhibition of a certain architect, which he stopped by to see on his way home from work. There were only a few people inside, as the gallery was getting ready to close, so Ryō decided to make it a quick tour. He entered the booth labeled "Kobe Reconstruction Plan" to find a woman standing in it, alone. Despite her casual attire, to him she looked for all the world like the geisha in Kaburaki Kiyokata's famous print *Tsukiji Akashichō*. Her soft hair fell gently about her shoulders, swaying in the still air as if by some unseen breeze.

Ryō perused the rest of the gallery, but found that she hadn't moved when he went back to the Kobe booth. He was already talking to her before he thought to stop himself.

She'd arranged to meet with a friend and see the exhibit, but he never showed up. That had been three hours before.

"I thought she'd been stood up. I only found out later her boyfriend turned back at Komae Station after an urgent call cajoling him into filling in for a home tutor. Since she didn't have a cell, he had no way of letting her know. It wasn't that she'd forgotten it, but that she didn't even own one. Knowing this made me like her even more."

The two of them left the gallery and parted ways at the Chūo ticket window. One week later, they ran into each other again quite by chance in the middle of Tokyo Station's Chūo concourse. She'd just finished seeing off her parents, who'd been visiting all the way from Shikoku. They exchanged slight bows.

"Let's meet again at the Kobe booth. No standing up this time," he'd said in a clear voice.

She came twenty minutes later.

"I'll be staying at her place. The address is . . ."

"No need. I'd rather not know. Still, I . . . well, just tell me her first name."

"It's Maiko."

"Maiko . . . We should get to bed. You're leaving tomorrow."

Ryō got up from the sofa.

"Tomorrow, yes. But first, we're going to do some major housecleaning. Once that's out of the way, I'll be off."

"That's okay. About the housecleaning, I mean. That nasty cold laid me flat last winter, so I never got around to it. You can do it when you come back."

Yet the following morning Ryō was up early, polishing every window to a shine. Once Mizue had filled him with bread, an omelet, and some spinach salad, he grabbed his suitcase and left, dressed in a sweater and brown zip-up jacket. After he was gone, she stood absentmindedly in the sun-flooded living room. She came back to her senses with a shudder before taking out the vacuum cleaner from the closet and easing into her housework. She opened the windows wide, letting in the breeze, which seemed to spur her on as she flitted through the house. In Ryō's study she discovered his favorite electric shaver, forgotten on the desk. She flipped the switch and placed it to her cheek.

Ryō was at Ōfuna, descending the stairs from the monorail to change over to the Tōkaidō line.

"Crap, I forgot my shaver," he said in spite of himself.

A few passengers shot him a backward glance. The train pulled in, departed. As the hulking white statue of the Ōfuna Kannon receded behind him to the left, he let out a hefty sigh. He noticed a couple who managed a restaurant in his neighborhood sitting three seats ahead of him, and ducked his head so as not to be seen. They got off at Kawasaki, at last allowing him to relax. Just as the departure chime signaled, he spotted them again on the opposite train. Ryō thought it curious. Both sets of doors closed almost simultaneously.

The train thundered its way across the Tama River. Ryō changed to the Yamanote line at Shinagawa and got off at Shibuya. He went underground and rode the Tōkyū Den-en-toshi line to Sangen-Jaya, navigating the undulating subterranean passage until he reached the station at Setagaya. This train was a two-car affair, colorful and small like a toy. The track intersected with Tokyo Metro Road, where a red light brought the train to a temporary halt. In the interim, Ryō watched as seemingly endless droves of cars and people passed before his eyes.

He got off at the third stop, went through the small railroad crossing, and turned left onto the first street.

"It's a cold one today, isn't it?" came a high voice from inside the bicycle shop. There was no answer. The road zigzagged, and at last Maiko's apartment building came into view. A silhouette moved behind the beige curtains swaying gently in her window on the fourth floor.

When he rang the doorbell, he heard the chain being unlatched on the other side. The door opened outward and there stood Maiko, all smiles. A vacuum cleaner bellowed in the background. Maiko stepped from the threshold toward the door. She leaned into the upper half of his body, arching over the concrete floor, put her forehead to his, and laughed softly.

"You really came. You're not a ghost, are you? Show me your feet."

She placed her hands on his chest and pushed herself away, looking down at the floor. Ryō kicked off his shoes and embraced Maiko, even as she continued to scrutinize his feet, before moving into the dining room. And for the first time they sat at her table in total relaxation. He stroked Maiko's hair and placed a gentle kiss on her neck. The vacuum cleaner continued its tirade, the accordion-like pipe snaking around of its own volition. They kissed before Maiko resumed her cleaning.

"In case you didn't notice, I was in the middle of something," she said, raising her voice above the noise. "I have to make this place livable for two, and the first step is to give it a thorough cleaning."

Her apartment was a two-bedroom rental, but modest all the same. Ryō's long stride could have easily traversed its length in a few steps. He grew fidgety, pacing around like a bear in a cage before he filled a bucket with water and set to work on the windows, just to give his hands something to do.

Later, they went out shopping for groceries and other essentials for his stay. For the next month, Ryō would be handling all the expenses. He looked for an electric shaver but his preferred model was nowhere to be found, so he decided to make do with a manual. At the local flower shop he bought two pots of poinsettias and a half dozen roses. The poinsettias were red and yellow; the roses two each of pink, yellow, and white. Ryō was something of an expert on the latter. He pointed to them, saying, "This is a double-flowered Old Garden Rose, and this one's a large-flowered variety."

He hung the poinsettias from the balcony parapet and put the roses in a Czech glass vase on the dresser. Maiko's dinner menu included miso soup, paella, mackerel stewed in miso, gratin, some Uwajima fish cake from her parents, and a spinach and pine nut salad.

"I know it's a bit unconventional."

"A regular smorgasbord, you might say, but it's absolutely delicious."

They opened a bottle of Chilean wine.

"I promised to make a call at nine," said Ryō, holding Maiko from behind as she did the dishes. "Do you mind?"

Maiko nodded. "Maybe I should turn the water off?"

"No, it's fine. Silence would make her even more uneasy."

Ryō called Mizue at nine o'clock sharp. She picked up on the third ring. The conversation was awkward at best. Maiko turned up the faucet at full blast. Ryō turned around, the receiver still pressed to his ear.

"I hear water," Mizue said.

Yet when Maiko turned it off, the sound didn't go away.

"Is your water running?"

Mizue peeked into her kitchen. Sure enough, it was. It had completely slipped her mind. She hung up the phone, went into the kitchen, and shut the faucet tight. Ryō got to his feet.

"Maybe our water lines are connected?" he quipped. Maiko said nothing.

As she applied her hand cream, she said, "I've got a kettle on. Be a dear and pour me some tea?" her voice cracking. They held each other again.

"Shall we watch TV?"

Maiko shook her head. "You sure you don't want to go back?"

"Don't be silly. I . . ." The kettle was ready.

Ryō switched off the gas. He turned back, hoisted Maiko up in his arms and carried her to bed. With the lights left on, he furrowed his brow almost angrily, and covered every inch of her body with kisses.

Afterward, they slept a little, their bodies intertwined. They woke up with a start and looked around.

"What time is it?"

Ryō glanced at the alarm clock. Only five minutes had passed. They showered, changed into their pajamas, and got back into bed, closing their eyes in the light of the bedside lamp. The phone was ringing in the living room.

"Your wife, I take it?"

"No. She doesn't know the number."

Maiko got up and went to answer it. It was her mother calling from Shikoku.

"Oh, the usual. Just making sure I'm still alive," she said, tangling her icy feet around Ryō's. "You're so warm. I'm really worried, you know."

"About?"

"How do I know you won't just go back to her tomorrow?"

Ryō warmly grabbed her tense shoulders and pulled her close.

"I'll stay here until you tell me otherwise."

"But you'll be gone in a month."

"Yes, I will. And you'll be going back to Shikoku."

"Say, tell me a story. The longest one you know."

Ryō moved his eyes in erratic circles as he wracked his brain.

"There must be something I can tell . . . Oh yes, but it's from way back in my student days. I once spent a summer vacation in East Germany and Poland, you know."

"Is it a long story?"

"It could be. If you get tired, go ahead and sleep."

"I won't. Is it a story about Germany?"

"No, it actually has nothing to do with my trip. It is a bit disturbing, though. I'm sure I read it in a book somewhere. Now, what was it? The title escapes me."

"Grimm, maybe?"

"No, it wasn't Grimm. I'll probably screw it up. I've never told it to anyone, and my storytelling skills leave something to be desired."

"I don't mind. Let's hear it, then."

" . . . Our tale begins with a young man. He has just returned from some faraway land to his native village in the German countryside. Let's see, one of the towns I visited in my trip . . . Wrocław, was a pretty nice place. All those Polish towns were. Until World War II, it was called Breslau, a name given by the early Germans who settled there. I guess Breslau's good a place as any. So, he had returned to Breslau to be with his fiancée. Although he no longer felt much love for this woman, he'd brought back a souvenir for her, a rare stone from his travels, and was hiding it in his pocket. After a lavish meal, he was just sitting down in his parents' parlor when the door opened and his fiancée called to him. Both families were preparing for an outing and she wanted to know what was keeping him so long. But he had absolutely no desire to go out. Angered by his silence, the girl slammed the door and left in a huff.

"Rudolf . . . yes, that was his name. It's slowly coming back to me now. Rudolf was strangely withdrawn, his attention captured by a picture on the wall he remembered from his boyhood. Seeing it again now after all this time made him feel all the more alone.

"In the foreground was a rococo garden, populated by courtly ladies and cavaliers out for a stroll. An elegant villa rose beyond the treetops, its vaulted stained glass windows glittering brilliantly in the sunlight. In one of the garden paths stood a solitary lady, holding a slip of white paper. Or was it a handkerchief? Rudolf had always wondered which. Was she reading a letter, or was she crying into her handkerchief?

"Rudolf stepped up to the painting for a closer look. Now that it was at eye level, he no longer had to crane his neck like he did when he was a boy. As he peered closely at the painting, immersing himself in its colors and shapes, the little men and women in the garden began to move. They gave off a light, pleasant fragrance as they passed him by. Rudolf felt his feet moving, and the crunch of the finely graveled promenade as he approached the lady in question. She lifted her concealed eyes and stared at him. It was then he realized the truth. She'd been reading a letter after all. A letter he had, in fact, written to her long ago.

"'At last, you've come, my darling.'

"The lady let her right hand fall, as if the letter's weight were too much to bear.

"'I've never stopped waiting for you, not for a single moment. Look, this is the letter you wrote me before your departure. Now that you are here, everything is going to be fine.'

"They kissed and disappeared into the deep forest. At sundown they returned to the castle, where a grand feast awaited them. All the knights and ladies of the land hailed the return of their lord. With bellies sated, the lovers retired to their extravagant chambers. As the enchanted evening broke into dawn, birds roused them from their dreams.

"So did many days pass, the moon waxing and waning through their slumber. The passage of time was forgotten in their games, feasts, hunting, and deep conversations; their youthful joy revived every palatial room grown dank in his absence.

"'Everything you see, it is all yours,' said his beautiful wife. 'Except,' she added, 'for one thing, and one thing only. You must never open that door. So long as it remains closed, we will lose nothing.'

"More time passed. But then, during a night as still as death, he slipped out of bed and stood at the window, gazing blankly at the leaves turning in the garden.

"Just then, he heard a voice calling someone's name. He vaguely recognized the name, but not as his own.

"His curiosity led him to the voice, which was coming from the only room he'd never entered. He opened the door. There was nothing inside. The chamber was completely bare, save for a single picture hanging on the wall from which the voice issued.

"The lord approached the painting and saw it depicted a single room. Like the voice, it seemed familiar, but he couldn't place it.

"In the painting was another painting hanging in the background, but the voice was coming from the door beside it. His amazement only increased as he strained his ears, and Rudolf suddenly found himself standing in his parents' parlor. The door, now quite real, flew open.

"'Aren't you coming, Rudolf? How long do you expect us to wait? The carriage is already here. Am I to waste my whole day because of your foul mood?'

"Rudolf awkwardly stood there for a moment before taking his fiancée's hand and leading her to the old painting.

"'Look closely, do you see that woman? She's crying. That's a handkerchief she's holding, not a letter. And the blue brooch pinned to her chest, I gave it to . . .'

"His fiancée only snorted at this.

"The end," said Ryō.

Maiko's eyes sparkled in the dim light.

"So it started off as a letter, then turned into a handkerchief?"

Ryō nodded.

"And where am I in your picture?"

"In the castle, no doubt."

"I guess I am. But even though you'll be gone in a month, I won't cry."

"No, I don't want you to cry."

"But you know I probably will. Maybe I should have a handkerchief ready, just in case. This story, did you ever tell it to your wife?"

"I can't remember."

---

*Author's note: The fairytale adapted herein originally appeared in Ernst Bloch's *Traces*.

"And what happens next?" Maiko propped herself on her elbows.

"That's where the story ends. There's no more. Nothing comes from nothing."

"But Rudolf's life must have been so empty after that. He must have tried to meet that noble lady again. Once she found out the truth, his fiancée might have asked Rudolf to take her with him."

"That's impossible. It was a one-time deal. There was no place for her in the castle."

"But what if your wife came here . . . ?"

"Ah, is that where this is going? That would never happen. First of all, she doesn't know this place, and doesn't want to know. She'd rather wait a month for me than come all the way out here. I think it's a wise decision on her part."

"But what if she *did* come . . . ?"

Maiko cowered as if out of fear. Just before they fell asleep, a police siren wailed in the distance.

Ten days went by.

Mizue forwarded her husband's mail to the company, and when his college orienteering club called to let him know about an upcoming reunion, she told them to call him at work. Ryō called every night on schedule. He usually did most of the talking, while Mizue only answered curtly. Still, the initial awkwardness was beginning to wear off.

"Strange," she said on the eleventh night. "It's almost as if we've always lived like this."

"What do you mean . . . ?" said Ryō, agitated.

"Don't get me wrong. We *are* husband and wife, of course, but we might as well have been brother and sister before that. At least, that's what it feels like. We're always so considerate of each other . . . wouldn't you say?"

"Yeah, but now I've . . ."

". . . 'but now I've got Maiko' . . . is that what you wanted to say? It's okay. No one can know of our promise, but I plan on keeping it all the same. Maiko is yours for one month and one month only. That was the promise you made to me. We may be separated, but we're both sticking to this."

For once, Mizue was dominating the conversation.

During these phone calls to Kataseyama, Maiko usually holed herself up in the bathroom, shut the door tight, and took a bath or shower. Other times, she did nothing and simply stood by Ryō's side, rigid as a pole.

It was the morning of the thirteenth day. Mizue jumped out of bed, only to find her underwear, pajamas, and sheets covered in blood. She was three days early. It was a heavier flow than usual, and had seeped down into the mattress. As she ran the washing machine, she daubed the mattress with cold water and scrubbed away the stains with a nailbrush. It was almost noon by the time she was done. As she stared blankly out into the sunlit garden, a tear rolled down her cheek. A small flock of birds alighted in the grass, scrounging for insects..

"It's almost like they're competing with each other, not that they'd know the difference," she said, as if someone were there to hear it.

She had three calls before nightfall. The first was from a high school classmate, inviting her for a girls' night out. Unfortunately, she and her husband had already planned a day trip to Hakone that day, she said. The second one she didn't answer. The third was from her mother. They were having the heaviest snow in ten years in Sasayama, her father was nursing a cold he just couldn't shake, and Kōji had just become PR officer for the local Junior Chamber. She told Mizue not to catch cold, asked that she pass on her best to Ryō, and wished them both good health. Mizue told her Ryō was on a business trip, but that she spoke with him on the phone every evening and would give him the message.

At nine, the phone rang. She had no idea how long she'd been staring absently at the ivory white device. Normally, she would have picked it up on the third or fourth ring, but for once she held off. After twelve rings, it stopped. When it rang again, she answered on the second.

"That's new. I called you a while ago, but it kept ringing."

Ryō sounded strangely nervous, as if holding back something.

"I'm sorry. Are you upset?"

"Not at all. Anyway, hello. It looks like I'm being transferred to a local subsidiary in Panama. Executive vice-president."

"Starting when?"

"April."

"That's a great opportunity, right? You're not going alone, are you?"

"Of course not."

Just then, she heard Maiko's tender voice in the background.

There was a moment of silence.

"So, Panama . . . Do they speak English or Spanish there?"

Mizue's voice was trembling slightly. Ryō covered Maiko's mouth with his hand.

"What did you say?"

"What's their official language?"

"Spanish, obviously, but I imagine they also use English."

"I guess I'd better brush up on my Español, then," she said jokingly.

Mizue hung up first. For a long time, Ryō and Maiko remained still in their nakedness.

That night, snow filled the air, leaving Kataseyama lightly dusted by morning.

Mizue left the house just before noon. The sunlight set the melting snow to sparkling. After killing some time with an Aki Kaurismäki film at the Yebisu Garden Place Cinema, she arrived at Tokyo Station at around five o'clock and walked down a side street toward Ōtemachi. At 6:15, Ryō emerged from his office building. She narrowed the distance between them as he was waiting for the intersection light to change and followed him down into the subway, navigating the serpentine underground passage to Hanzōmon Station. She boarded the train bound for Chūō-Rinkan. The train was extremely crowded, worsening with every stop.

At Sangen-Jaya she transferred to the Setagaya line. She got off at the third stop, and when she saw with her own eyes the apartment building Ryō was temporarily calling home, Mizue turned on a heel and went back: from Shibuya to Shinagawa on the Yamanote line, from Shinagawa to Ōfuna on the Yokosuka line, and lastly by monorail to Kataseyama Station for exactly one hour and forty minutes of travel. Mizue broke into a run as she climbed over the hill. She left the door open and flew through the hallway into the living room.

"What's wrong with you, you're panting."

"I was in the garden."

"In this weather?"

"The stars are beautiful."

"You'll catch cold."

"No, I won't. Really. You all right?"

"I'm feeling a little under the weather myself."

"Take care of yourself, okay? Good night."

As she went to close the front door, she leaned out over the porch and looked up at the sky. There were no stars out. She shrugged her shoulders with a shudder and went into the kitchen to boil some water. She poured herself some tea, lacing it with a few drops of brandy. She spread out a map of Setagaya Ward on the coffee table and marked the apartment complex in red.

The next day, she woke up and dressed. She didn't like the way her hair looked, and left three curlers in until she was out the door. From the monorail she changed to the Yokosuka, Yamanote, Den-en-toshi, and Setagaya lines, and by noon was exiting the last station. She passed the railroad crossing and made her first left between the pharmacy and the convenience store. There was a bicycle shop, a laundromat, and a small playhouse. At last the road veered, and again she was standing in front of the same apartment complex as the night before.

Each floor of the white four-story concrete building, which stood across the street from a five-story complex, was outfitted with a row of five verandahs enclosed in white-latticed iron handrails. The taller complex faced the street and was nothing short of an eyesore. Its concrete walls were painted a faded and peeling green, making the entire monstrosity look as if it were covered in moss.

A plate mounted at the entrance of the white building read "Shōin Flats."* The green complex was branded as "Shōin Court."

Mizue located Maiko's name on one of the Shōin Flats mailboxes. Number 404. She went outside and looked up at the window of what she assumed was 404. The parapet was hung with red and yellow poinsettias. A pale lace curtain filled the window.

She was on her way back to the station when she spotted a sign for a real estate agency just beyond the railroad crossing. The double glass doors of the one-room office were plastered with so many condo and

---

* Shady Pines Flats

apartment flyers that she couldn't even see inside. She hesitated at the door.

She then heard the scampering of sandals behind her. A tall, slender woman yanked the door open and walked in. Mizue followed her inside.

The woman sat behind the counter and glared at her. Mizue took off her coat to reveal a bright orange cashmere sweater. She felt the woman's eyes on her chest.

Mizue said she was looking for a place suitable for a single lady such as herself. The woman's breath whistled through a gap in her teeth. She reeled around, took out a thick file, and dropped it on the counter with a thud.

"How about Shōin Flats?" Mizue asked.

"No rooms at the moment," the woman answered brusquely as she continued flipping pages.

"Could you show me anyway?"

The woman opened to the Shōin Flats spread and held it out for her inspection. Mizue fixed her eyes upon the diagram and confirmed the floral verandah as belonging to 404.

"Oh yes, this room will be vacant in March, actually."

"That's okay, thank you. I was hoping for something sooner. What about across the street? Any rentals there?"

"Yes. Shōin Court. We do have some available, but I should warn you: they're old and dirty."

"No problem. I don't need anything fancy. I've just gotten a divorce and I need to work."

The woman laughed sardonically through her nose. Mizue smiled in return. The woman opened to Shōin Court. Mizue looked it over and inhaled slowly.

"Is this empty, number 507?"

"Are you sure? It's more like an office, really—too big for one—and completely unfurnished. It hasn't had a tenant in two years."

"May I see it?"

The woman twisted around abruptly and shouted to the back area.

"Hey boss, a customer wants to check out Shōin Court! Number 507."

From the shadows appeared a short fat man in his fifties with a tooth-pick in his mouth.

"Excellent. Allow me to give the grand tour," he said in a relaxed, self-important tone. Mizue stood up as he reached for his jacket on the wall. When the key to 507 was nowhere to be found, an argument broke out between the secretary and her boss. By the time they'd aired their griev-ances, the key was found to have been on the first key ring all along.

The woman was right: the apartment was dingy and utterly desolate. There weren't even any curtains or kitchen appliances, just a room with ordinary wooden floors and a simple square window, but no verandah. Still, it provided a slightly angled view of apartment 404. Not only that, but being one floor higher gave her a convenient vantage point to look down from.

They went over the terms of contract. Rent was $600. She would also need to put down a security deposit plus two months' rent and a one-month service charge. The lease was renewable every two years.

"When can I move in?"

"Anytime you want."

"All right, then. I'll be moving in today."

"Are you sure?" The man rubbed his hands together. "In that case, why don't we go back to the office and get the paperwork in order. You'll need a co-signer."

"That could be a problem. I don't have any relatives."

"That is a problem."

Since Mizue was half a head taller than the realtor, she saw past his balding pate to the dirty window behind him, through which she had a spotty view of Shōin Flats. Maiko's beige curtains were firmly drawn.

"But hasn't this place been empty for the last two years, anyway?" said Mizue slyly as she looked down at him.

The man took a step back and attempted a feeble wink with his left eye.

"All right, madam. We'll worry about the co-signer later. Let a thief catch a thief, as they say."

"And just what is that supposed to mean? How rude."

"Now don't get upset, madam."

Mizue walked away from the man with a hardened expression on her face and went over to the window. Seeing she was having trouble opening it, the man all too happily accommodated and a moment later the wind came rushing in, churning the air in the room.

That night, she was back in Kataseyama, but didn't bother answering Ryō's nine o'clock call. He tried back at 9:30 and again at 10. At 10:30 he finally heard his wife's voice. When Ryō pressed her for an explanation, Mizue blamed a late movie for her absence.

"I guess now that I'm alone, my life is taking on a rhythm of its own."

"Well, sure, that's to be expected. What movie?"

"Some Swedish film."

"What was it about?"

" . . . Something about a bunch of kids. Robert Mitchum was chasing them on a horse."

"Chasing who?"

"The children."

"You sure it was a Swedish film? Robert Mitchum's an old Hollywood star. Now that I think of it, didn't we see one of his films a long time ago . . . *Cape Fear*, wasn't it?"

"Different film. The main character loses his memory, only to regain it when he's whacked over the head by a burglar at the end. The man's love was so beautiful when he didn't know who he was. Oddly enough, his lover was always hiding a vial of rat poison in her purse. Every time she saw a beautiful flower, she'd kill it by sprinkling a little of the poison on it."

Ryō was silent.

"How's Maiko?"

"She'll be out late in Harajuku for a going away party with her classmates."

"So that's why you sound so relaxed."

"Am I always in such a hurry?"

Mizue chuckled. "It feels that way to me."

"I'm sorry, Mizue, I really am."

Mizue briefly fell silent. "I have a cell phone now. Just bought it today."

"Oh? I thought we were against them."

"Maiko still doesn't have one?"

"No."

"I'll give you my number."

Mizue repeated the eleven-digit number, which Ryō jotted down in the margin of his evening paper. They hung up and Ryō called Mizue back on her cell.

"Now I don't have to call you at nine."

"Why not? A promise is a promise. One month means one month, nine o'clock means nine o'clock."

"I know. Hey, look, it's snowing outside."

With her cell phone still in hand, Mizue opened the terrace door. The cold wind ushered a few snowflakes inside. "Here, too. Only a little, though. Let's hang up now."

"I'd like to come home, if only for a change of clothes and some of your cooking . . ."

"No. We made a deal . . . We still have ten more days until we've fulfilled our vow."

"When you put it like that . . ."

"Are you getting tired of her?"

"It's not that," said Ryō, shaking his head. "By the way, it looks like I won't be going to Panama after all."

"Oh, that's too bad. I was looking forward to living there."

" . . . I think she's home now. I'd better go."

Maiko's cheeks were flushed from drink. As Ryō was dusting off the snow from her hair and coat, Mizue went out on the terrace and gazed for a while at the sky. Snow fell into her eyes, melting before she could blink.

The snow didn't stick. Mizue left the house at seven the next morning, arrived at Shōin Shrine by eight, and settled her paperwork with the realtor. She cleaned the window and put up some lace and beige curtains. She bought a space heater and a metal folding chair from a nearby supermarket.

She opened the curtains slightly and looked down out at Maiko's dining room window, only slightly askew from her own. With the lace curtains closed, she couldn't see inside with the naked eye—only an occasional silhouette that looked like it could be her husband's mistress. Mizue grabbed her binoculars.

Maiko was sitting at the table, reading a book. She had on an angora sweater that matched her beige curtains. A mass of soft curls fell about her shoulders. Her beautiful lips moved occasionally. Flowers sat atop the dresser just behind her: two stems each of yellow, pink, and white, all slightly wilted.

When Maiko stood up, Mizue caught sight of her burgundy flare pants before she disappeared from view. Fifteen minutes later, she came walking through the dining room with her shoulder bag.

Maiko left the building and walked leisurely along the street below on her way to university. Mizue stayed put. She paced the empty room, sometimes stopping to stare into space. Eventually, she poured herself some coffee from a thermos and drank it in her chair. She looked about the room indifferently. Nothing. She read a book. She knit a scarf. Then she left.

At the flower shop in front of the station, she bought one pot of red poinsettias and one of yellow, as well as some roses. She put the poinsettias on the windowsill and the vase of roses in a corner.

A knock at the iron door filled the room with its deep metallic boom. Mizue bit her lip and ignored it. She heard her last name being called.

"I know you're in there. Make sure you get a co-signer soon."

Mizue stopped her breath short, listening as the man's grumbling receded. Darkness began to creep in all around her. Mizue continued her lookout from the window, lit only by the orange glow of her space heater.

Ryō and Maiko came back after seven, walking hand-in-hand. As they set the table for dinner, Mizue followed every plate with her binoculars and watched them enjoy their leisurely meal.

At exactly nine, Ryō turned to the phone on the dresser. Mizue's cell rang. At the same time, Maiko disappeared from view. It was an incoherent exchange, peppered with Mizue's clumsy replies.

"Where are you now?"

"At home, where else?" she said, looking around her. Her eyes went to the roses in the corner.

When they were done, she left in a hurry and took the five trains required to get her back to Kataseyama. The next few days of monotonous stakeouts continued without incident. She braved the rush hour crowds in the mornings and endured the vulgar words whispered into her ears by drunkards at night.

One day, in the middle of the railroad crossing, she bumped into the realtor, who inquired once again about the co-signer situation. Mizue avoided eye contact and would have brushed him off had he not taken her by the arm.

"How about a coffee?"

He escorted her into a nearby coffee shop.

"They make a good cup here. How's the job hunt?"

"Still looking."

"Seems like the whole world's in a recession."

"Can't you wait just a little longer for me to find that co-signer?"

"How about you work for me instead? That would kill two birds with one stone. I could be your co-signer."

"But don't you already have an assistant?"

"That's just it. After all these years, she still doesn't know what she's doing. Plus, she's a bit shady. I was planning on firing her anyway. What do you say?"

The man's beady little eyes, nestled in an oily face, nervously took in their surroundings. With his pinky extended, he lifted the coffee cup and slurped down its contents.

"Look, madam . . . Actually, I suppose I should call you Miss, now that you're single," he said, lowering his voice. "I like slender, flat-chested types like you. I know my way around a woman, and I'm not afraid to say it. Unconventional beauty really turns me on, and you've got it, all right. You must have a damn good reason for wanting that room so badly . . . but since you've clearly got your heart set on the place, I'm willing to put in the money to fix it up. Anyway, just leave everything to me. It's not such a bad plan, is it?"

With this, the man stretched out a hand under the table and touched her knee. Mizue sprang out of her chair.

"Not bad at all. But on one condition: get rid of that woman. I'll give you a week. One week. Until then, don't come near me. Can you do that for me?"

"I can, and I will."

"Good, then. One week from now, right here."

"You got it."

The realtor scooped up the check and paid at the register.

"Okay, then. Next week, Friday. Same time, same place," he said with a wave and lumbered into the great outdoors. Mizue ordered another cup of coffee. She took her time to savor it before heading out.

That night, beyond the lace curtains, she saw Ryō and Maiko in the nude, their bodies entangled on the dining room carpet. Ryō stood up and drew the curtains, after which he called right on schedule.

The next day was quite chilly and developed into a full-blown snow-storm by late morning. The snow made for poor viewing. Having no use for her binoculars, Mizue called it a day and was home by evening to find that the storm had also hit Kataseyama. For the first time in weeks, she made a proper meal for herself and ate in solitude.

The clouds cleared by morning, leaving Kataseyama and Setagaya covered in white. The Sunday air was still and quiet. She opened the window to the sound of melting snow dripping from the treetops. The sparrows were chirping, flying about from branch to glistening branch.

"I got a letter from him," said Maiko.

Ryō was absorbed in his morning paper.

"Are you listening?"

"Yes, I'm listening."

"I haven't been answering his calls lately. He's worried I might be sick, or so he says. But I bet he's really . . . he probably suspects I've got a man in Tokyo."

"He doesn't suspect nothing."

"I hate it when you use double negatives. Can't you stop it? . . . Anyway, he says mom and dad are sending Hisao to Tokyo."

"Hisao?"

"My little brother. Apparently, he gave Hisao a cell phone to pass along to me, so we can have our own private 'hotline,' so to speak."

"Spying on you, is he? Welcome to the mobile world. Wait, when's he coming?"

"Tomorrow. He wants to know if he can stay here."

"That's sudden. What about me?"

"Will you go back to Kataseyama?"

"I can't do that. We've only got five days left together."

This put Maiko in tears. Ryō came around the table and held her close.

"What's wrong?" he said, looking into her eyes.

Maiko looked out the window with a start.

"I thought we agreed not to count the days."

"I'm sorry, but what little time we have is so precious. It's just . . . What are you looking at? The curtain?"

"It looks like someone's finally moved in on the fifth floor across the street. Look, they've got curtains up."

Ryō turned around and went up to the window.

"You're right. They're the same color as yours."

"That's strange. I don't see any laundry out to dry, and they never turn on their lights."

"Maybe they're still moving in?"

"But I've seen a faint light on at night. Could be a heater. Someone's there, for sure. I'm going to change the curtains."

Ryō turned back to face her, puzzled.

"Just because they've got the same ones as you? Whatever for? Besides, you'll be out of here soon."

"But I want to change them."

"As you wish."

He picked Maiko up with a laugh and carried her into the adjacent bedroom, filled with sunlight intensified by the snow. Maiko lay face up on the bed. As he made love to her, she focused her attention on the snow melting on the edge of the gabled roof outside her window, and soon her body went into little convulsions.

Mizue was looking through the curtain, training her binoculars from the tree branches to the hedges, from the fence to the roofs of cars, before settling on the softening snow. She boldly widened the curtains and swung her binoculars to the right, watching the thick snow clinging to the edge of the gabled roof. Maiko gasped at the falling snow.

Mizue held her breath as she tracked the same patch of snow as it fell to the ground.

She returned her binoculars to the empty living room, focusing on the now dried roses on the dresser. It was quiet. Mizue kept her eyes firmly on the flowers.

Suddenly, a single pink petal separated from its stigma. It held its shape and turned a bit to the side before being guided by air resistance onto the chair on which Maiko had been sitting.

Another petal, this one yellow, soon followed. Within seconds, they were falling all around. Mizue watched as the final swath of pink landed on the edge of the carpet.

She quickly turned to her roses, as yet supple, in the corner of her room. She put down the binoculars and stared at them.

One of the pink petals fell lightly. She kept her eyes locked as a yellow petal overlapped the pink. One, two, three more followed. Before she knew it, the floor was a mosaic of pink, yellow, and white.

Mizue jumped at the ringing of her cell. It was completely dark outside. Maiko's roses had wilted at three in the afternoon, which meant that Mizue had been watching hers for six hours straight.

She heard Ryō's voice on the other end.

"Where are you right now?"

"At home, of course."

"But I called your home phone."

"I'm upstairs. We get so many calls these days and, seeing as you're not here, I've decided not to answer them anymore," she said, fingering open the curtain and staring absently at Ryō's silhouette. "I'm so tired. I don't know if I can keep this up until you come back home."

"I wish you would . . ."

"It's okay. I'm sorry. Don't worry. Stay warm."

By the following morning, Maiko had put up new curtains. A blue jacquard weave embroidered with tropical plants now graced her window. The lace was also different. At 10 a.m., a pajama-clad Maiko opened them gracefully. At 11:10, she closed them and left the apartment.

Mizue read a book by the heater and made some progress on her scarf. Before long, the darkness began to fill the room like water. She stood up. She went to the window, gnawing her lip, and opened the curtain to see Maiko's figure circumscribed by her own reflection in the dark glass. Maiko was looking at her. Mizue hid herself in the curtain's shadow.

At around eight that evening, a young man shouldering a backpack walked into Shōin Flats and soon appeared in Maiko's living room. The two of them sat across from one another at the table, exchanging pleasant conversation, when Maiko suddenly began to cry. The man took out a white handkerchief from his pocket and handed it to her. Maiko daubed her eyes and nose, unable to staunch her tears.

Mizue's cell rang.

"Where are you right now?"

"Why do you ask?"

"Your phone sounds different."

"That would be because I'm calling from a hotel room."

"Oh, get kicked out did we?"

"Something like that. Her little brother's come to Tokyo. And it's not like I can come home, either. We still have four days left . . ."

Mizue bit her lip gently.

"She even has a cell phone now. Her fiancé hotline, she says."

Mizue said good night, locked the door, and left. A balmy wind whipped around her face. She failed to notice the realtor coming from the opposite direction on his bicycle. When their paths intersected at the railroad crossing, he put on the brakes, wedged one foot in the crossing sign, and cupped a hand around his mouth.

"Only four days left," he whispered. "Four days!"

And with a jerk, he pedaled unsteadily into the darkness. A warning sound signaled an oncoming train.

Due to trouble with the overhead lines on the Tōkaidō line, the return train from Yokosuka was twice as crowded as usual. Mizue held her tongue as some nameless groper fondled her chest and thighs. The young, foul-breathed man got off at Hodogaya.

On Thursday, the secretary from the realtor's office was pacing back and forth on the street below, firing an occasional look up at Mizue's window. Eventually, she disappeared into the Shōin Court entrance. Mizue turned around and kept her eyes on the door. The footsteps stopped just outside her apartment, but there was no knock. Five minutes passed, then ten, before the footsteps retreated.

Mizue returned her attention to the window, keeping an eye on the front entrance. But no matter how long she waited the woman didn't show. Maiko's younger brother left Shōin Flats not long after. In addition to his backpack, he was cradling large department store bags in both hands.

Mizue curled herself up in a blanket and slept a little.

Ryō settled three buyer negotiations in the morning, with four more in the afternoon, and took a much-deserved stretch. He refused an invitation to a client's party that evening and left work at six. He met up with Maiko at the lobby of the Tokyo Station Hotel, where she'd put up her brother, then grabbed a taxi to an Italian restaurant in Minami-azabu.

"I'm going to cook for us tomorrow. We'll go all out. Our very own Last Supper. Are you relieved, Ryō?" asked Maiko as she chewed her duck, sliced paper-thin. Ryō merely stared back in silence.

They left the restaurant and strolled arm-in-arm down Aoyama Antique Street. Though some of the shops were closed, others had a variety of decorative items spread out in dazzling illuminated displays. Ryō moved his right hand to check his watch, but Maiko held him back.

"Just for tonight, don't call."

And so, the two of them walked on. A dim hanging lamp lured them into a charmstone shop.

When Ryō asked about the stones, an old man wearing a long Chinese gown plucked a lapis lazuli from one of the display cases. The large almond-shaped stone was flecked with pyrite that glittered like a sky full of stars against a rich, deep blue.

"Have you ever seen the stars in the steppes of Central Asia?"

"No."

"You haven't . . . ? Then look no further, for now you can have a piece of the night sky in your very hands. Behold." He held the stone up with his papery hand. "Do you see where it says 'AAA' on the back? That means it's vintage grade, from Azerbaijan."

He handed the stone to Maiko, who stared at it.

"The color really pulls you in. Lapis brings good luck, you know," she said, leaning against Ryō.

"Indeed it does. However, when choosing the right lapis, you must be calm and pure of mind."

Maiko clenched the stone tightly.

"Then again, I see that one has already chosen you."

"How much for it?" asked Ryō.

"Three thousand dollars," the old shopkeeper replied.

"I'd like it in a brooch, then. Do you do your own casting here?"

And just like that, he set it into an oval of silver.

"There, a perfect fit ... The power spot is right here." The old man pointed to a cluster of stars at the stone's edge.

"It's wonderful. But too expensive."

"Don't worry about it," said Ryō, turning back to the shopkeeper, who shook his head.

"Ten percent off. That's as low as I go."

They left the shop and hailed a taxi to Daikan-yama, where, at a cocktail bar under a large elm tree, Maiko drank a Blue Moon, and Ryō, a scotch.

"That brooch looks beautiful on you. Is it lapis?" said the bartender. Maiko smiled, twisting her glass by its thin stem, and straightened the slightly crooked brooch.

"I remember it now," said Ryō.

"That young man in the story, he must have gone to Azerbaijan."

From behind the counter, they heard the sound of rain beating on the leaves of the elm outside.

"They didn't predict rain for today."

The bartender nodded in agreement.

Mizue was waiting for the Yokosuka train at Shinagawa Station. No trains had come in a while. Finally, the station PA announced that the trains had been halted because of fatal accidents on both the Shinagawa and Tōkaidō lines. As if on cue, the rain began to fall violently onto the steel canopy.

"No one said anything about rain," yelled a staggering drunk man.

"You can't predict an accident," someone said.

The passengers made their way over to the Keihin-Tōhoku platform. Mizue merely stood there on the Yokosuka side, only climbing up to the overpass when she noticed the crowd thinning around her.

A few rough shoves from a station attendant later, she found herself on the Keihin-Tōhoku line. From Yokohama she merged into the Nigishi line, and finally arrived in Ōfuna, where the monorail sped through a spray of rain.

By the time she was in Katasesyama, the storm had lifted. Mizue slowly climbed the sloping path. Above her head, the clouds parted, revealing a pitch-black sky studded with stars. A waning gibbous moon revealed its face before disappearing behind the clouds. A breeze shook the curls hanging over her forehead. She heard a whoosh from above as the monorail sped past.

She followed the path to the top, where she directed her gaze to the sea as she so often did. Mizue's breath stopped short.

From behind Mt. Kamakura, a rainbow painted its bold arc over the valley and into the sea. She counted the colors from bottom to top: violet, indigo, blue, green, yellow, orange, and red.

Mizue's eyes reflected the rainbow's sparkle, which bathed her face in rose. A smile came to her lips, and for a long time she didn't move. This rare evening rainbow disappeared into the countless surrounding stars as if receding into the distance.

Saturday evening. Wearing the same clothes as when he left, Ryō came down the hill rolling his luggage and stood at the front door. When no one greeted him, he took off his shoes in silence and went into the living room, announcing he was home. The house was just as he'd left it one month before. He could still smell the Kilimanjaros they'd drunk that morning hanging in the air.

"Welcome back," said Mizue calmly. She was wearing a bright orange cardigan. Ryō breathed a heavy sigh and collapsed into the sofa.

"I didn't sleep a wink," she said.

"She didn't come home last night." Ryō buried his head in his hands. "I waited all day today, and she still didn't show. But I came home because I promised to. I have no idea where she's gone."

Mizue picked up her unfinished scarf from the rocking chair and sat down, skillfully manipulating her knitting needles.

Ryō took his hands from his forehead and lifted his face.

"What am I going to do? She . . ."

He got that far before he swallowed his words, staring at the brooch pinned to her cardigan. Cast in a finely filigreed silver, it held a large almond-shaped lapis lazuli stone.

"What's wrong? Is it crooked?" she asked calmly, holding the brooch in her fingers.

Glossary

Amuro: Namie Amuro (1977–). Japanese pop and R&B singer from Okinawa. She reached stardom in her teens and her signature look at the time (long, dyed hair, tan skin, mini-skirt and boots) inspired many fans to adopt her style. She is still producing big hits and going on tours, and the tabloids also pursue her as a celebrity single-mom.

Bundansha: fictional publishing house with a name that implies the literary realm comprised of writers, editors, etc.

chu-hi: the term is coined by putting *shochu* and highball together and refers to an alcoholic drink using spirits (*shochu*, sometimes vodka) as the base and adding fruit for flavor and carbonated water. Often considered an inexpensive, low-alcoholic drink popular in pubs, the canned versions can have a higher alcoholic percentage.

happoshu: beer-like beverage with less malt and lower tax than beer.

kotatsu: a knee-high table with an electric heater attached to the underside. A comforter covers all four sides and retains the heat. A flat board is placed on the very top.

Marui: a department store geared towards the younger crowd.

nabe: a dish with a variety of vegetables, tofu, fish or meat in an earthen pot, often cooked on the dining table on a portable gas stove.

OL: short for "office lady" or women who work at an office.

purikura: short for "print club," a fun photo booth that allows you to take instant, tiny sticker-photographs. They come with a wide variety of playful frames and other add-ons to choose from before printing.

PHS: short for "personal handy-phone system," a relatively cheaper alternative to cell phones that uses weaker electromagnetic waves. Though with about a four-million subscriber base, there's only one company left offering PHS services and even they have filed for bankruptcy. PHS was well-received initially for its flat rates and substantial transmission even underground, but cell phones now share these advantages as well, and the difference between the two has become less apparent.

seppuku: literally meaning "stomach cut;" *seppuki* is also known as *hara-kiri*, though in Japan the word *seppuku* is typically preferred. *Seppuku* was originally reserved only for samurai. It is a ritualized suicide by self-disembowelment with a sword.

Takarazuka theater: the all-female troupe Takarazuka has two elegant theaters. Their main theater was built in Hyogo Prefecture in 1924 and houses both the grand theater and a smaller hall. The other one built in 1934 is in Hibiya, Tokyo. Both locations went under major reconstruction in the 1990s, Hyogo again in 2005. To fill in the void created by the all-male *kabuki*, the troupe was founded by Ichizo Kobayashi, the original head of the railway company Hankyu, for single women. The actresses play male characters (as well as androgynous ones), and their performances have been perceived as a symbol of female liberation from restrictive gender roles. Ironically, however, the troupe is also known for its patriarchal, military-like hierarchy.

About the Editor

HELEN MITSIOS IS THE EDITOR OF *NEW JAPANESE VOICES: The Best Contemporary Fiction from Japan*, a Morgan Entrekin Book with an introduction by Jay McInerney, which was twice listed as a *New York Times Book Review Editors' Choice*.

She has contributed feature articles and book reviews for magazines and newspapers including *The Washington Post Book World, The Washington Times World & I Magazine, The Philadelphia Inquirer*, and *the San Francisco Chronicle*. In addition, she co-authored the memoir *Waltzing with the Enemy: A Mother and Daughter Confront the Aftermath of the Holocaust*. She lives in New York's Greenwich Village with her husband who is the principal of Pentastudio Architecture.

About the Translators

Brian Bergstrom is a Ph.D. student in the East Asian Languages and Civilizations Department at the University of Chicago, completing a dissertation examining representations of youthful criminals in Japanese literature and popular culture. It was in the course of this research that he first came across the work of Tomoyuki Hoshino, specifically his 1998 novella *Treason Diary* which provocatively re-imagines the futures of two real-life young criminals of the 1990s. Brian has also published articles on prewar Japanese proletarian writer Takako Nakamoto and contemporary "Gothic Lolita" author Novala Takemoto. In his spare time, he enjoys listening to Kyoto/Osaka garage-punk bands and watching horror movies.

Jessiqa H.W. Greenblatt is native to Long Island, New York. Her interest in languages found its roots in her childhood fancy for hieroglyphs and later blossomed into a reverent admiration for Asian logograms. Jessiqa first came to Japan to participate in a summer exchange program at Hokkaido University during her undergrad at the University of Massachusetts Amherst. She spent the next summer in Shiga Prefecture learning Japanese puppet theatre and completed her junior year abroad at Nanzan University in Nagoya where she graduated with a degree in Japanese and Linguistics. Jessiqa currently works in Kofu City as the Prefectural Advisor and Consultant for Assistant Language Teachers at the Yamanashi High School Board of Education.

Tyran Grillo, a California native, was born in 1978. He developed an interest in the Japanese language in high school, where his friendship with an exchange student led to a discovery of Japanese rock music and a desire to learn what his new favorite bands were singing about. Language studies at the University of Massachusetts Amherst, interrupted by a brief musical career in Japan, fostered an intense interest in translation, a topic that has dominated his studies ever since. After publishing his first two translations as an undergraduate—Sena Hideaki's *Parasite Eve*

and Suzuki Koji's *Paradise*—with Vertical Inc., he went on to complete his Master's. An accomplished singer, blogger, illustrator, and composer, Tyran is currently pursuing a Ph.D. in East Asian Languages at Cornell University.

Jonathan W. Lawless first developed his love of Japanese history and culture in high school and started his study of the language as an undergraduate at Union College. His life as a Japan-enthusiast truly started, however, when he studied abroad in Osaka during his junior year. There he learned important life lessons, such as how to speak Osaka-ben, how to eat every single grain of rice in a bowl with chopsticks, and how to break dance. Completely enthralled by nearly every aspect of modern Japanese culture, he continued to visit Japan regularly and even did a three-year stint as an English teacher in Tokushima (on the island of Shikoku). Returning to the States, he received an M.A. in Japanese from the University of Massachusetts Amherst, married a wonderful woman, and now finds himself in Northern Virginia with his wife, where he teaches Japanese language and culture to high school students.

Jay Rubin received his B.A. in Far Eastern Studies in 1963 from the University of Chicago and completed a Ph.D. in Japanese literature there in 1970. He has taught at the University of Chicago, the University of Washington, and Harvard University and translated the fiction of Doppo, Soseki Natsume's *Sanshiro* and *The Miner*, Ryunosuke Akutagawa's *Rashomon and 17 Other Stories*, and Haruki Murakami's *The Wind-Up Bird Chronicle* and *Norwegian Wood* among others. He is currently translating Murakami's latest novel *IQ84*.

L. Hale Sterling first encountered Japanese culture in the summer of the year 2000, while on a trip to visit a friend in Tokyo. He began his love of Japanese literature and translation while an undergraduate at the University of Massachusetts Amherst under the tutelage of Professor J. Martin Holman, his mentor and dear friend. He received his B.A. in Japanese language and literature in 2005, and his M.A. in Japanese literature from the University of Massachusetts Amherst in 2007. He is a former JET Program Participant (2007–2008). L. Hale Sterling currently resides in Tokyo, Japan. He is employed at Mizuho Corporate Bank, Ltd. as a financial translator and interpreter.

Stephen Snyder is Professor of Japanese Studies in the Department of Japanese Studies at Middlebury College in Vermont. He is the author of *Fictions of Desire: Narrative Form in the Novels of Nagai Kafu* and has translated works by Yoko Ogawa, Kenzaburo Oe, Ryu Murakami, and Miri Yu among others. His translation of Natsuo Kirino's *Out* was a finalist for the Edgar Award for best mystery novel in 2004. His translation of Kunio Tsuji's *The Signore* won the 1990 Japan-U.S. Friendship Commission translation prize. His most recent translation, Yoko Ogawa's *Hotel Iris,* was published by Picador in March 2010.

Tyler Tape is a graduate of the department of Japanese language and literature at the University of Massachusetts Amherst. He lives in Isahaya City, Nagasaki Prefecture, and has one of the best jobs in the world teaching English to elementary and junior high school students there. When not in class or on the playground, he can sometimes be found mangling his favorite songs on the piano. He is currently preparing to continue his studies as a research student in Japan.

Tomoko Nagaoka-Kozaki is a Ph.D. candidate in English literature at the University of Tokyo Graduate School. She lives in New York with her husband and two children. Her published translations include *Emperor Meiji and Empress Shoken* (2007), multiple sections from *Masterpieces in Japanese Photography* (2005–06), and footnotes in *Textbook for Japanese III* (2003). While in Tokyo she interpreted for Kenzaburo Oe and once translated his script for a keynote speech, but her passion for literary translations was rekindled when Masahiko Shimada asked her to translate segments of his novels during his stay in New York.

Credits

Toshiyuki Horie, "The Bonfire." "Okuribi" originally appeared in *Yukinuma To Sono Shûhen*. ©2003 by Toshiyuki Horie. First published in Japan in 2003 by Shinchosha Publiching Co., Ltd.

Hitomi Kanehara, "Delilah." Reprinted by permission of the author.

Masahiko Shimada, "Diary of a Mummy." Reprinted by permission of the author.

Maki Kashimada, "The Female Novelist." Reprinted by permission of the author.

Natsuo Kirino, "The Floating Forest." Copyright 2005 by Natsuo Kirino. Reprinted by permission of the author.

Ira Ishida, "Ikebukuro West Gate Park." Copyright 1998 by Ira Ishida. First published in Japan in 1998 by Bungei Shunju Ltd. Reprinted by permission of the author.

Yoko Tawada, "To Khabarovosk." Reprinted by permission of the author.

Tomoyuki Hoshino, "The No Fathers Club." Reprinted by permission of the author.

Yoko Ogawa, "The Sea." "UMI" copyright 2006 by Yoko Ogawa. First published in *UMI* by Shinchosha Publishing Co., Ltd. English translation rights arranged with Yoko Ogawa through Japan Foreign-Rights Centre/Anne Stein.

Noboru Tsujihara, "My Slightly Crooked Brooch." Reprinted by permission of the author.